GENETICS AND
SOCIETY

GENETICS AND SOCIETY

An introduction

ALISON PILNICK

OPEN UNIVERSITY PRESS
Buckingham • Philadelphia

Open University Press
Celtic Court
22 Ballmoor
Buckingham
MK18 1XW

email: enquiries@openup.co.uk
world wide web: www.openup.co.uk

and

325 Chestnut Street
Philadelphia, PA 19106, USA

First Published 2002

A catalogue record of this book is available from the British Library

ISBN   0 335 20735 9 (pb)   0 335 20736 7 (hb)

Library of Congress Cataloging-in-Publication Data
Pilnick, A.
   Genetics and society : an introduction / Alison Pilnick.
     p. cm.
   Includes bibliographical references and index.
   ISBN 0-335-20736-7 (hardcover) – ISBN 0-335-20735-9
   1. Genetics – Social aspects.   2. Human genetics – Social aspects.
   I. Title.

QH438.7.P54   2002
576.5–dc21   2001054494

Typeset by Graphicraft Limited, Hong Kong
Printed in Great Britain by Biddles Limited, Guildford and Kings Lynn

This book is dedicated to my parents, Irene and Mike, with thanks

CONTENTS

LIST OF FIGURES

ACKNOWLEDGEMENTS

Many people have contributed, either directly or indirectly, to the work contained within this book. For most of the time of writing the text, I was on a research secondment to the Genetics and Society Unit (now renamed the Institute for the Study of Genetics, Biorisks and Society) at the University of Nottingham. I gratefully acknowledge the financial support of the Unit in getting this project started and the intellectual support of colleagues during the task of writing. In particular, Robert Dingwall provided encouragement and insightful comments on draft materials. The help of Rachael Williams, in sourcing and collating material while on an internship with the Unit, was invaluable. The aid of colleagues elsewhere was also much appreciated, in particular Lindsay Prior's incisive comments on a first version of this text. Thanks are also due to the Galton Institute, who were kind enough to allow me access to their archive at the Wellcome Institute, and to the archive staff who assisted my search. Davina Allen read and commented on an early part of the text – both her constructive criticisms and her support, as always, helped immeasurably. Last, but by no means least, I would like to record my thanks and love to Mark for drawing Figure 1.1, but more importantly, for providing diversion, support and latterly sanity as the deadline for this manuscript approached.

Permissions for the figures are as follows:

Figure 1.3 Autosomal dominant inheritance.
Reproduced by permission of Progress Educational Trust.

Figure 1.4 X-linked inheritance.
Reproduced by permission of Progress Educational Trust.

Figure 2.1 Pedigree of the Wedgwood-Darwin-Galton family, as used by the Eugenics Society.
Reproduced with the permission of the Galton Institute and the Wellcome Library, London, © The Galton Institute, London.

INTRODUCTION

Just as the genie escaped from the bottle, the gene is now out of the test tube, and we cannot put it back.

(Lenaghan 1998: 129)

This is a book about contemporary developments in the scientific understanding of genetics, and the ways in which these developments are transforming the possible relations between humans and their natural environment. Since the discovery of the structure of the DNA molecule in the 1950s, the science of molecular genetics has developed rapidly and has had far-reaching consequences. Recent advances in the applications of genetic science, often termed 'the new genetics', raise important sociological issues and have significant policy implications. This text uses a series of examples to draw out these issues and implications, beginning with some of the lessons to be learned from recent historical applications of biological information and ending with contemporary developments such as cloning and genetically modified food. The focus is mainly, although not exclusively, on human genetics; there is some consideration of animal and plant genetics as appropriate in specific areas.

Although the focus of the text is on key issues raised by the application of new genetic technologies, it does not necessarily cover all the developments that a biological scientist would see as being at the cutting edge of scientific research. Instead, it focuses on those that are most significant in terms of public perceptions, social impact or public policy. The substantive applications of genetic science that are covered are organized as a series of case studies. These case studies (for example, genetic testing, antenatal screening and pharmacogenetics) are used to address both the specific issues that the implementation of these particular technologies raise and the underlying sociological themes that are relevant to understanding their impact. Where possible, empirical data are used to illustrate points so that the discussion of theoretical debates can be related to contemporary research.

By beginning with a consideration of how genetic knowledge has been used in recent history and moving to look at contemporary developments, the importance of social context is stressed. Placing genetic knowledge in its social context also requires an exploration of how that social context affects the development and implementation of genetic research. Throughout the text, examples are drawn from both US and UK perspectives and, where appropriate, comparisons are made between the two.

Aims of the book

This book has two key aims: to encourage readers to critically examine social issues that relate to genetic science and practice, and to encourage readers to explore the links between social theory and the research and practice of genetic science. It is not intended as a complete survey of the rapidly growing literature on the applications of new genetic technologies. Instead, it aims to focus on key debates, issues and concepts to provide the reader with a foundation from which to tackle this literature on their own.

Special features

To make the book as accessible to readers as possible, several special features have been included in the text.

- *Boxes*. These are used throughout the substantive chapters. Boxes contain text that is additional to the core chapter, for one of three reasons. First, they provide examples drawn from empirical research to illustrate points that are raised in the text. Second, they examine specific points in more depth. Third, they provide different viewpoints on matters considered in the main text.
- *Summary points*. At the end of each chapter there is a list of summary points. These are intended as a reminder of the key points that have been covered in that chapter. They are not intended to stand alone and are best used as a way of checking understanding after reading the chapter.
- *Further reading*. In the text itself, references have been kept to a minimum. Suggestions for further reading in each substantive area are included at the end of each chapter. These suggestions include key works in the field, as well as recent empirical research, and are intended as a starting point for readers interested in following up a particular theme or topic.
- *Accessing up-to-date information*. With any book that attempts to address a rapidly changing and developing area, becoming out of date is a

problem. To address this, readers are encouraged to supplement this text with their own, up-to-date materials. In the text, the web addresses of resources such as the Wellcome Trust and the Human Genome Project are included, so that current information on new developments and debates can be readily accessed. It is also recommended that readers keep a file of clippings from newspaper, magazine and journal articles covering genetic 'stories' that appear while they are reading this book. One easy way to access news stories related to genetics is to subscribe to the Progress Educational Trust's weekly news service at http://www.progress.org.uk/news. Throughout the text, historical and cross-national examples are drawn on and used as part of the case studies, to illustrate how the development and impact of genetic science is linked to social and cultural factors at particular times. In the same way, these news items will provide a resource for examining how and why particular applications of genetic knowledge may be reported and received in different manners.

Intended readership

Reading the text requires no previous biological knowledge. However, although technical terms and jargon are avoided where possible, some basic understanding is necessary to grasp fully the significance of some of the debates that are discussed. For this reason, the text includes a very brief introduction to genetics, explaining the terminology used in the course of the book, alongside the basic mechanisms of genetic inheritance. For those readers with some biological knowledge, but who may wish to refresh their understanding of particular terms, there is also a glossary at the end of the book.

Although no prior biological knowledge is necessary, the book does presume a very basic grounding in sociology. It draws on the resources of the social sciences to develop a critical perspective on advances in genetic science and to examine the impact these advances have on relationships between humans and the world in which they live. Rather than beginning by outlining key sociological themes, these themes are drawn out of the examples in the chapters. By allowing these themes to emerge from the debates, and by using sociological theories and concepts to explicate topical issues, it is hoped that the relevance of the text to a wide audience will be maintained.

Structure of the book

The book is divided into ten chapters. Chapter 1 gives a very brief introduction to genetics, explaining what the terms 'gene', 'chromosome' and 'DNA' mean, and how genes can be implicated in determining the inheritance of disease. It sets these explanations alongside a brief history of genetic science, charting its ascendance over the twentieth century and its rapid developments since the 1950s.

The remaining chapters focus on substantive areas within the field of genetic science. Chapter 2 provides a brief overview of the recent history of social discrimination based on biology, considering how this is derived from an individualist view of human nature. It introduces the principles of reductionism and biological determinism, to which we will return throughout the book. It also gives a brief introduction to the sociological study of science and technology. The development of the Eugenics Society in the UK is used as a case study to examine how the history of discrimination is entwined with both biological and social sciences.

Chapter 3 returns to the present day, considering the contemporary evidence for the biological basis of human traits and behaviours. It focuses on four areas: aggression, alcoholism, homosexuality and intelligence. In the case of the first three, the evidence to date, and the potential social consequences of pursuing these kinds of research programmes, are examined. The fourth area, intelligence, is examined in more detail with reference to one very famous (and controversial) piece of social science research. This case is used to illustrate how contemporary biological research may become entwined with social and political agendas.

Chapter 4 considers the practice of antenatal screening and testing, and the issues it raises at both individual and wider societal levels. It begins by outlining the kinds of procedures that are commonly used and the ways in which these are integrated into health care practice. It also considers the relationship between antenatal screening and testing and the way in which disability is viewed at a societal level, linking this relationship to long-standing debates over eugenics. This chapter also introduces one of the key themes that we will return to throughout this book in relation to the applications of new genetic technologies that are considered here – that is, risk. Risk and the assessment of risk have become increasingly important issues in modern society, but from a sociological point of view, some of the prevailing assumptions that are involved, such as the idea that any given risk is discoverable and subsequently measurable, are fundamentally flawed. In particular, these assumptions ignore the way in which risks are socially constructed. Nevertheless, risk communication has come to be seen as having particular importance for health care, both in terms of explicating the risk of particular medical procedures, such as surgical operations or diagnostic testing, and in encouraging individuals to make informed decisions based on personal risk. Both of these aspects have particular implications for the sociological study of new genetic technologies and will be explored in relation to specific applications of these technologies in the subsequent chapters.

Chapter 5 focuses on genetic testing, outlining the different types of test that may be used and some of the specific difficulties associated with these different types. It concentrates on the issues raised by testing individuals for disorders that evidence suggests may be present in their families. Questions of confidentiality, autonomy and informed consent are considered, together with the possible implications of test results for insurance and employment. These issues are considered in the context of the health care services that are intended to support genetic testing and, in particular, the process of genetic counselling. The chapter concludes with a discussion of the relevance of sociological and anthropological studies of family and kinship to genetic practice, in terms of understanding how individuals come to make decisions in relation to genetic testing.

Chapter 6 examines the development of the Human Genome Project, its aims and its likely impact on medicine and medical practice in the near future. It then moves to look specifically at two of the developments that are predicted for medicine as a result of the Human Genome Project: gene therapy and pharmacogenetics. The development of pharmacogenetics is dependent on large-scale biological sample collection and this chapter draws on the Icelandic experience of collecting this kind of database to explore the potential issues in a UK and US environment.

Chapter 7 shifts the focus from medicine to agriculture, considering the area of genetically modified (GM) foods. Since the debate over GM foods has largely been constructed in oppositional terms, the proposed advantages and disadvantages are examined. However, it is suggested that this oppositional construction is potentially counter-productive in terms of understanding public reactions to GM foods. The chapter goes on to consider reactions in both the US and UK in the light of the sociological debates around risk, trust and the social significance of food.

Chapter 8 looks at cloning. It begins with a description of the process and a summary of the aims that lie behind the pursuit of cloning research. It moves on to look at two potential applications of cloning: reproductive cloning and therapeutic cloning. Some of the differences between these applications, as well as differences in the ways in which they have been perceived, are explored. The final section of the chapter focuses on public responses to cloning, examining the role of narratives and the media in informing these responses.

Chapter 9, which addresses the rapidly growing field of bioethics, is written by Robert Dingwall. This chapter looks at some of the ethical issues raised by the new genetics and their implications for the way in which we make individual and social choices about how technologies should be used. It also examines the social construction of the dominant approach in bioethics, asking whether its philosophical principles both arise from and reinforce a particular view of citizenship.

The final chapter, Chapter 10, looks to the future. It begins by examining the results of surveys of public attitudes towards new genetic technologies and exploring how these vary across different applications and between economic and cultural circumstance. Concern over the regulation of genetic research and practice is a key theme arising from these surveys and possible models of regulation are presented and explored. The chapter ends with a summary of the sociological critique of the advances promised by the new genetics, drawing on themes that have been discussed throughout the book.

Although genetic science continues to progress at an amazing rate, the science itself cannot give us answers to the social questions raised by the new genetics. This book represents an attempt to begin to define and explore these questions.

1

A VERY BRIEF INTRODUCTION
TO GENETICS

Introduction

This chapter outlines the basic concepts of genetic science, assuming no prior knowledge on the part of the reader. It is intended as a simple introduction, to allow those without a biological background to put the issues that will be considered in the later chapters of this book into context. For those with some biological knowledge, there is a short glossary of terms at the end of the text that may be more useful.

Alongside the basic concepts, this chapter also provides a brief summary of the history of genetic science, beginning with the work of Charles Darwin and working through to the Human Genome Project.

The development of genetic science

Observing the similarities and differences between living organisms is not new, but the development of the branch of biological science concerned with genetics is relatively so. The beginning of modern genetic science is often considered to be the publication of Charles Darwin's *Origin of Species* in 1859. Darwin had developed his ideas about evolution through the process of natural selection over many years, stimulated by his five-year journey on *HMS Beagle*. During this time he observed a wide variety of organisms in their natural habitats and noted the adaptations that had occurred in particular environments. The different species of finch of the Galapagos Islands, for example, had beak shapes that matched the feeding habits of the birds. Darwin proposed that these adaptations were the result of natural selection: that individual birds with particular characteristics that were advantageous were more likely to reproduce and pass these characteristics on to their offspring. This theory is discussed in more detail in Chapter 2. However, while it formed the basis for much debate, and was strongly attacked on religious grounds, it was not presented or considered a genetic theory, since the precise mechanisms by which advantageous characteristics might be passed on were yet to be discovered.

Six years later, in 1865, Gregor Mendel turned the study of the way in which traits are inherited into a science. Mendel was a monk who studied the peas that he grew in the monastery garden. Between 1856 and 1863, he carried out a series of careful experiments with these pea plants, documenting his results in detail. His technique was to use straightforward crossing experiments between plants and then to look for regularities in the resulting offspring that might point to general principles or rules. In this way he pollinated pea plants, saved their seeds to plant separately and then analysed the succeeding generations of plants.

Mendel recognized the need to start his experiments with groups of plants that displayed a uniform set of characteristics within the group. For this reason, at the beginning of his experiments he self-pollinated plants so that they 'bred true', giving rise to similar characteristics generation after generation. The characteristics that he chose to study in his subsequent crossing experiments were easily observable ones, such as flower colour and height.

Examining the results of these experiments led Mendel to realize that, when plants that differed in flower colour or height were crossed, the result was not a plant with a height or flower colour that was a combination of the originals. Crossing a purple flowering plant with a white flowering one gave a plant with purple flowers, and crossing a standard plant with a dwarf one gave a standard plant. In each case, the offspring showed only one of the parental traits; the other was absent. Mendel named those traits that were visibly present (or 'expressed') in the hybrid plants **dominant** traits and those that were not visibly present **recessive** traits.

Mendel's next step was to self-fertilize the offspring produced by these experiments. When he did so, he discovered that there was often a 3:1 ratio of characteristics in the second (or F2) generation, so that, for every three tall plants, for example, there would be one short one, and for every three plants with purple flowers, there would be one white one. This ratio is illustrated in Fig. 1.1.

The popular concept of heredity at the time of Mendel was that the traits of parents became blended in their offspring, so that a short and a tall parent would give rise to offspring of medium height. Mendel's results directly disproved this, showing two things:

- Traits are discrete and do not mix – they are inherited discrete and remain discrete. A plant with purple flowers may contain a white flowering trait. Since purple flowers are dominant, the trait may not be expressed, but can still be passed on.
- The determinants of heredity are transmitted in pairs – each plant has two elements that determine flower colour, height, and so on.

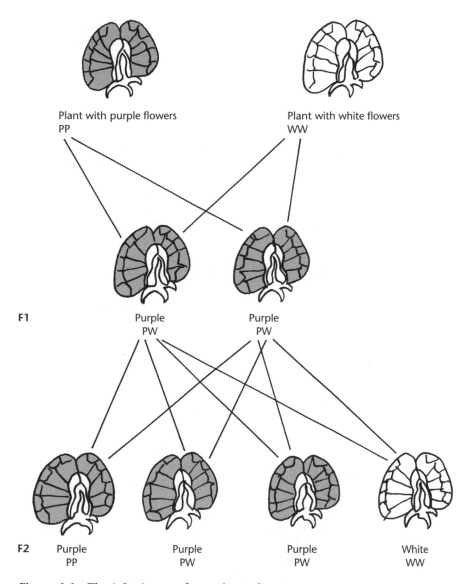

Figure 1.1 The inheritance of recessive traits

The rules of hereditary transmission that could be inferred from Mendel's results are often referred to as Mendelian genetics. Although they were not instantly appreciated, they subsequently became recognized as the first explanation of transmission genetics.

Following Mendel's work, genetic science began to develop in earnest. It was not until 1909, however, that the term 'gene' was coined to describe

Mendelian units of heredity, by Wilhelm Johanssen. The word comes from the Greek 'genos', meaning 'birth'. It was also Johanssen who made the distinction between an organism's outward appearance, or **pheno-type**, and its genetic traits, or **genotype**.

What is a gene?

The fundamental concept of genetics is that inherited traits are deter-mined by the elements of heredity that are transmitted from parents to offspring in reproduction. These elements of heredity are called **genes**.

Our bodies are made up of different cells which perform specific tasks, and genes provide the instructions for how each cell should operate to carry out these tasks effectively. This begins when they provide the instruc-tions for our development into a baby from a fertilized egg, and continues as they provide instructions for the everyday maintenance and function-ing of our bodies. Genes are sections of **DNA** (or deoxyribonucleic acid) and they are contained in the chromosomes passed on from our parents at conception. They are found in the **nucleus** of the cell (see Fig. 1.2).

Cytoplasm

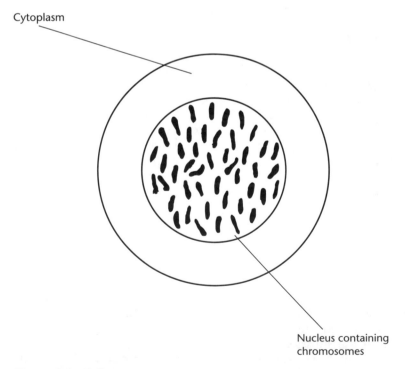

Nucleus containing
chromosomes

Figure 1.2   Cell structure

What is a chromosome?

A chromosome is a linear structure found in all cells of an organism that contains the DNA of that organism. Chromosomes are arranged in pairs; each chromosome is formed from a single DNA molecule that has many genes along its length. In 1879, Flemming observed how animal cells divided; by staining chromosomes, he established how they behave during division. This formed the basis of the chromosomal theory of inheritance. In 1955, it was established that there are 46 human chromosomes. Most human cells have two sets of 23 chromosomes, making 46 in total. The only exception to this is the cells from which sperm or eggs develop; these have 23 chromosomes. When the sperm and egg come together at fertilization, the full complement of 46 chromosomes is produced, containing a more or less random and equal contribution of genes from each parent.

Chromosomes also determine the sex of any offspring. All but one of the 23 pairs of chromosomes are the same for males and females and are called **autosomes**. The exception is the pair of sex chromosomes, which determine the sex of an individual. Females have two X chromosomes, whereas males have one X and one Y. All eggs contain an X chromosome, but sperm may contain either X or Y, and so this is what determines the sex of the child.

What is DNA?

In 1869, **DNA** (deoxyribonucleic acid) was first isolated by Friedrich Miescher, a cell chemist. He called the substance 'nuclein'. By the 1900s, other scientists had begun to work on it in much more detail. In 1944, work on bacteria showed that DNA was the agent that was responsible for transmitting genetic traits; in 1952, it was established that genes were made of DNA. Then, in 1953, Crick and Watson famously established the double helix structure of DNA.

DNA consists of two molecules joined in a double helix, held together by a string of four possible bases: guanine (G), adenine (A), thymine (T) and cytosine (C). This basic structure is the same for all organisms; the differences are in the length of the code and the order of the letters. What this means is that human DNA, for example, is not fundamentally different to viral DNA, except in the way these four bases are ordered and repeated. Just as words only make sense in phrases or sentences, a length of DNA becomes meaningful when it makes up the recipe for a gene. The length of code instructs a cell to make a protein. Humans are the result of a length of code that contains the instructions for around 30,000 genes.

Genetics: an analogy from cookery

A helpful way to understand how DNA, genes and chromosomes relate
to one another is, as R.E. Sockett suggests, to consider the relationship in
terms of a cookery analogy. In this analogy:

- DNA is like a series of code words for each ingredient.
- Genes are like the recipe.
- Chromosomes are like a cookery book, containing a wide range of
  recipes to make a particular creature.
- Proteins are the finished dishes coded for by each gene recipe.
- Living creatures are like the whole dinner party – a complex mixture
  of dishes that work together.
    (Reproduced with the kind permission of R.E. Sockett, Institute of
        Genetics, University of Nottingham, personal communication)

Recent developments in genetic science

From these basic building blocks, the late part of the twentieth century
saw rapid developments in genetic science, with the cloning of the first
single animal gene, the development of DNA sequencing methods to
'read' genetic sequences and the first **transgenic** animals (animals which
have had new genetic material added to their genome). In 1983, a major
development, the polymerase chain reaction (PCR) was invented; this is
a technique for copying DNA. The ability to rapidly copy sequences led
to an increased pace of genetic research. In 1990, the Human Genome
Project was officially launched. By 1999 there was the first full-length
sequence of a human chromosome (chromosome 22), by June 2000 a
working draft of 90 per cent of the human genome, and by 2001 the first
full draft had been announced. The implications of the Human Genome
Project are discussed in more detail in Chapter 6, but it is anticipated
that a greater understanding of how particular genes function will bring
great advances in the diagnosis and treatment of disease.

What causes genetic disease?

The inheritance of disease was first observed by Garrod in 1902, who
saw that the disease alkaptonuria was inherited by Mendelian rules. In
humans, with 46 chromosomes and upwards of 30,000 genes, there is
huge potential for things to change slightly as the reproductive process
takes place. Some changes can be beneficial, making individuals better
adapted to their environment, but others can be harmful. Most of the
differences we inherit are not associated with disease; they may just
make us taller, for example. It is also important to realize that everyone

carries some genes that potentially associate with disease, so it is unrealistic to think of anyone having a 'perfect' genetic profile.

Since Garrod's initial observation, we have come to understand the role genetics plays in some human diseases and disorders. In 1956, the cause of sickle cell anaemia was traced to a genetic alteration and, in 1959, the fact that Down's Syndrome was caused by three instead of two copies of chromosome 21 was identified. Two years later, in 1961, the first testing for a metabolic defect was identified: phenylketonuria (PKU). PKU is a recessive disorder, characterized by an inability to metabolize the amino acid phenylalanine. In sufferers, exposure to phenylalanine can cause severe learning disabilities, but early identification means that dietary exposure can be avoided. The identification of PKU led to the first mass screening programmes being introduced.

Modes of inheritance

Whether or not any individual inherits a particular disease depends on what is called the 'mode of inheritance' of that particular trait or disorder. Each individual inherits two sets of chromosomes, each with a full set of genes. As Mendel's work with pea plants showed, this means that genes are also inherited in pairs. So with any gene, an individual may inherit two affected copies, two unaffected copies, or one of each. Whether an individual with only one affected copy inherits a disease depends on how a particular disorder is inherited. For disorders caused by a single gene, there are three common types of inheritance patterns.

1 Autosomal dominant disorders

With dominant disorders, a person will be affected by inheriting a single copy of the faulty gene. An example of a dominantly inherited disorder is **Huntington's disease**, a degenerative disease of the central nervous system that usually has its onset around the age of 35 years or later. Those who have the disease will have one affected copy of the gene and one unaffected copy. (Affected genes have a mutation that causes an excessive repetition of a particular DNA sequence within the gene. This repetition causes the production of abnormal proteins and is responsible for the development of the disease in individuals.) In the case of a couple with a father affected by the disorder and an unaffected mother, there is the possibility that they may have affected or unaffected children. This is because the father will produce both unaffected and affected sperm. However, every child who inherits the affected gene will be affected by the disorder. As Fig. 1.3 shows, the risk of a couple with one affected member of having an affected child is 50 per cent.

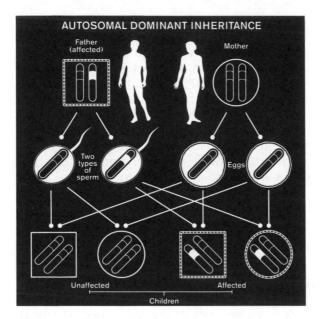

Figure 1.3   Autosomal dominant inheritance

2 Autosomal recessive disorders

In the case of recessive disorders, two copies of the affected gene are needed to develop the disorder, since one unaffected copy will override the other. An example of a condition that is inherited in this way is cystic fibrosis. Those with one affected and one unaffected gene are known as **carriers**; they will usually be unaffected themselves. The probability of inheriting a recessive condition is shown in Fig. 1.1. If a person carrying a recessive gene has children with another carrier, the chance of inheriting two affected genes is 25 per cent. The chance of inheriting one affected gene, and also being a carrier, is 50 per cent. There is also a 25 per cent chance of inheriting two normal genes and not being affected in any way.

3 X-linked inheritance

The third mode of inheritance for single gene disorders is known as X-linked inheritance. These disorders, such as muscular dystrophy, are caused by mutations on the X chromosome. Most X-linked disorders are recessive; therefore, an unaffected copy of the X chromosome will cancel it out. However, males only have one copy of the X chromosome, inherited from their mother. Females who have one copy of the affected

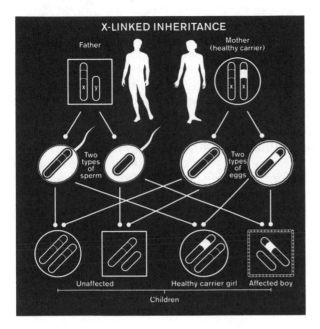

Figure 1.4 X-linked inheritance

gene will be carriers and usually show no effects themselves. As shown in Fig. 1.4, a carrier mother and an unaffected father have a 50 per cent chance of passing on the faulty gene. However, it is usually only boys who are affected by the disorder.

These three modes of inheritance are the ways in which **monogenic** disorders, or disorders caused by single genes, are inherited. However, by no means all disorders are caused by single genes; most are the result of mutations on several genes (**polygenic** disorders) or of genetic mutations in combination with other factors (**multifactorial** disorders).

Polygenic and multifactorial disorders

Many common disorders, such as cancer and heart disease, are known to have a genetic component. However, these are not caused in any straightforward way by single genes, but by mutations on several genes and the interactions between them. Often, the disorder is caused by a combination of genetic and environmental factors. Since there is no straightforward diagnostic test for multifactorial disorders, these raise specific questions about how genetic knowledge is to be applied in these cases. The particular issues raised by polygenic and multifactorial disorders are discussed in more detail in Chapter 6.

Using genetic knowledge

As the subsequent chapters of this book will aim to illustrate, our ever increasing genetic knowledge – and the way in which it is used – has important social implications. Most fundamentally, with new genetic knowledge comes an increasing risk that, because we now know so much about the science, too much emphasis will be placed on it, to the extent that we begin to see ourselves and others simply as the sum of our genes. This kind of genetic determinism is extremely problematic for social scientists, since it minimizes the role of social factors in explaining the characteristics of individual members of society. It also has the potential to change the way we view health and illness. As Blom and Trach (2001: 1006) caution: 'Though we are all virtually biologically identical, each of us is also unique'. This theme of biological determinism will be examined in detail in the next two chapters, both historically and in relation to one very famous contemporary study.

2

'GOOD' GENES AND 'BAD' GENES: A HISTORICAL PERSPECTIVE

Introduction

This chapter looks at the recent history of social discrimination based on biology. It considers how this is derived from an individualist view of human nature and introduces the principles of reductionism and biological determinism. The ways in which scientific developments, particularly Darwin's theory of natural selection, have given weight to individualist theories are examined, and key sociological approaches to the study of science and technology are introduced. Finally, the development of the Eugenics Society in the UK is used to demonstrate how the history of discrimination is entwined with both social and biological sciences.

Historical perspectives

Recent developments in genetic science, often termed 'the new genetics', have made many people anxious about their potential applications. The 'new genetics' has been equated with a 'new eugenics'.

Popular notions of **eugenics** have their roots in nineteenth-century racial science and these interpretations were reinforced after the Second World War when the role of large-scale, state-led eugenic ideas in the Holocaust was revealed. One way of thinking about the social implications of the new genetics identifies this with the 'old eugenics' represented by these relatively recent historical events. Critics suggest that the new genetics facilitates an ideological shift in the perception of social problems: these are no longer to be seen as issues of culture and social structure that can only be solved by collective action, but individual failures, reflecting a defective personal biological inheritance (e.g. Conrad 1997; Rothman 1998; Willis 1998). Instead of changing a society to make it fit for all its people, whatever their biological inheritance, people will be made to fit the society into which they are born.

Although the technologies may be new, this individualist view of human nature is, however, very old. Its roots can be traced to the beginnings of bourgeois society in the seventeenth century, represented by Hobbes's argument, made in the introduction to *Leviathan* (1651), that the natural condition of human existence was a war of all against all. Hobbes argued that any account of human action must be consistent with the fact that all individuals are essentially self-serving. It follows that people created society to control their own nature in the interests of survival. It is important to recognize here, as Rose *et al.* ([1984] 1990) point out, that Hobbes's view of the human condition derived from his understanding of human biology: human nature was *biologically given*. It is also important to recognize that Hobbes's position incorporates two philosophical elements that are still central to current debates: *reductionism* and *biological determinism*.

Reductionism

Reductionism is 'the name given to a set of general methods and modes of explanation both of the world of physical objects and of human societies' (Rose *et al.* [1984] 1990: 5). The defining feature of reductionism is its attempt to explain the properties of complex objects or systems – whether biological, physical or social – in terms of the units that make up those objects or systems. Rose *et al.* give the following example:

> A reductionist would argue that the properties of a protein molecule can be determined and predicted in terms of the properties of the electrons, protons, etc. of which its atoms are composed. Using the same process of inference, they would also argue that the properties of a human society are no more than the sum of the individual behaviours and tendencies of the individual humans of which that society is composed.

If societies are aggressive then, a reductionist argues that this is because the individuals who compose them are aggressive: the units (individuals) and their properties (aggressiveness) exist before the whole (the society), which is no more than the sum of the component parts.

Biological determinism

Biological determinism may be viewed as a special case of reductionism. Biological determinists believe that human lives and actions are the consequences of the biochemical properties of the cells that make up an individual (Rose *et al.* [1984] 1990). These biochemical properties are, in turn, determined by the genes that each individual possesses. All human behaviour – and, according to the principles of reductionism, all human society – is governed by the chain of determination set out below:

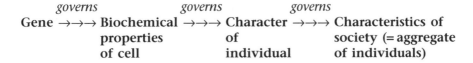

governs	*governs*	*governs*
Gene →→→ Biochemical →→→ Character →→→ Characteristics of
properties	of	society (= aggregate
of cell	individual	of individuals)

According to biological determinists, all social behaviour can be explained in terms of the biological make-up of the individuals involved in it. One example of this kind of explanation will be considered in more detail in the next chapter, when we look at a study that explains the poorer performance of African Americans in standard IQ tests by reference to proposed differences in hereditary aspects of intelligence.

The attraction of biological determinism for some interests in a society lies in the way that it presents human behaviour as *inevitable* rather than as a matter of *choice or circumstance*. Nature has given people unalterable biological endowments: if genes cause behaviour, then bad genes cause bad behaviour. The social claims of biological determinism can be summarized as follows (after Rose *et al.* [1984] 1990):

1 Inequalities in society are a direct consequence of the differential inherited ability of individuals. Any individual may succeed, but whether they do so or not is the result of their biological endowments rather than their cultural capital or the opportunity structures open to them.
2 The genetic basis of social achievement means that the capacity for achievement can be passed on from one generation to another, particularly if successful people tend to have children with people of the same status.
3 The inter-generational transmission of 'good' genes by selective reproduction among the genetically advantaged means that social hierarchy is the *natural* result of biological differences rather than stemming from differential access to cultural or material resources.

These three assertions depict society as a biological meritocracy. Social inequalities are both inevitable and fair, because they are *natural*. As an explanation of social inequality, this kind of deterministic account is claimed to be as legitimate as those accounts that see inequality as determined by cultural or economic circumstances. They are simply rival determinisms, although their policy implications are rather different. (All of these can, of course, be contrasted with those accounts of society that stress the role of human agency.) However, biological determinists argue that their case is grounded in the Darwinian principles of natural selection and can derive additional credibility from the achievements of this approach in other scientific domains.

The scientific context: Darwin's theory of natural selection

According to Darwin, **evolution** occurs through the conversion of variation *within* populations into differences *between* populations. Individual members of a population – whether animal, human, plant or whatever – differ. Darwin himself did not have the concept of genes available when he carried out his research, but subsequent work has shown that some of these differences have a genetic basis. This may be the result either of the mixing of genes in sexual reproduction or of random changes (**mutations**) caused by natural exposure to radiation or chemicals. Natural selection preserves those differences that favour the survival and reproduction of some individuals better than others under changing environmental conditions. A widely quoted example is that of Kettlewell's work in the 1950s on the peppered moth (see Kettlewell 1973). In the early 1800s, peppered moths were predominantly light grey in colour, with some black scales interspersed. Darker specimens, with more black colouration, were occasionally found. The light grey moths were able to camouflage themselves from their bird predators against tree bark. However, in 1848, an entirely black form was collected in Manchester, UK and, over the next hundred years, the black 'melanic' form came to make up more than 90 per cent of the population in the local area. With the advent of the industrial revolution and the heavy pollution that ensued, the melanic moths were better able to camouflage themselves against the now discoloured treebark. As a result, they were more likely to survive and reproduce. Their higher survival rate meant that they represented an increasing proportion of the population and were increasingly likely to mate with each other, increasing the proportion of moths with the gene for darker colouration in the next generation.

Box 2.1: Evolution as a continuous process

More recently, changes in industry combined with restrictive legislation have led to a decrease in the soot-based pollution that caused discolouration of tree bark. Lighter tree bark meant that the survival advantage for the black melanic moths was reversed. As this process has occurred, lighter moths have once more begun to thrive and once again form the predominant group. This process illustrates how advantageous characteristics are dependent on the environment and how they can change over time.

Although not illustrated in the example of the peppered moth, the concentration of genes produced by selective mating between organisms with particular characteristics can eventually lead to the emergence of a species related to, but distinct from, the original species. One example of this would be the way that woolly mammoths eventually evolved from early elephants.

Reproduction is the important element in natural selection. Although evolution is often described as the 'survival of the fittest', this phrase was actually coined by Herbert Spencer, later a pioneer of English sociology, in his *Principles of Biology* (1865) and only adopted by Darwin in a late edition of *Origin of Species*. Natural selection has its strongest effects on those characteristics that appear before and influence reproductive maturity. A modern example is sickle cell anaemia. This genetic condition can result in disability and early death but its high incidence in regions where malaria was prevalent led a British biologist, Anthony Allison, to consider the possibility that it was associated with a selective advantage. He discovered that having the sickle cell trait conferred resistance to malaria. In environments where malaria is prevalent, carriers are more likely to survive childhood and reproduce, so this genetic variant has been preserved by natural selection despite its associated disadvantages (Allison 1954). The speed with which natural selection operates is affected by the speed with which an organism can reproduce – a few hours for a bacterium and upwards of thirty years for an average woman of the professional classes in the developed world.

The Darwinian account of evolution is inherently amoral. Natural selection is a mechanism that operates on the basis of *random* genetic variation within populations to favour the perpetuation of some characteristics over others. It is also a fluid scheme. If we take a snapshot of any group of organisms at any particular moment, we simply see the current accommodation between them – each is constantly changing and, in doing so, changing the environment for the others. However, Darwin himself

---

Box 2.2: The 'selfish gene'

In recent years, some commentators have suggested that it is the *amoral* aspect of Darwinian theory that we find unsatisfactory in relation to human characteristics, rather than the theory itself. Richard Dawkins, a prominent evolutionary biologist, describes this in his book *The Selfish Gene*. He argues that although we may behave selfishly as individuals, in our societies we admire those who put the welfare of others first. Group-based theories of natural selection appeal to us because they are in line with the moral and political ideas that many of us share, or at least aspire to. For individual genes, however, evolutionary success is simply a matter of getting copied through reproduction (Dawkins 1976).

took a great interest in the way that humans had intervened in the process of natural selection in respect of some organisms that they valued. He made a close study of the work of dog and pigeon breeders, for example, who had deliberately manipulated variations within the species to emphasize characteristics like the shape of tails or colour markings. Although Darwin did not have the concept of a gene available to him, his work began to provide a theoretical basis for the genetic management of organisms.

Darwin himself was very cautious about the possible extension of his work to human populations, recognizing the extent to which humans could control their environments in ways other species could not. However, some of his followers were much less restrained. They saw a potential for realizing a human dream that was at least as old as the Ancient Greeks, namely a basis of legitimation for the management of populations. As Gould (1997) notes, Socrates had suggested that Citizens of the Republic should be educated and selected by merit into three classes – rulers, auxiliaries and craftsmen – symbolized by the metals gold, silver and bronze. He proposed to found this on a complex system of oracles and prophecies to ensure that these ranks were honoured and a stable society ensued. The extension of Darwin's ideas to social organization, however, borrowed from the prestige of their contribution to science. If you believed that England under Queen Victoria, the United States before the Great Crash of 1929 or Germany under National Socialism offered the perfect environment for human life, then natural selection meant that those who were less 'successful' were genuinely less fitted to existence in this utopia. Moreover, if we could manage the reproduction of animals, so that cows grew bigger, quicker and gave more milk, for example, why could we not manage the reproduction of humans in the same way? We might not easily be able to produce a 'better' human with the knowledge available at the time, but we could at least prevent the genes of the less fit from being perpetuated. The 'scientific' basis of these arguments gave them a weight in modern societies comparable to that of oracles or prophesies in Socrates's world.

Scientific knowledge and cultural context

In defending their viewpoint, biological determinists often invoke the prestige of science as objective knowledge, free from social and political taint. However, we have already noted determinism's value for powerful groups within a society, as an argument that legitimizes their privilege and enables them to represent inequality as unavoidable. Gould (1997) describes this linkage of power and policy as making nature an accomplice in the crime of political inequality.

Science is a socially embedded activity, carried out by people and funded by particular institutions, agencies or interests within particular social and cultural contexts. Its course of development is not independent of these social arrangements, although there is considerable debate about the extent and means of their influence on discovery. In a recent survey of sociological thinking on science and technology, MacKenzie and Wajcman (1999) conclude that scientists do not simply discover what is 'already there'. Discovery arises from an interaction between the material world and the metaphors, conceptual schema, experimental traditions and models of understanding that are available in any particular social and historical context. The results of scientific research are subject to interpretation in the light of these same contexts.

Constructing scientific knowledge: the sociology of science

Over recent years, science and its technological applications have increasingly become the subject of sociological study. This body of research is sometimes divided into two areas: what is referred to as the 'weak programme' of the sociology of science and the 'strong programme' of the sociology of scientific knowledge. The weak programme, often represented by the work of Merton (e.g. Merton 1973), has as its focus the study of science as a social institution and may simplistically be categorized as the study of the 'scientific community', examining the professionals working within it, the prescribed norms of the community, socialization into the community, and so on. The strong programme, by contrast, has developed more recently and focuses on the way scientific knowledge is arrived at. In this way, as Elston (1997) notes, sociologists have turned their attention to the processes through which scientists make judgements about the value of scientific representations of nature. This approach implies a sceptical stance towards scientific discovery in general, as opposed to the 'naïve' perspective that views it as a progressive process of discovery that gradually becomes closer and closer to an accurate representation of the natural world (Atkinson *et al.* 1997).

Elston (1997) describes how studies in the sociology of scientific knowledge (SSK) have tended to make their claims through detailed qualitative study and empirical example. The most influential study in the field is widely considered to be that of Latour and Woolgar (1979), based on Latour's extensive period of fieldwork in a French biochemistry laboratory. Latour aimed to follow closely the processes of scientific work, following not only what scientists did and how, but also the reasons and explanations that were given for these actions – the 'social construction' of science. He illuminated how this construction was a slow practical process, by which accounts were backed up or dismissed and through which statements gradually became transformed into scientific objects or facts into artefacts. As a result, he argues, reality in science is best viewed as the settlement of a dispute through which a fact becomes an accepted artefact. The SSK programme, as seen by Latour (1987), requires no preconceptions of what constitutes knowledge. In addition, social context and technical content are both essential to a proper understanding of scientific activity. This approach tends to be categorized as social constructionism.

Subsequent work in this field has built on Latour's approach, while bringing other perspectives to it. Gilbert and Mulkay's (1984) discourse analytic approach to scientists' discourse, for example, examines how scientists' accounts of their work are organized and how they portray themselves. In this sense, as the authors describe, it documents some of the methods used by scientists as they continually construct and reconstruct their world. Lynch (1985) takes an ethnomethodological approach to the study of the laboratory, interested not in explaining facts with reference to the social context of their production, or understanding discovery as a matter of social construction, but instead in the everyday practices and competencies through which scientists carry out their work, as collaboratively produced and coordinated actions.

Box 2.3: Key concepts from studies of scientific knowledge: actor-network theory and 'black boxes'

Actor-network theory is an approach to the study of scientific knowledge that 'focuses on the strategies scientists use for building networks to make findings into facts' (Fujimura 1996: 238). Within this approach, as Elston (1997) describes, the sociological task is to follow actors as they construct these networks. Analysis centres on the different work that actors do and the consequences that these have in advancing or undermining scientific claims. In this context, non-human entities can also be actors, for example computers, or scientific techniques such as DNA sequencing, which allow particular lines of research to be carried out.

A 'black box' is a concept used by cyberneticians whenever a piece of machinery or set of commands is too complex for straightforward description. In its place, they draw a little box, about which they only need to know its input and output (Latour 1987). An everyday example might be a personal computer. However, as Latour describes, the black box of a personal computer contains within it all the uncertainty, scientists at work, decisions, competition and controversies in the past of its development. Creating a black box makes an item of equipment, or of knowledge, distinct from the circumstances of its creation.

The relationships between science, technology and society

As Elston (1997) describes, studies of the sociology of scientific knowledge have tended to study 'science in action' rather than ready-made science or technology such as the use of novel treatments. However, since the early 1980s, the sociology of scientific knowledge has increasingly focused on technology as well as science. Where past work has tended to keep the concepts of science and technology analytically as well as conceptually distinct, there has been an increasing consensus that scientific knowledge and its technical applications are mutually constituted and cannot be artificially separated. For this reason, the term 'technoscience' is now often used to describe the subject of study.

MacKenzie and Wajcman (1999: xiv), in the introduction to their collection of essays examining aspects of the social shaping of technology, argue strongly against the rise of the paradigm they describe as technological determinism – the viewpoint in which technology is seen as 'a separate sphere, developing independently of society, following its own autonomous logic, and then having "effects" on society'. Clearly, developments that work technically (for example, GM food or genetic testing) will fail if they are too costly, unattractive to consumers, and so on. However, they also caution that social construction, or the social shaping of technology, is at too high a level a vacuous notion. We need to understand *how* and in what ways technology is socially shaped and what this tells us not only about technology, but also about society. Scientific theories are co-constructed along with social relationships and social structures.

Scientific procedures in the study of genetic inheritance

Two particular scientific procedures play an important role in the interpretation of, and meaning given to, studies of genetic inheritance, especially the studies of intelligence that will be considered in more detail in the next chapter. These are *reification* and *ranking* (Gould 1997).

Before we can measure anything, we first have to define what it is. Sometimes this is relatively unproblematic. The method for answering the question 'how tall are you?' is widely agreed upon, even if there might be some debate about the units of measurement to be employed – Imperial or metric, perhaps. However, as Gould notes, answering the question 'how intelligent are you?' is much more difficult. Since we recognize the importance of mental competence in our lives, we often wish to characterize it. Our ordinary language has a host of words for describing the relative intellectual capacities of the people around us – who is smart and who is stupid. These characterizations may then be used to make and justify distinctions within society – who goes to a regular school and who goes to special education, who gets to write software in Silicon Valley and who gets to clean the offices, who plays violin with the Berlin Philharmonic and who busks outside the concert hall. If we want to give these distinctions a scientific basis, however, whether taking advantage of the explanatory power of science or borrowing legitimacy from its cultural prestige, we have to find a way of defining and measuring them with as much agreement as we do about height.

In this case, though, there is nothing material to work with and to discipline our approach. We simply have a set of everyday concepts and distinctions that seem to capture *something* important to us. We can only handle these scientifically if we can find a way to treat them as if they were the same kind of material object as our bodies are when we measure their height, by *reifying* them. We generally do this by *operational definition*. What does this involve? Formally, it means that, rather than defining something in terms of its properties, we define it in terms of the procedures we use to measure it. With something like intelligence – or aggression, assertiveness or other behaviours – we identify a group of people who appear as a matter of common sense to show what we are looking for. We can then try to develop a measurement procedure that produces appropriate scores for people in this group. Many intelligence tests, for example, were originally devised for people with learning disabilities and designed to produce scores that distinguished them from the 'normal' population. Having created this procedure, 'intelligence' can be defined as the score on the test, since that score simply reflects 'what everybody knows' about people and gives it a numerical expression.

There is no intrinsic reason why mental competence should not be treated as contextual and measured in a variety of ways for a variety of purposes, as occupational psychologists do on an individual basis for many commercial organizations. In modern societies, however, much of the demand for testing is linked to an agenda of social discrimination, of a demand for *ranking* on an apparently objective, impersonal and scientific basis. Mass testing requires much simpler tests and is less accommodating to complex notions of individual or contextual variation in capacity. It reduces intelligence – or other behaviour – to simple terms so that it can be represented as a standard entity.

The end result is a kind of circularity: intelligence *is* what intelligence tests measure. Those tests are required to show a high degree of consistency in results from day to day because intelligence is defined as if it were a material object that should not be expected to vary. Tests that do not show this are likely to be discarded as unreliable. Tests are also expected to correlate highly with each other, since they are just different ways of looking at the same thing. Again discrepant tests are likely to be discarded. The correlation that results from this selection, however, is widely treated as some general capacity that underlies the specific dimensions being tested, usually labelled g for *general intelligence*. The g factor is often identified with the genetic component of intelligence, but it is important to understand that it is purely a statistical artefact for which no material reference has ever been established. The use of g in intelligence testing is discussed in more detail in Chapter 3.

Arguments about the relative merits and ranking of individuals have a long history and have used many bases of legitimacy. The acceptability of slavery in the eighteenth and nineteenth centuries, for example, was founded in part on Biblical interpretations that defined black people as a separate and unequal species. In this context, hierarchy between and within social groups was seen as part of the Christian God's plan for the world, as the verse from the hymn 'All things bright and beautiful' illustrates:

The rich man in his castle
The poor man at his gate
God made them high or lowly
And order'd their estate

These views never went unchallenged. There were also readings of the Bible that emphasized the common humanity of all people and inspired popular protest and social activism from medieval times onward. However, the argument was always in terms of the way in which particular texts were to be read and the relative importance to be given to conflicting Biblical messages.

The early nineteenth-century scientific developments in biology and geology that culminated in Darwin's *Origin of Species*, first published in 1859, meant that such traditional justifications for discrimination on the basis of race, class or gender had to be reviewed. Science overtook religion, but it did not eliminate the demand for discrimination. Instead, the debate about social hierarchy was carried on in scientific language and founded on 'scientific' justifications.

Darwin and Galton

Darwin's cousin, Francis Galton, made an important contribution to the application of this new biological thinking to human societies. Believing that mental qualities were inherited just as much as hair or eye colour, he concluded that they could also be affected by selective breeding.

Galton coined the term 'eugenics' in 1883 (from the Greek, meaning 'good in birth') to describe the active management of human reproduction according to the principles of racial science in order to favour the reproduction of the fittest and to discourage the reproduction of the less fit. As we note later, Galton's ideas attracted interest across a wide political spectrum. However, their policy impact in Britain was limited. In 1904, for example, the Interdepartmental Committee on Physical Deterioration, which had been set up to examine claims that the poor health of recruits to the army during the South African wars reflected a decline in the quality of the British racial stock, dismissed this argument and blamed the soldiers' conditions squarely on poor environments, nutrition and health care.

Elsewhere, however, hereditarian biology had a strong influence on public policies. In 1913, for example, the United States began intelligence testing of immigrants arriving at Ellis Island to determine who would be allowed to enter the country. Groups such as southern Europeans performed poorly, on average, in these tests, and the results, seen as evidence of hereditary incapacity, were used to justify legislation that made it more difficult for such groups to gain entry to the USA. From 1920 onwards, 24 states in the USA, several Canadian provinces and some European countries such as Sweden passed laws authorizing the compulsory sterilization of various groups. In the state of Virginia, for example, more than 7500 people were sterilized between 1924 and 1972, having been defined as 'feeble minded' or antisocial in other ways that were believed to have a biological basis. This included prostitutes, unwed mothers and petty criminals. Attempts to pass similar laws in Britain failed, but voluntary sterilization was widely advocated and the medical superintendents of some institutions for the mentally ill or handicapped do not seem to have been quite as scrupulous about consent as modern standards would require.

Kevles' (1995) comprehensive history of eugenics describes how the justification for these laws linked the greater public good to the management of biological inevitability. Oliver Wendell Holmes, delivering the Supreme Court's decision upholding the Virginia sterilization law in 1927, stated:

> We have seen more than once that the public welfare may call upon the best citizens for their lives: it would be strange if it could not call upon those who already sap the strength of the state for these lesser sacrifices . . . three generations of imbeciles are enough.
>
> (cited in Kevles 1995: 111)

The rationale for these policies only began seriously to be questioned after the Second World War, when the full scale and horror of the German National Socialists' eugenics campaign, beginning in the 1930s and culminating in the 'Final Solution' of 1941, became apparent. Less drastic versions of the same practices had been widely accepted in Europe and North America, partly on economic grounds and partly as encouraging general public welfare. Again, it is important to acknowledge that many of the advocates of eugenics in these countries would have seen themselves as compassionate and progressive men and women who were bringing a humane benefit to those who were the object of the policy as much as benefiting society in general.

At the end of the Second World War, however, the best defence against the atrocities committed by the Nazis was seen to be a renewed emphasis on the human rights of individuals in the face of the claims of science or the wider society. This is exemplified in the Nuremberg Declaration on the rights of medical research subjects and the European Convention on Human Rights, signed in 1950. These rights could not be abridged or infringed in pursuit of some higher good.

However, this view has recently been challenged, by the suggestion that focusing on the good of the individual, rather than the good of society, may itself be unethical. Contemporary China is sometimes cited as an example: its population exceeds 1.2 billion and its geneticists broadly support eugenic policies. It is argued that the grief of those who are prevented from reproducing is likely to be less than the pain created by the addition of their potential descendants to a population that is already thought to be unsustainable. Individual choice should not be privileged over the greater good of society as a whole in the area of reproduction any more than it is in terms of, for example, criminal behaviour. Since new genetic technologies provide more sophisticated methods of distinguishing between 'good' and 'bad' genes and may, in the future, provide the opportunity to turn bad genes into good ones, they are increasingly invoked in this argument by both sides.

The Eugenics Society in the UK

The distinctive British experience of eugenic policy and practice has already been mentioned. The final part of this chapter examines the formation of the Eugenics Society in the UK to demonstrate more specifically how the history of genetics and the history of social science are entwined.

The Eugenics Society, originally called the Eugenics Education Society, was founded in 1907 in Britain by followers of Francis Galton, with the objective of promoting those agencies under social control that might improve the human race. As this definition shows, its interests lay in both human biology and social problems and, in particular, in Galton's theories of the heritability of intelligence. Its members were mainly biologists, social scientists and social activists.

Mazumdar's (1992) comprehensive history of the Society highlights a common misconception. Reflecting present-day uses of hereditarian biology as discussed in Chapter 3, it is often assumed that the Society had a conservative political agenda. In reality, its formation owed more to the efforts of middle-class reformers to improve the lives of their social inferiors. These efforts long pre-dated the appearance of the hereditarianism associated with Galton, but this approach seemed to offer a new method of dealing with the apparently intractable problem of the pauper class. Membership of the Eugenics Society overlapped with others in a network of activists: eugenics had many supporters in the Fabian Society, where the management of reproduction formed part of their general approach to social reform through the enlightened and scientifically based action of a progressive elite.

As Mazumdar (1992) notes, the appeal of Galton's theories for the Eugenics Society was that its members saw the pauper class not only in terms of its dependency on the Poor Law, but also as a self-contained breeding group. If the breeding of this class, which was prolific relative to the middle class, were not controlled, pauperism and its associated undesirable qualities would continue to increase. The end result would be that the evolutionary direction of the human race was reversed.

To persuade audiences to accept this principle of 'negative selection', the Society's lecturers used pedigrees of pauper families. These attempted to show how pauperism, together with other undesirable qualities such as alcoholism, was passed on through inheritance. These examples of social undesirability were contrasted with other pedigrees showing inheritance of desirable characteristics such as intellectual ability. The model family most often chosen was that of Darwin and Galton, whose pedigree is reproduced in Fig. 2.1. The pedigree claims to show the inheritance of brilliance, and scientific ability, with men represented by squares and women by circles. Despite the general prevalence of brilliance in the family, it appears that these characteristics failed to be transmitted to any of its female members!

As a method of persuasion, the pedigrees worked well, although of course their scientific validity is entirely dubious; what the findings represent is merely the recognition of a pattern that has not been proven to have a biological cause. That these pedigrees were so influential despite this serves to demonstrate the extraordinary power of scientific 'knowledge',

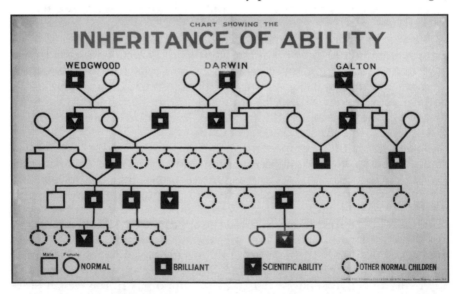

Figure 2.1 Pedigree of the Wedgwood-Darwin-Galton family, as used by the Eugenics Society. Reproduced with the permission of the Galton Institute and the Wellcome Library, London.

and the enthusiasm with which it was received, at this time. Mazumdar (1992) describes how, in the presentation of these pedigrees, there was often no analysis in terms of any theory of transmission, but instead a simple presentation of the claim that like produced like.

As we have seen already, from its beginnings in Britain located in the work of Galton, the eugenics movement spread to many other countries. In each country, the ideal type, who were to be encouraged to breed, and its negative image, to be discouraged, were different, reflecting national background and historical context: in Britain, those to be discouraged were casual labourers, paupers and the feeble minded; in the USA, immigrants from southern Europe; in Germany, at least initially, psychotics and psychopaths, and later the feeble minded. It is interesting to note that there was no element of social class included in the German programme, given that National Socialism itself was in part a revolt against the German aristocracy.

Members of the Eugenics Society campaigned to legalize voluntary sterilization and to promote birth control; for them, pauperism was a hereditary biological defect unconnected to the distribution of property, status or power. In other words, their research and campaigning emphasized heredity at the expense of environment and nature at the expense of nurture. In the course of this effort, they made major contributions to the development of statistical methods for social science and the emergence of the academic discipline of social policy: Richard Titmuss's first post, for example, was as a research assistant with the Society.

The eugenic movement finally fell apart in the 1950s. In part, as we have seen, this resulted from the stigma of Nazi racial science. However, it was also widely believed that post-war social and economic reconstruction would eliminate pauperism through social justice and economic growth. Biological theories were seen as irrelevant and obsolete. Ironically, advances in the science of genetics itself were also showing up the weaknesses of the eugenicist's simple models.

Where does this leave us now?

The forced sterilization of 'undesirables' has now been replaced by individuals actively seeking genetic screening and testing for themselves. However, developments since the 1980s in human genetics have revived some old fears. This is particularly true of biological determinism. The last 30 years have borne witness to incredible scientific advances in molecular biology, with the discovery of genes that cause disease, such as Huntington's disease and cystic fibrosis, and the mapping of whole chromosomes and even the whole human genome. There are undisputable benefits to the new genetics. Gould (1997) demonstrates the humane value of identifying biological bases for particular conditions, using the example of autism. Autism was once thought to be psychogenic and blamed on parents: we can now avoid that distressing imputation. More broadly, the knowledge of a genetic contribution to common diseases, such as coronary heart disease, offers the opportunity for carriers of the gene(s) to take preventative action. However, we need to remain wary of fatalistic genetic explanations. When eugenicists attributed diseases of poverty to the inferior genetic constitution of poor people, their only answer was sterilization. But, as Gould (1997) argues, when Goldberger proved that pellagra (a disease common in poor families) was not a genetic disorder, but a vitamin deficiency resulting from poor diet, he could cure it.

However, and despite technological advances, we have not found genetic answers to all, or even many, of the questions to which they have been sought. Although frequencies for different states of genotype differ between human populations, we have failed to find any 'race genes' that are fixed in certain races and absent from others. By contrast, studies of genetic variation show that there is more genetic variation within populations than there is between them, making any genetic explanation for race unsustainable. Equally, despite the impression media reports may give, we have no gene 'for' criminality or homosexuality. Moreover, the existence of a genetic contribution to a condition such as coronary heart disease does not mean that it is inevitable or cannot be modified in any other way.

Ultimately, the arguments of biological determinism are undermined by biological determinists themselves, because of the features they call upon in justifying distinctions between groups. These features are usually *cultural* products rather than biological ones – for example, performance in intelligence tests, attitudes, and so on. Societies change because social, economic and cultural activity alters the physical, social and cultural conditions under which these activities occur. As the Sociobiology Study Group (1978) note, feudal society did not decline because of an evolved increase in the frequency of entrepreneurs in the population. The economic dynamic of Western feudal society itself changed economic relations. Serfs became peasants and peasants became landless industrial workers as part of vast changes in other social institutions.

The decline of sociobiology as an explanatory paradigm for human behaviour, however, has not meant the end of Darwinian explanations in this context. The late twentieth century has seen the development of a new discipline, evolutionary psychology, that brings with it some sociobiological principles. As Malik (2000) describes, sociobiology was seen not only as a biological endeavour, but also as a political one, and was often criticized on political grounds in terms of the inequalities it sought to reinforce. Evolutionary psychology may be seen as the modern version of sociobiology, in that it also aims to develop an improved Darwinian science of human nature. However, the key object of study for the evolutionary psychologist is, as the name suggests, psychology rather than behaviour. In particular, it is argued that we need to distinguish between *proximate* and *ultimate* causes for behaviour. Although

---

Box 2.4: Evolutionary psychology and the mind

Leda Cosmides, one of the founders of evolutionary psychology as a discipline, offers the following analogy for the mind. The mind is best conceptualised as a Swiss Army knife, with a different blade (or 'module') for every task. Each of these modules is an adaptation that has come about through natural selection, in order to solve a particular problem faced by our ancestors. This analogy illustrates the two basic claims of evolutionary psychology: that the mind is composed of modules, each designed for a particular task; and that these modules have been 'designed' by natural selection.

(Cosmides, cited in Malik 2000: 194)

---

the ultimate cause may be genetic, proximate causes incorporate individual desires, beliefs and attitudes.

Although evolutionary psychology has been criticized from a sociological point of view for the emphasis it places on biological factors, it has not been treated with the same widespread hostility that sociobiology began to receive in the mid-twentieth century. Malik (2000) argues that this is inextricably linked with societal change. Darwin's theory of evolution emerged in an intellectual climate that was already open to biological ideas – for example, the widely held belief that there were biological differences between races. Malik suggests that there is a similar process at work today, because changing social concepts of freedom have come to focus firmly on the individual. This individual focus in turn makes us more receptive to a mechanistic view of what it is to be human. In making this point, the synergy between changing political and social ideas of the human self and biological depictions of human nature becomes clear once again.

This is not to say, however, that some biological constraints are not fundamental to our lives, such as the relatively narrow range of adult size in humans or the ageing process. However, as Gould (1997) indicates, sociobiologists – and, more recently, evolutionary psychologists – always seem to be tempted to seek the genetic basis of human behaviour at the wrong level: Jane's homosexuality or Paul's aggression rather than the cultural constructions of sexuality and violence in the society where Jane and Paul live. Warfare is often used as evidence for the alleged innate aggression of humankind. But if people can also be peaceable, then aggression cannot be directly coded in our genes: at best we can only talk about a potential for aggression under particular environmental conditions. The concept of aggression only has meaning as a contrast with a concept of peaceableness. The question 'What is the basis of aggression?' is far more complex than most sociobiologists allow.

In Gould's (1978) critique of sociobiology, he argues that human behaviour is not a straight division between nature (what we are born with) and nurture (what we acquire from our environment, upbringing, culture, etc.). The real polarity is between determinism and potentiality: the genetic potential or possibility for people to develop or acquire certain traits in certain contexts or environments. As Ramsay (1994: 258) puts it:

> If we reduce societies to individuals, and individuals to their genes, we cannot put the pieces back together again and expect to understand them, for we deny the interaction between genes and the environment, the individual and society.

Summary points

- Although the 'new genetics' is sometimes equated with the 'new eugenics', the philosophical roots of an individualist view of social problems go back much further.

- The principles of reductionism and biological determinism allow explanations for social phenomena to be located in the biological make-up of individuals.

- Darwin's theory of natural selection provided scientific weight for the proponents of eugenics and was used to justify social hierarchies as a *natural* occurrence.

- From a sociological point of view, the results of scientific research are not pure 'discoveries', but are informed by and interpreted within the social and cultural context of a society.

- In the first half of the twentieth century, eugenic policies were widespread in the USA and Europe. The Eugenics Society was founded in the UK in 1907.

- The formation of the Eugenics Society in the UK can be traced back to the efforts of the reforming middle classes to improve the lives of their inferiors. In this sense, it was informed by a much more liberal policy agenda than is commonly acknowledged.

- The new genetics again raises the spectre of biological determinism. It is suggested here that the argument should not focus on nature *vs* nurture, but rather on determinism *vs* potentiality.

Further reading

Badcock, C. (2000) *Evolutionary Psychology: A Critical Introduction*. London: Polity Press.

Farrell, L.A. (1979) The history of eugenics: a bibliographical review, *Annals of Science*, 36: 111–23.

Kevles, D. (1995) *In the Name of Eugenics: Genetics and the Uses of Human Heredity*. Cambridge, MA: Harvard University Press.

Thom, D. and Jennings, M. (1996) Human pedigree and the 'best stock': from eugenics to genetics?, in T. Marteau and M. Richards (eds) *The Troubled Helix: Social and Psychological Implications of the New Human Genetics*. Cambridge: Cambridge University Press.

Wilson, E.O. (1980) *Sociobiology: The Abridged Edition*. Cambridge, MA: Harvard University Press.

3

GENETICS AND BEHAVIOUR

Introduction

This chapter considers the evidence for the biological basis of human traits and behaviours, with reference to four areas: aggression, alcoholism, homosexuality and intelligence. Although there is a historical tradition of debate as to the causal factors of all these conditions, all four have also been the subject of recent research and high-profile media reporting. In the case of the first three, the evidence behind the reporting of 'a gene for' aggression, alcoholism and homosexuality will be considered. The fourth area, intelligence, will be examined in more detail as a case study of the potential implications of this line of scientific research and the ends to which it may be used. The chapter concludes with a consideration of the ways in which contemporary biological research may become entwined with social and political agendas.

In considering the body of research in this area, one of the fundamental questions to be asked is 'Why search for a gene "for" a particular behaviour?' Social scientists have argued that, with the major advances in genetic science at the end of the twentieth century, the gene has become a kind of 'cultural icon' and has given rise to genetic essentialism, where individuals and their traits and characteristics are reduced to genes (Nelkin and Lindee 1995). In the same way, the social problems that may be created by these particular traits and characteristics can be reduced to genes. This reductionism is attractive, as we have seen in Chapter 2, because it offers a way of viewing social problems as discrete and controllable, arising as a result of problematic individuals rather than more widespread societal problems.

This distinction between private problems and public issues is not, of course, a new one. In *The Sociological Imagination*, C. Wright Mills (1959) identifies it as a key area for sociological endeavour. He argues that what may seem to be private troubles are the result, at the individual level, of the working out of the problems of the society that an individual lives in. One example of this is unemployment: although unemployment may be viewed solely as a problem for the unemployed individual, it cannot realistically be divorced from the social and structural arena in which that unemployment occurs. Mills concludes that sociologists must use 'the sociological imagination' to look at personal troubles as public issues, a view that is in direct conflict with that of genetic reductionism.

How is research into human behaviour carried out?

Although much genetic research relies on the selective breeding of laboratory animals, it is obvious that this kind of highly controlled experimental process cannot be used in the investigation of human traits and behaviours. The selective breeding or raising of children in highly controlled environments is unlikely to be seen as ethically acceptable in any circumstances (Renfrew 1997). In these circumstances, **monozygotic** (identical) twins, who share the same genetic identity, have provided researchers with a natural opportunity for study. Since they share the same genetic components, any differences in traits or behaviour can potentially be linked to environmental factors. Traditionally, these studies have used monozygotic twins who have been separated at birth, in an attempt to separate out the effects of environment and genetics. The goal of these twin studies is heritability estimates, based on the similarities and differences that are exhibited between twins. However, this research population has always been small and has become increasingly so with the advent of better social welfare systems and adoption policies that aim to place and keep siblings together. For this reason, as McGuire (1995) points out, it has become more common to study **dizygotic** (fraternal or non-identical) twins as a comparison group. If both types of twin have experienced the same environments, then heritability estimates can also be made as a result.

Twin studies have been criticized on methodological grounds for several reasons. In particular, before the advent of sophisticated DNA technology, it is possible that fraternal twins who simply happened to look similar were included in these studies. The low numbers of subjects are potentially problematic in terms of generalizability of results. Since there are so few potential subjects in the first place, it is difficult to exclude them, for example in trying to ensure a representative sample or to exclude potential bias. Additionally, as Renfrew (1997) observes, experimenter bias is not always taken into account or controlled for. If the experimental results from one twin are known, this might influence the reported outcome from the other twin.

Although these studies form the historical basis of the work into the genetic basis of behaviour, in recent years advances in molecular biology have led to a different kind of research programme. Increasingly, there has been an attempt to identify specific genes, or genetic variations, which can account for the behavioural differences seen in individuals. These two strands of research will now be considered in relation to the four areas identified at the beginning of this chapter.

Aggression

Renfrew (1997) suggests that we may suspect genetic influences on aggression for two reasons. First, if an individual from a 'normal' family is especially aggressive, then the shared environment of the family members may suggest a biological basis in this individual. Second, if many members of a family are aggressive, a genetic link may be suspected. Paradoxically, these two reasons potentially cover all eventualities, meaning that the presence or absence of aggression in other family members may be taken as evidence for a biological basis in an individual! Early studies in this area tended to focus on families (e.g. the 'Kallikak' family; Goddard 1912), many of whom were involved in crime and socially undesirable activities. The framework surrounding this kind of work is highlighted in the following description by Renfrew (1997: 26): 'Interestingly, the Kallikaks had a normal or superior branch, descended from a formal marriage, and a troubled branch, descended from a liaison with a woman of subnormal intelligence and questionable morals'. Renfrew goes on to describe how the problems of this second branch of the family were thought to have come about through the contamination of a 'good' gene pool by 'bad blood' from the second woman, as illustrated in Fig. 3.1. Although these conclusions were in line with the preconceptions of the time (cf. Galton's pedigrees of feeble mindedness discussed in the previous chapter), there is little consideration given to the potential impact of social or environmental factors such as poverty, lack of education or social exclusion on these findings.

In terms of the biological evidence for a genetic basis for aggression, key early work revolves around twin studies. Mednick (1981, cited in Renfrew 1997) reviewed evidence from many twin studies and suggested that, for identical twins, there was a 60 per cent rate of concordance for problems caused by their aggression. For fraternal twins, this figure was 30 per cent. However, the twin studies on which these estimates were based were problematic, essentially because larger numbers of twins than seemed likely to exist had been included in some of the study populations. In addition, as Renfrew (1997) notes, several of these studies had been undertaken in Nazi Germany with the attendant likelihood of political bias in the context of justifying an ongoing programme of eugenics. In 1973, taking a slightly different approach, Hutchings and Mednick examined the criminal records of biological and adoptive fathers of 143 criminals. They found that there was evidence of criminal convictions in

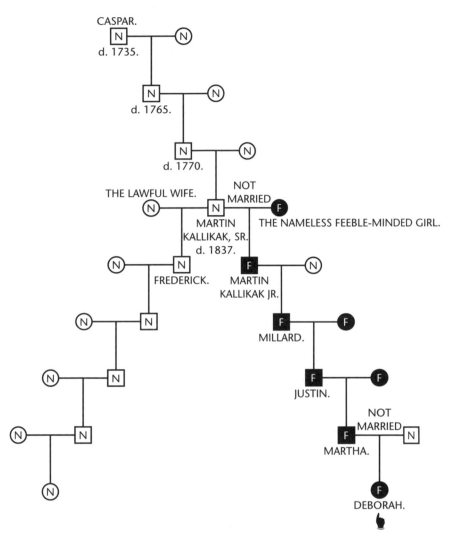

Figure 3.1 The Kallikak family pedigree showing the 'normal' (N) and 'feebleminded' (F) branches of the family

70 of the biological fathers but in only 33 of the adoptive ones. Interestingly, in a mixed group of adoptees both with and without criminal records, they found rates of criminality highest in adoptees where both biological and adoptive fathers had criminal records (36 per cent), followed by biological father alone (21 per cent) and adoptive father alone (10–11 per cent). What this indicates is a correlation between criminality in biological parents and their children, but it does not provide evidence of any genetic causality. Other work suggests a similar pattern of evidence where biological mothers are concerned.

The most recent and perhaps most famous attempt to locate a genetic basis for aggression is the study of XYY syndrome. Individuals with this disorder have an extra male sex chromosome (Y). As Renfrew (1997) describes, since males are generally thought to be more aggressive than females, the rationale for research into this disorder was that the presence of this extra male chromosome might lead to extra aggression. The original work that suggested a correlation was carried out by Jacobs *et al.* (1965), using biological samples from inmates of an institution for the criminally insane. The higher than expected incidence of XYY individuals in the institution (estimated to be approximately 300 times greater than in a normal population) suggested a causal role in criminality. Physical differences and lower intelligence in the XYY sample were also found. The theory was widely publicized and gained such common currency that it began to be used as a criminal defence.

Subsequent research, however, began to discredit this apparently straightforward link between XYY and aggression. Limited sample sizes, varying estimates of the incidence of XYY in the wider population, and the use of newborn babies who had a limited exposure to environmental factors as a control group were all grounds on which the original study was criticized. Others have drawn different conclusions to those of Jacobs *et al.* For example, Witkin (1976) concluded that the extent to which XYY individuals are disproportionately found in the prison population might simply reflect the association of XYY with lower than average intelligence. It is not that they are inherently more likely to commit crime than any other group, but that if they do commit crime they are more likely to be caught and subsequently to be convicted. The only certain conclusion to be drawn, then, is that the effect of XYY syndrome on aggression is uncertain. Renfrew (1997) makes an important point in describing the alternative explanation – that if XYY individuals tend to be larger and less intelligent than the male population in general, differential social treatment in terms of the way that society reacts to a large, unintelligent male may be just as important. Nevertheless, research continues and suggestions of a causal link of some kind are still common, since the hypothesis has not been definitively rejected by the scientific community.

Proving scientific claims

In the previous chapter, we examined the sceptical stance that sociologists of scientific knowledge have taken towards scientific discovery, rejecting naïve accounts of science as a progression towards ever more accurate representations of the natural world. Atkinson *et al.* (1997), in considering the stance of the sociology of scientific knowledge (SSK) programme, argue that popular accounts of science actively promote this naïve imagery and, as a result, controversy between scientists, the process of laboratory practice and the ways in which findings are interpreted and represented become marginalized. From a sociological perspective, however, these 'discoveries' do not establish themselves unequivocally, but must go through a process of recognition and legitimization. By way of example, they state that the reported discovery of a particular gene

> is not an event in itself. The discovery is not merely a claim entered by particular groups or individuals, it is a process of accounts and constructions. The discovery claim itself must be entered and supported through various modes of accounting and representation, and its status as a discovery is subject to processes of definition and redefinition – on the part of the scientists themselves and by others in the scientific community.
>
> (Atkinson *et al.* 1997: 123)

The 'discovery' and subsequent disconfirmation of the link between XYY individuals and aggressive behaviour is a clear illustration of the way scientific 'knowledge' can be constructed, represented and pass into common use, only to be subsequently rejected. As we have seen in the previous chapter, these constructions and representations may be bound up with wider social and political agendas and prevailing views of human nature.

The implications of 'a gene for' aggression

If the search for a genetic basis for aggression is successful, what are the likely consequences? A tendency to aggression is not a discrete disorder that can be controlled or treated in the way that disease states such as haemochromatosis or cystic fibrosis can. Raising the question of what societies might practically do with this knowledge poses some uncomfortable answers. If aggression is linked to genetics alone, aggressive behaviour may be condoned or seen as inevitable. The principle of the individual's responsibility for their own behaviour is undermined. This type of outcome has already been seen in the 1970s in the attempted use of XYY syndrome as a defence in criminal trials.

The second potential consequence relates to reinforcing gender stereotypes. Research has suggested that males are more genetically aggressive than females. Some commentators have argued that this knowledge may be used to discriminate, for example, against women working in the armed forces or in management positions, and against men in positions where these characteristics are undesirable (e.g. in childcare work or professions such as nursing).

The third potential consequence relates to much wider issues and can itself be identified by posing a question. If the search is successful, what happens to the civil liberties of those identified with a gene for aggression? What kind of 'preventative measures' might be taken? Restrictions on freedom, in the form of surveillance or detention, are one obvious possible scenario. Nelkin and Lindee (1995) recognize the appeal for policy that lies in predicting and preventing crime by identifying those thought to have 'criminal genes'. However, on the basis of this kind of genetic screening, there is no way of distinguishing those who carry the genes and do go on to commit a criminal act and those who do not. As a result, innocent people may be categorized on the basis of an apparent violent *potential*.

Box 3.1: Fictional representations of biological determinism

In Philip Kerr's (1992) novel, *A Philosophical Investigation*, the central premise is that, by the year 2013, the biological determinants of crime are readily identifiable. A small percentage of men are born lacking the structure that helps to regulate violent impulses. These men (called 'VMN negatives') are likely, although not certain, to become serial killers. There is a test for the condition, the results of which are released only to the individual and to a computer system that will inform the criminal justice system if he is involved in a criminal investigation. However, the security of this system becomes compromised and those in the system begin to be killed themselves. The novel raises questions of the effects of labelling individuals as potential criminals, of confidentiality of information and of the uses and abuses of biological knowledge.

Clearly, the scale of possible abuses of this kind of solution will potentially increase as the interest in behavioural genetics increases. Social perceptions and social stereotyping are key factors here, reminding us of how, in the past, some of those interested in the study of heredity have found evidence to support the preconceptions they began their research with. Galton's pedigrees (discussed in the previous chapter) showing the undesirable characteristics of impoverished slum-dwellers owe as much to his desire to promote a selective breeding programme and to the social circumstances of the individuals in question as to any evidence that these characteristics were innate or inherited. In the same way, Nelkin and Lindee (1995) describe a scenario of selective testing of black males for criminality genes, as a result of current stereotypes associating crime with race.

Alcoholism

Although research interest in the biological basis of alcoholism is more recent than that of aggression, Ball and Murray (1994) suggest that it is generally accepted that alcoholism runs in families. Like aggression, however, alcoholism is not a homogenous disorder but a subjective definition, and studies often provide little information about how they are using the definition (e.g. frequency of drinking, quantity).

Box 3.2: Alcohol and behaviour

Evidence from anthropological studies suggests the strong influence of social and cultural factors, and individual expectations, on
the effects of alcohol. MacAndrew and Edgerton's (1969) systematic
analysis of the empirical evidence relating to drunken behaviour
(for example, aggression and promiscuity) demonstrated a profound
difference between the conventionally accepted effects of alcohol
upon comportment and the empirical evidence of how people
actually behave when drunk. In some societies, drunkenness does
not result in 'disinhibited' behaviour; in others, its effects appear to
have varied over time.

Family studies demonstrate an association between genetics and
alcoholism, but also confirm a significant environmental component.
Cotton's (1979) review of 39 family studies concluded that alcoholics as
defined by these studies were six times more likely than non-alcoholics
to report parental alcoholism. At the same time, however, she demonstrated the high proportion of alcoholics without a parental history of
alcoholism, with the studies she reviewed reporting this figure as any-
where between 47 and 82 per cent. Therefore, although there is clearly a
familial component involved, the source of this component is much less
clear. Examining pedigrees of families affected by alcoholism indicates
that simple single gene models of inheritance cannot explain inheritance patterns. For example, more men than women are affected, but
whether an affected relative is male or female does not appear to alter
the risk for other relatives (Ball and Murray 1994). Another complicating
factor is the link between alcoholism and psychiatric symptoms. In some
studies, samples have been drawn from attendees or inmates of mental
health institutions, suggesting that what is presented as evidence for the
genetic basis of alcoholism may actually represent a genetic component
of psychiatric disorders.

The strongest historical evidence for a genetic component to alcoholism comes from adoption studies, which have tended to show an increased rate in alcoholism in those adoptees with an alcoholic biological
parent. More recently, evidence for an actual genetic link was presented
by Blum *et al.* (1990). Using cadaver brains from alcoholics and non-
alcoholics, they identified an area on the D2 dopamine receptor that
they believed was involved in severe cases of alcoholism. Much media
attention followed, although their results were subsequently disconfirmed
by researchers at the US National Institute on Alcohol Abuse and Alcoholism. Holden (1991) has suggested that scientists are now beginning to
suspect that there are no genes 'for' alcoholism as such, but instead a

general susceptibility to compulsive behaviours of which heavy drinking is only one possible manifestation. The specific way in which this behaviour expressed itself would depend on environmental and temperamental factors.

The implications of 'a gene for' alcoholism

As with studies on aggression, it is worth considering what the end result of successful research in this area might be. If a genetic influence on alcoholism is conclusively found, then this may offer opportunities for treatment. Since current thinking links alcoholism to other types of compulsive behaviour, these opportunities may extend to other compulsions, such as eating disorders or gambling. However, there are similar issues in relation to those raised by aggression as to how this knowledge might practically be used. Identification itself will not help in management, without further steps that might curtail an individual's liberties. How, and by whom, would these be imposed and policed?

Homosexuality

Although the search for a biological basis for alcoholism may be relatively recent, biological theories of homosexuality can be traced back to the discourse on reproduction and sexuality that began in the nineteenth century. Herrn (1995) describes how these theories were attempts not only to explain the cause of homosexuality, but also to maintain the social exclusion of homosexuals as 'other' and to propose medical 'cures'. The influence of Darwin's work on sexual selection led to a prevailing view of the individual measured by useful contribution to reproduction; non-reproducing individuals were seen as 'unfit'. This dichotomy, between those who consider homosexuality to be simply an alternative state and those who view it as a pathological disposition, has continued. With the advent of the first genetic theories of homosexuality around the turn of the nineteenth century came the beginnings of the eugenics movement, and genetic theories were used as justification for the eradication of homosexuals in Nazi Germany. However, there was no tangible biological evidence for these theories (the numbers of twins potentially available for study here were even less than in other cases) and certainly none at a genetic level.

The popular currency of the idea of a gene 'for' homosexuality can be traced back to media reporting of the work of Hamer et al. (1993). In an attempt to examine the inheritance pattern of homosexuality, the authors recruited 114 homosexual male volunteers and questioned them about the sexual orientation of their fathers, sons, brothers, uncles and male cousins. The pedigree charts that were subsequently assembled indicated that the men's brothers, maternal uncles and maternal cousins had a significantly higher probability of being gay than would be expected by comparison to the incidence of homosexuality in the general population. By contrast, fathers and paternally related relatives had average or less than average rates of homosexuality (the average was estimated as 2 per cent). One explanation for this apparent pattern of maternal transmission of a trait is linkage to the X chromosome, which male children inherit from their mother. Laboratory analysis of the X chromosomes of 40 pairs of homosexual brothers found a cluster of identical markers in the region known as Xq28 in 64 per cent of the pairs. However, the Xq28 region contains several hundred genes. Hamer *et al.* were careful to report that what they had found through their research was a genetic predisposition, rather than a genetic determination, and that multiple genes might be involved. In addition, not all of the homosexual men in their sample carried the X-chromosomal region they had identified. However, as Wilkins (1993) describes, the press was sometimes content to report this as a finding of either 'a gay gene' or 'the gay gene' and over the next two or three years the term became common currency. This kind of reporting is a clear illustration of common misconceptions about the genetic determination of complex human traits. To quote Conrad (1997: 142), 'For most people, the reality of science is what they know from the press'.

The implications of 'a gene for' homosexuality

Researchers continue to investigate the link between genetics and homosexuality, but in this case opinion is strongly divided as to what the likely outcome of a successful search would be. Some believe that the successful search for a biological basis of homosexuality will advance the search for equality and be a further cause of gay liberation, since if it can be established as a biological, and hence natural, variation, it will be seen as more acceptable to society at large. This view is particularly important in cultures where there is strong religious opposition to homosexuality, as in some parts of the USA. The opposing argument, however, is that by ascribing homosexuality to a genetic variation or mutation, it will come to be viewed as a disease or disorder in the same way as those caused by other types of genetic mutation. Just as parents may use **pre-implantation** or prenatal diagnosis in choosing not to have a child with cystic fibrosis, so they may opt for 'orientation selection' to ensure the sexual orientation of their child.

From a sociological point of view, there is a particular criticism to be made of biological research into sexuality. Researchers often assert a homosexual–heterosexual dichotomy, but there are not necessarily such clear distinctions to be made. Sexual behaviour can be difficult to put into such distinct categories, and sexuality may be viewed better as a continuum than as a dichotomous state. Interestingly, there has been little research into any genetic causal factor that might exist in gay women, perhaps because, historically, they have tended to be viewed as less socially problematic or threatening.

The case of homosexuality, and the very real oppression and murder of homosexuals in Nazi Germany, illustrates more than any of the other cases considered so far the way in which medicine can be used, willingly or unwillingly, as a political instrument and how scientific theories can become ideologies. Every theory to date concerning the supposed causes of homosexuality has resulted in suggested attempts for cure or prevention. This is perhaps best summed up by quoting Herrn: 'The social acceptance of homosexuality is not to be found in science' (Herrn 1995: 50). Scientific research will not guarantee social equality for any group within society, and an accepted genetic explanation might just as easily lead to another round of eugenics as to an alleviation of discrimination (McGuire 1995). However, the case of homosexuality highlights the importance of taking into account the broader societal context of scientific research. Establishing a biological identity for gay men and women has the attraction of accommodating the gay minority into an otherwise unchanged social order (Fernbach 1998). Society is not required to make any major adjustments, gay men and women remain not only a minority but a clearly delineated one, and any potential threat to the underlying social order is defused.

Intelligence

Perhaps the most controversial attempt to identify a biological basis for a human trait or behaviour has been in the area of intelligence. In the latter part of the nineteenth century, Charles Darwin had asserted that the transmission of inherited intelligence was a key step in evolution, setting our ancestors apart from other apes. Francis Galton, Darwin's cousin, seized on this and set out to demonstrate its continuing relevance by using British families as a source of data. Galton's work and its implications are discussed in more detail in the previous chapter, but, put simply, his aim was to present evidence that intellectual capacity of various sorts (as well as characteristics such as alcoholism, feeble mindedness and destitution) ran in families. As a result, it is in Galton's work that the controversial debate over the correlation between intelligence and heredity really begins.

To substantiate his assertions, Galton realized that he needed a precise, quantitative measure of what it was he was trying to analyse, and began an attempt to develop the first 'intelligence tests'. He did not succeed, but the ideas of others were more readily accepted and tests began to be commonly used in the UK, USA and Western Europe at the beginning of the twentieth century. By 1908, the concept of mental level, or mental age, had been developed by Alfred Binet, followed in 1912 by the Intelligence Quotient, or IQ. At first this was just a measure of a child's mental level relative to his or her contemporaries, but later it came to have more general use. Binet, who developed the first widely accepted measure of what came to be called IQ, was careful to distance himself from hereditarian assumptions. However, some of those who used his tests were, as Gould (1997) describes, pioneers of hereditarianism. This was particularly true in the US context, where, over the first half of the century, drawing on the work of Goddard, Terman and Yerkes, intelligence testing became an accepted part of public policy, used for example in assessing immigrants for entry to the country and in deciding military placements for recruits to the US army.

By the 1960s, however, a behaviourist view of human intelligence had come to be more prominent. This view stressed the importance of environmental influences and, as a result of its popularization, the focus on IQ testing and on genes as the sole determinant of intelligence became less universally accepted.

Box 3.3: Behaviourism

The behaviourist school of psychology was founded by John Watson in 1913, building on the work of Pavlov on animal behaviour. Watson's aim was to control and predict behaviour; by the 1920s he was also applying his experimental techniques to humans. Some of his experiments are shocking by modern ethical standards: in one experiment, for example, a baby was conditioned to cry in the presence of a rat, by associating the presence of the rat with an unpleasant noise. Behaviourism became widely accepted among psychologists from the 1920s onwards and, by the 1950s and 1960s, popularized by the work of B.F. Skinner, was the dominant psychological paradigm. Since Skinner's interest, like Watson's, was in determining how behaviour was shaped by external forces, the work was in sharp contrast with the biological determinist argument that stressed the importance of heredity.

In terms of the behaviourist viewpoint, some of the causes of differences in human intelligence lay outside the individual, for example poverty, education and medical care. Then, in 1969, Jensen, an American educational psychologist, reopened the debate with an article on remedial education programmes in the USA. In it, he claimed not only that these programmes failed because they were targeted at children whose low IQ scores were largely inherited, but also that they were targeted at disproportionately black populations and these populations historically had lower average IQs than white populations. Predictably, Jensen's work provoked a huge reaction, from supporters and critics. As a result of the ensuing debate, and the sharp contrast with the previous work of the behaviourists, in the early 1970s the use of testing by US employers and schools was limited and sometimes banned. Behind these restrictions were fears that testing would discriminate unfairly against socially disadvantaged groups

The Bell Curve

The most visible contribution to the debate over the heritability of intelligence in recent years is undoubtedly *The Bell Curve*. *The Bell Curve* is a US work published in 1994, which purports to describe the relationship between class structure and intelligence in American society. Of the two authors of the book, one, Richard Herrnstein, was a psychologist, and the other, Charles Murray, is a political scientist. The release of the book fuelled a media frenzy in the USA, not least because it was suggested that the distribution of advance copies favoured those who were known to be supportive of the ideas it contained, whereas those seen as likely critics were unable to make criticisms grounded in the actual substance of the book. Even today, it is still a highly controversial work, which divides public and political opinion, and it is also one of the most commonly cited studies in discussing the potential dangers of new genetic research.

Although the publication of *The Bell Curve* is an important landmark in the debate over the relationship between genetics and intelligence, it is important to recognize that it differs from the work discussed in the previous three sections. In itself, it does not represent any contribution to biological knowledge or research. Instead, the authors seek, through the use of social science methods, to provide a justification for assuming the biological basis of intelligence. In this respect, their book is one of the most visible and divisive products of social science in recent years. Another important point is that *The Bell Curve* is sometimes referred to as a study, but in actual fact what it presents are data from a number of studies, none of which were carried out by Herrnstein and Murray. However, they do sometimes carry out additional statistical analyses of data from these studies.

One of the fundamental issues underlying the debate over the book becomes clear at the outset. To assess the relationship between intelligence and any other variable, a researcher would need to have a clear idea of both what is meant by intelligence and a satisfactory method (to them at least) of *measuring* intelligence. Herrnstein and Murray state 'That the word *intelligence* describes something real and that it varies from person to person is as universal and ancient as any understanding about the state of being human'. But they also go on to say that 'for the last 30 years, the concept of intelligence has been a pariah in the world of ideas' (Herrnstein and Murray 1994: 1), which goes some way to illustrating that the acceptance of this idea is not quite as universal as they might like us to believe.

On the one hand, it is certainly true that studies of variation in intelligence in its broadest sense have been carried out for many years. These were stimulated in particular by Charles Darwin's theory of evolution in the latter part of the nineteenth century. However, as suggested in the previous chapter, the acceptance of any kind of concrete and real measure of intelligence as a unitary concept is far less widespread. It was not until 1904 that Charles Spearman put forward evidence for a unitary mental factor, named 'g' for general intelligence. Although the evidence for this may have been persuasive, it is worth noting again that it was entirely circumstantial, based on statistical analysis rather than direct observation.

Spearman hypothesized that g is a general capacity for inferring and applying relationships, drawn from experience. Herrnstein and Murray give the following examples of what g might mean in practice and how it might be measured: 'Being able to grasp, for example, the relationship between a pair of words like "harvest" and "yield", or to recite a list of digits in reverse order, or to see what a geometrical pattern would look like upside down, are examples of tests that draw on "g" as Spearman saw it' (1994: 4).

The first modern intelligence tests drew heavily on Spearman's work, and questions of the kind described by Herrnstein and Murray can still be seen in IQ tests today. However, as we have seen in the introductory part of this section, the fact that IQ tests became widely used did not mean that they were universally accepted. They were highly controversial, particularly where mental tests were used to support immigration or sterilization policies. The popularity of the behaviourist viewpoint and the restriction on intelligence testing meant that, by the early 1980s, the idea that intelligence was a bankrupt concept, which was too complex and diverse to be readily defined, had become more common. To use an analogy that the authors of *The Bell Curve* pick up on, intelligence was thought to be a concept that had more in common with justice or beauty than something readily measurable and describable like height or weight. So while, of course, there were still researchers who clung to hereditary explanations, it was into this kind of climate, where many took for granted the diverse nature of intelligence, that *The Bell Curve* came.

What The Bell Curve *asserts*

The Bell Curve makes several assertions about the correlation of particular social factors with intelligence, as measured by intelligence tests. To examine these social factors, the US population is divided into five 'cognitive classes' on the basis of IQ. As Fig. 3.2 shows, this is where the book gets its name: the pattern of intelligence follows a normal distribution, with very few people at either end and most in the middle. The authors divide their classes at the 5th, 25th, 75th and 95th percentiles,

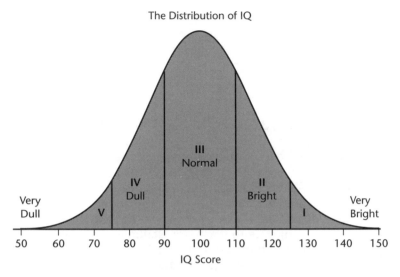

Figure 3.2   The five 'cognitive classes', as defined by IQ distributions

to give five classes in total. In terms of this distribution, they describe Class 1 as the cognitive elite. They go on to state that, put bluntly, high cognitive ability is generally associated with socially desirable behaviours and low cognitive ability with socially undesirable ones. More specifically, using this normal distribution, the authors of *The Bell Curve* assert that several variables are correlated with IQ: poverty, employment, illegitimacy and welfare recipiency.

The data used to support these assertions are taken from the National Longitudinal Survey of Labour Market Experience of Youth. This began in 1979, when all the participants were aged 14–22 years, and continued to follow them at regular intervals. About 12,000 participants in total are included in the survey, but of course all the analyses that are performed do not apply to them all, for example those specific to gender or ethnicity.

Considering poverty first, and specifically white poverty in relation to cognitive class, the data are used to demonstrate a clear relationship between cognitive class and poverty. The lower the cognitive class an individual is in, the more likely they are to be in poverty, and the ratio of classes V : I is 15 : 1. Importantly for the authors, the most marked differences in this increasing ratio are where cognitive ability falls below the average as measured by intelligence tests.

The figures presented in relation to white employment show a similar pattern, although less marked. What the authors call 'dropout' from the labour force, which is characterized by a month or more of unemployment in 1989, rises as cognitive ability falls. The ratio here of class V to class I figures is less spectacular though: 2.2 : 1. Nevertheless, once again the differences are most marked where cognitive ability falls below the average.

Turning to illegitimacy, which is the term used by the authors, the same relationship is shown: as cognitive ability falls, the percentage of white women who have a baby outside of marriage increases. The patterns are the same, but the difference here is marked again: 16 times as many women in cognitive class V as in class I fall into this category.

Finally, welfare is examined. This analysis takes two parts: first, it looks at the percentage of white women who went on welfare within a year of first birth; it then goes on to consider the percentage of mothers who went on to become chronic welfare recipients. Once again, there are the same patterns: an increase in both categories from class I through to class V. The differences here are the most noticeable of all the analyses: 55 per cent of mothers in cognitive class V went on welfare within a year compared with only 1 per cent of class I and, in terms of chronic recipience (which is counted as five years or more of welfare), there are 31 per cent of mothers in class V but none in class I.

In all of these cases, the link is made between a particular factor (for example, welfare recipiency) and IQ. However, as many sociologists have argued (see Duster 1995; Hauser 1995; Taylor 1995), the possible relationship of social factors to the rates of employment, poverty, and so on, and the interrelationship between these variables is never considered. Leaving aside the debate over IQ score as a valid measure of intelligence for the moment, the fact that the four indicators used by the authors are not independent variables is clear. If we know, for example, that there are more of what the authors call 'illegitimate' births in cognitive class V, an alternative way of looking at these data might suggest that these are women who may be less likely to be in a partnership where the other partner can assist with financial provision for the child, or less likely to be able to juggle work and childcare themselves. If this is the case, then why should we be surprised that these women are disproportionately represented among welfare recipients, or among those in poverty? A causal relationship between 'illegitimate' births and receiving welfare is at least as plausible as the inference of two separate relationships between IQ and illegitimacy and IQ and welfare recipiency.

In other words, it can easily be argued that it is social factors that explain these differences, or at least an interplay between social factors and IQ, rather than IQ alone. What the authors have to say about the influence of socioeconomic variables is very interesting: they suggest that to include these factors would make the analysis so complex that it would be a 'bottomless pit' (Herrnstein and Murray 1994: 123). They also say that if social or economic variables were considered, this would necessitate the inclusion of further variables such as religious background. The problematic nature of an argument which suggests that, since all possible influencing factors cannot be easily considered, those that seem most likely will be totally discounted, speaks for itself.

Ethnicity and intelligence

Thus far, all the data we have examined have been in relation to white Americans. However, arguably the most controversial part of *The Bell Curve* is what it has to say about ethnic differences in cognitive ability. To state this baldly, the authors say that ethnic groups differ in intelligence (ethnic is the term they use, since they say that race is too difficult to explore in the US environment). These differences are described as follows (the capitalization is that used in the original):

- Asians have higher IQs than Whites by about 2–3 IQ points (this difference is said to be small and poorly understood).
- Whites have higher IQs than Blacks by a much larger margin.
- The Black mean in the IQ test is 85.
- The White mean is 100.
- Standard deviation in IQ is about 15 points.
- And this is also the difference between average Black and average White IQ.

Herrnstein and Murray represent this graphically, using data from the NLSY (see Fig. 3.3):

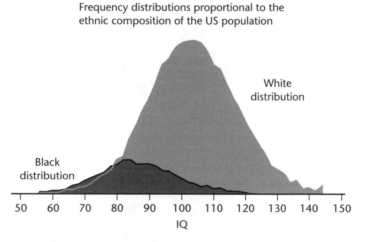

Frequency distributions proportional to the ethnic composition of the US population

Figure 3.3 The difference between Black and White IQ distributions, as calculated from the National Longitudinal Survey of Youth

Having stated these differences at the outset of their analysis of ethnic differences, the same kinds of correlations are then drawn as for the White study group. Specifically, the relationship between IQ and poverty, welfare recipiency, employment and illegitimacy is examined. In this case, however, the data are then submitted to further manipulation: controlling for IQ.

Considering the data on employment, Herrnstein and Murray note that higher rates of black male unemployment have been a policy concern in the USA. However, their data purport to show that there is very little disparity in employment rates if IQ is controlled for. The probability of being unemployed for a month or more before controlling for IQ is 10 per cent for the White sample, 14 per cent for the Latino sample and 21 per cent for the Black sample. After controlling for IQ, the figure for both Whites and Latinos is 11 per cent and that for Blacks falls to 15 per cent. In other words, the authors imply that higher black male unemployment is a function of lower intelligence, rather than of discrimination or any other social factor.

The same kinds of analysis are carried out in relation to poverty and income and similar results are presented. The only marked differences from this pattern are in the areas of illegitimacy and welfare recipiency, where controlling for IQ does not significantly narrow the Black–White gap. For illegitimacy, the Black figure before controlling for IQ is 62 per cent and for Whites it is 12 per cent. After controlling for IQ, these become 51 per cent and 10 per cent respectively. For welfare recipiency, the figures show a slightly more marked decrease but a substantial difference still remains.

Despite the possible links suggested here between being a lone parent and being a welfare recipient, the authors conclude that the reasons for these remaining differences transcend IQ or poverty. The following shows what they are much less tentative about:

> The evidence presented here should give everyone who writes and talks about ethnic inequalities reason to avoid flamboyant rhetoric about ethnic oppression. Racial and ethnic differences in this country are seen in a new light when cognitive ability is added to the picture.
> (Herrnstein and Murray 1994: 340)

The underlying premises of The Bell Curve

Having briefly summarized the key findings presented in *The Bell Curve*, this section considers the underlying premises behind the work. Some of these are explicitly stated by the authors, whereas others can be inferred from their treatment of the data they present.

Taken as a whole, the study makes five main points regarding the relationships in society among social class, race/ethnicity and measured cognitive ability (after Taylor 1995):

1 That past or present IQ tests accurately measure intelligence.
2 That intelligence is unidimensional, having one general factor (g).
3 That g, and its presumed indicator, IQ, are heavily determined by genes (and that genetic heritability of intelligence is as high as 80 per cent).
4 That various groups in society differ significantly in average IQ. Since IQ is largely heritable, they therefore must differ in genes for intelligence.

There are two kinds of extension to this line of thought. One is that lower social classes, those in poverty, and so on are, on average, in possession of genes for lower intelligence. The other is that Blacks, Hispanics and Native Americans (among other US minority groups) have genes on average for lower intelligence than Whites or Asians. These lead on to a fifth point:

5 That those who are disadvantaged in society are disadvantaged because of their own genetic inadequacy. The converse is that, while the cognitive elite may seem to consist disproportionately of white upper-class males, this too is as a result of genetic predisposition rather than social factors.

The assertions made by the authors of *The Bell Curve*, then, appear a long way advanced from a variable, *g*, and a method of testing, which is so contentious in the first place. How these results would look with a less narrowly defined concept of intelligence is never discussed. Equally, the suggestion that intelligence is 80 per cent heritable is not one that receives a great deal of support in the literature: a more common *upper* estimate is 40–50 per cent. The authors do give some perfunctory discussion to the notion of cultural bias in intelligence testing, using one famous test example:

RUNNER : MARATHON
(A) envoy : embassy
(B) martyr : massacre
(C) oarsman : regatta
(D) referee : tournament
(E) horse : stable

The correct answer to this question, (C), depends on the person taking the test understanding what kind of event a regatta is, which is an example of culturally dependent knowledge. However, the authors conclude that this kind of bias does not have a significant effect on test results. In drawing this conclusion, they choose to ignore the growing body of sociological and anthropological work which demonstrates what Duster (1995) calls the contingent and contextual nature of intelligence. For example, Lave's (1988) work with street children in Brazil showed that they could do complicated maths on the street, but failed to do the same problem in a classroom. In other words, the authors never fully address the following question: Might the testing process somehow give rise to these results as an artefact?

Rose *et al.* ([1984] 1990) suggest that, to test intelligence, we must have some prior notion of intelligence against which the results can be compared. People who are generally considered 'intelligent' must do well, and those who are obviously 'stupid' must do badly, or the test will be rejected. In other words, tests were constructed to correspond to teachers' and psychologists' *a priori* notions of intelligence. They were standardized so that they became consistent predictors of performance.

Test items that differentiated girls from boys, for example, were removed, since the tests were not meant to make that distinction. Differences between social classes, or ethnic groups, however, have remained, precisely because it is these differences that the tests are meant to measure.

The implications of a genetic basis for intelligence

As with the previous discussions of aggression, alcoholism and homosexuality, the results presented in *The Bell Curve* beg the question of why the relationship between genetics and intelligence has been the subject of so much research and debate. It can be argued that research on intelligence might offer ways to increase the intelligence of children who might otherwise have low intelligence or learning difficulties. More broadly, it might be beneficial in terms of improving our understanding of higher brain function and neurobiology.

In the case of *The Bell Curve*, more than in any of the other work discussed, however, an alternative agenda is very clear: the opportunities such research may offer for influencing policy development. In their conclusion to the book, Herrnstein and Murray suggest the elimination or curtailment of affirmative action programmes (in education and employment), since these are based on the supposition that minorities have historically been held back by social environment, not genes. Welfare programmes also come under attack, since these are seen as costly manipulations of environmental variables, which will have little effect, given the unchangeable genetic nature of the recipients. These recommendations are particularly interesting in the light of the timing of the publication: in 1994 the USA was near the beginning of the Clinton administration. Clinton was the first Democratic president for some years and, at that time, he was an extraordinarily popular president, particularly among what are generally considered to be the more socially disadvantaged groups in US society. He was also a strong supporter of initiatives targeted at these groups.

In summary, the recommendations set out at the conclusion of *The Bell Curve* grow out of poorly substantiated conclusions about the genetic inability of minorities to be educated or trained or benefit from welfare. The political scenario at the time of publication sheds light on the political reasons for making these recommendations, but it is the appearance of scientific justification that makes them particularly dangerous. The issue of the privileged nature of scientific discourse is discussed in more detail in the previous chapter, but *The Bell Curve* is a clear example of the way in which biology can become ideology.

Using genetics as a source of explanation

The four cases presented in this chapter have illustrated the breadth of the research programme that seeks to identify a biological basis for human traits and behaviour. Potentially, this research has the power to create a better public understanding of how genes and the environment interact and hence help to undermine media misconceptions. Indeed, if research finds that there is little significant impact of genetics on behavioural traits, the role of the environment may come to be taken more seriously and the importance of the interaction between genes and the environment may be more widely understood. There might also be a more widespread understanding of the fact that these traits are complex and many genes may be involved.

The danger of a disproportionate focus on genetics as a source of explanation, however, is that we see life as unchangeable – 'genetic fatalism'. If genetic causes are found, the only way to be sure of controlling these will be prenatal screening and testing and selective abortion. In cultures where sections of the population hold negative attitudes to homosexuality, for example, abortion may be seen as a desirable solution. These decisions may be made in a broader context; by parents wanting their child to avoid the intolerance and discrimination that can be associated with homosexuality, for example, but the end result is the same. As Stein (1998: 22) suggests, 'the primary negative features of being a lesbian, gay man or bisexual have to do with societal attitudes towards these sexual orientations, not with intrinsic features of them'. Unfortunately, the potential for abuse of this kind of scientific knowledge is shown by history. All the traits discussed here are to a greater or lesser extent socially stigmatized or may be seen as socially problematic in some way, which perhaps raises more profound ethical questions about why this research is being carried out at all. McGuire (1995: 141) recognizes this issue in commenting that 'Researchers working with traits that are stigmatized must be even more rigorous in their methodology and extremely careful in generalizing their data'. There appears to have been less scientific interest, for example, in the possibility of finding a gene for traits that tend to be more positively viewed in some societies, such as altruism or pacifism.

Throughout this chapter, media reporting of the new genetics has been shown to be important in determining public perceptions. This raises one final question: Why is there an oversimplified view of genetic association in the media and among the public? Conrad (1999a) uses the term O-GOD (one gene, one disease) to describe the way in which a one-to-one relationship is perceived between genetics and behaviour. The news media contribute to these perceptions by adopting a frame of what Conrad (1997) calls 'genetic optimism'. Within this frame, there are three assumptions. The first and most fundamental is that there is a gene responsible for a particular trait (e.g. alcoholism). The second is that this gene will be found, if not in the particular research that is being reported, then at some future stage. The third is that this discovery will have a positive impact, so that potential adverse consequences such as discrimination or selective abortion are rarely considered (Conrad 1999b).

This 'genetic optimism' means that subsequent disconfirmations of genetic research, such as the link between XYY individuals and aggression, go unreported or are not reported with the prominence of the original 'discovery'. The end result is a privileging of genetics in public discourse. This is potentially problematic not only because of the simplistic associations that are likely to be made, but also more broadly, as Gill and Richards (1998) point out, in that they result in unrealistic expectations of disease prevention and treatment by the public. Traits, behaviours or conditions with a multigenetic basis are highly unlikely to be simply treatable.

These issues are concerns not only for sociologists but also for biological scientists, as the following comment from the editor of the prestigious science journal *Nature* illustrates: 'Most geneticists will probably argue that nurture still has a place. But to fail to say as much, explicitly, may generate more disbelief and even more resentment than ethical worries have yet engendered' (Maddox 1993: 107).

Although explanations based on straightforward causal links may appeal in their simplicity, they fail to emphasize the intertwined relationship of nature and nurture on human traits and behaviour. However, with the continued rise of the genetic paradigm, and the further developments of the Human Genome Project, we are likely to see more of these explanations.

Summary points

- Evidence for a biological basis for human traits and behaviours has been sought for many years, but it is only recently that this search has been carried out at an explicitly genetic level.

- Opinion is strongly divided over the consequences of these research programmes. Some commentators claim that it will lead to behaviours such as aggression, or characteristics such as homosexuality, being seen as natural and therefore inevitable.

- Others argue that, by ascribing characteristics such as homosexuality to a genetic variation, they are more likely to be viewed as abnormalities or disorders.

- Identifying a biological basis for undesirable traits or behaviours will not in itself help in managing these traits. If a gene 'for' aggression is identified, the civil liberties of individuals with the gene may be threatened in an attempt to pre-empt any aggressive behaviour.

- Asserting a biological basis for characteristics viewed as socially undesirable may be an attractive stance for policy makers. Many welfare programmes are based on the idea that certain groups in society are held back by their social environment. If genes rather than social environment are the determining factor in behaviour, these programmes can be curtailed.

- The attractive nature of genetic fatalism as an explanation for social problems means it is unlikely to go away. The recent resurgence of biological determinism is linked not only with advances in genetics, but also with social and political factors.

Further reading

Conrad, P. and Markens, S. (2001) Constructing the gay gene in the news: optimism and skepticism in the US and British press, *Health*, 5(3): 373–400.

Conrad, P. and Weinberg, D. (1996) Has the gene for alcoholism been discovered three times since 1980? A news media analysis, *Perspectives on Social Problems*, 8: 3–25.

Duster, T. (1990) *Backdoor to Eugenics*. London: Routledge.

Fischer, C.S., Hout, M., Sanchez Jankowski, M. *et al.* (1996) *Inequality by Design: Cracking the Bell Curve Myth*. Princeton, NJ: Princeton University Press.

Jencks, C. (1980) Heredity, environment and public policy reconsidered, *American Sociological Review*, 45: 723–36.

Nelkin, D. (1987) *Selling Science: How the Press Covers Science and Technology*. New York: W.H. Freeman.

Rothman, B.K. (1998) *Genetic Maps and Human Imaginations: The Limits of Science in Understanding Who We Are*. New York: W.W. Norton (especially 'Rates and Races' and 'For whom the Bell Curves').

4

ANTENATAL SCREENING
AND TESTING

Introduction

This chapter considers the practice of antenatal (or prenatal) screening
and testing, and the issues it raises at both individual and wider societal
levels. It begins with an outline of the differences between screening
and testing procedures, and a consideration of the kinds of screening
and testing that are commonly used. It moves on to look at the ways in
which these procedures are integrated into heath care systems, focusing
on the issues of medicalization, routinization and informed choice. It
introduces the theme of risk in relation to the application of new genetic
technologies, which we will continue to explore in subsequent chapters.
Finally, it considers the relationship between antenatal screening and
testing and the way that disability is viewed at a societal level, analysing
the ways in which these technologies have been linked to long-standing
debates over eugenics.

It should perhaps be stated at the outset that most antenatal screening
does not itself specifically use genetic technologies. However, it is commonly used to decide which women should be offered testing for genetic
abnormalities such as Down's syndrome. Since it represents the most
common means by which individuals come into contact with ideas of
genetic disorders or abnormalities, it is also an important area in terms
of the accusations of eugenics that are sometimes levelled at new genetic
technologies.

One reason why antenatal testing and screening is where the greatest
fears about a eugenic agenda have been expressed is because of the use
to which information gained from these tests may be put. Testing for an
adult onset disorder like Huntington's disease may provide an opportunity
to diagnose and, subsequently, manage a disorder more effectively. It may
also raise questions for the reproductive plans of affected individuals,

who may decide that they do not wish to risk passing on affected genes to any offspring. Antenatal screening and testing, however, offers a different kind of preventative aim: in this case, the risk of genetic disorder can be eliminated through termination of an already existing pregnancy. The nature of this preventative aim has been used to argue that antenatal screening and testing programmes have important differences in terms of their social and ethical implications.

Screening and testing

Thus far, the terms 'screening' and 'testing' have been used together; in other contexts, they are often used interchangeably. However, there are some important differences between the two procedures. The Nuffield Council on Bioethics (1993) makes the following distinctions. Genetic testing provides information about an individual for whom there is some prior indication of a genetic condition being present. This prior indication may be symptoms of a disease or disorder, or it may be the presence of a family history of a particular genetic disease. Genetic screening, on the other hand, is carried out in the absence of any particular risk indicators. All members of a population – for example, all pregnant women – are screened to identify those who are either affected by, or at increased risk of developing, a genetic disorder. As Wood-Harper and Harris (1996) note, the results of screening tests often require confirmatory diagnosis.

Antenatal screening and testing procedures, however, are something of a special case in relation to these distinctions. The initial screening procedures, as discussed above, are not themselves genetically based. Instead, they identify those women whose pregnancies are at higher risk for developmental disorders, of which only some are genetic. Diagnostic testing can then be carried out to identify these genetic abnormalities. Antenatal screening procedures are used to identify those women for whom both the financial and psychological implications of diagnostic testing are thought to be justified (Green and Statham 1996). However, these procedures will not exclude all possible fetal abnormalities.

What is the aim of antenatal screening and testing?

Critics of antenatal procedures, as well as some supporters, argue that most antenatal diagnosis is performed to prevent the birth of children with severe disabilities, as predicted by abnormalities detected during pregnancy. The development of diagnostic techniques for the detection of fetal abnormality began in the 1960s and 1970s, with the use of **amniocentesis** to assess rhesus disease in the fetus. Rhesus disease causes complications in late pregnancy, which can be prevented by early delivery; the technology was used in these circumstances to assess whether there were likely to be any problems and, if so, to prevent them without any ill effects for mother or child. However, as testing procedures have developed, they have come to be used in a rather different preventative capacity, which has led critics of prenatal testing to suggest that there is a rather curious anomaly at work here. Medical diagnosis is usually used to promote the health and well-being of the individual being assessed, but this principle does not hold for fetal screening and testing. Some conditions that may be revealed can benefit from maternal medication during pregnancy – for example, some metabolic disorders – but most abnormalities that are identified by testing cannot be treated or cured. In most cases, then, the only possible intervention is to terminate the pregnancy. However, the notion of 'abnormality' is a contentious one, and how the term is defined is fundamental for the practical application of antenatal screening and testing, particularly in defending against accusations of eugenics.

Current screening and testing policies: an overview

Antenatal screening and testing differs from the genetic testing procedures described in the following chapter, in that it is largely carried out by midwives and obstetricians, rather than by genetic counsellors and clinical geneticists. Although specific families or cases may be referred to specialist genetic services, routine screening generally occurs within the antenatal clinic. At least part of the rationale for this is the rare nature of any specific genetic problem for which there is no family history. Most babies are born 'normal' as judged by medical opinion, with only a small percentage (about 2 per cent) being born with anything that might be classed as an abnormality. About half of these abnormalities will not affect the baby in any serious way and include things such as extra toes and birthmarks. However, the other half are more serious and can lead to severe disability or even death of the baby. Routine screening procedures and follow-up tests are increasingly offered to pregnant women to exclude the presence of one of the more common and serious abnormalities. In this context, however, it is important to bear in mind that not all abnormalities can be excluded through testing and that no test can guarantee a 'normal' baby.

At present, there are no national guidelines for antenatal screening procedures in the UK beyond those issued by the Royal College of Obstetricians and Gynaecologists, which recommend that all antenatal units should have a written statement of their policy (Lane *et al.* 2001). In the USA, policy differs on a state by state basis; in the UK, current policies also vary in specific timing and in tests that are routinely offered on a local and regional basis. Individual hospitals also vary in their policies when women specifically ask for particular tests that are not routinely offered. However, in most cases, the screening and subsequent testing procedures that are offered are similar to the model described in Box 4.1.

Box 4.1: An antenatal screening model

A typical model of antenatal screening in the UK might include the following:

- week 12: transabdominal ultrasound scan
- weeks 15–18: blood serum screening (to measure maternal serum **alphafetoprotein** concentration). MSAFP levels may also be combined with two other hormonal measures (human chorionic gonadotropin, and unconjugated oestriol) to produce what is known as the 'triple test'
- week 20: transabdominal ultrasound scan

Dependent on the results of the screening, the following *tests* might be offered:

- week 11 onwards: **chorionic villus sampling**
- weeks 16–18: amniocentesis

For most women, initial information about antenatal screening is likely to come from a community midwife or doctor. The woman will also be referred to an antenatal clinic, where this screening, if she accepts it, will take place. In the UK, a first visit to the clinic may be arranged for 12 weeks into the pregnancy, where a transabdominal ultrasound scan will be carried out. From a medical point of view, this scan is used to confirm three things: that it is a viable pregnancy, that it is a single pregnancy and that the gestational age of the baby has been estimated accurately (this helps to give an accurate date for delivery). However, the scan can also be used to estimate the risk of the fetus having Down's syndrome; other problems or developmental anomalies may also be evident. As Green and Statham (1996) argue, ultrasound occupies a slightly ambiguous position in relation to the distinctions previously made between screening and testing, for two reasons. First, the results are apparent during the scan and, second, although it is commonly used to establish possible abnormalities that merit further investigation, it may also give definitive information, for example fetal death.

Although, like other routine medical procedures, ultrasound scanning requires informed consent, practice in the UK might sometimes best be described as operating on a principle of informed refusal. In reality, this means that unless the scan is specifically refused, it is likely to be carried out, since consent is assumed unless otherwise stated. One reason for this is that it is clearly important, from a health professional's point of view, to establish whether a pregnancy is single or multiple, and also to put an accurate date on the pregnancy, to arrange for further testing and for delivery. Another reason, discussed in more detail below, is the slightly ambiguous nature of ultrasound scanning – for many women, it provides a widely recognized first opportunity to 'see the baby', and they may be less aware of its ability to detect abnormalities and of the potentially negative information it can highlight. It is of course possible to refuse the scan, but in practice this refusal may be quite complicated, because of the practical reasons for scanning listed above. What sometimes occurs is that women accept the scan for dating purposes, but choose not to be told of any abnormalities it might show. Evidently, there are ethical issues here concerning rights to information, since the end result may be that medical staff are in possession of knowledge that the mother is not.

In the USA, ultrasound is a less routinely used technology and many pregnancies will be scanned only once, or only on the specific request of the mother. However, both the USA and UK share common use of a second screening procedure, serum screening. In some US states (e.g. California), it is mandated that it should be offered. It is also widely routinely offered in the UK; in a large-scale survey carried out by Green (1999), it was found that it was offered on some basis by virtually all obstetricians in England and Wales. Serum screening is carried out through a blood test at around 15–18 weeks (ideally at around week 16) to measure maternal serum **alphafetoprotein** (MSAFP) concentration. MSAFP levels may be combined with two other hormonal measures to produce what is known as the 'triple test'. This test can then be used to *estimate* the risk of spina bifida, Down's syndrome and other abnormalities. However, this test is predictive, not diagnostic, and so will not in itself confirm whether or not a fetus is affected. Its use is further complicated by the fact that it only identifies 60–65 per cent of Down's syndrome babies, so it can give false reassurance. It can also give false-positive results, suggesting that a healthy fetus is at risk. These complications illustrate why the test is commonly used as a screening test, as a basis for deciding which women should be offered subsequent diagnostic testing.

The third procedure routinely offered in the UK is a second ultrasound scan at around 20 weeks. Women often remark on what a different experience this is to the first ultrasound, as by this time a heart beat and movement can usually be clearly seen. However, this examination can also be used to exclude certain serious abnormalities, such as hydrocephalus, spina bifida, heart defects and kidney and bowel abnormalities. As with all antenatal procedures, though, not all abnormalities can be excluded on the basis of this 20 week ultrasound examination.

As mentioned above, these routinely offered procedures – in particular, serum screening – are often used to decide who should be *offered* further diagnostic testing (although other women may also *request* it). This may be calculated according to risk factors that are expressed as a 1 in x number, with a typical threshold being 1 in 200. On this basis, if the risk of abnormality is calculated as 1 in 200 or greater, women will be offered an opportunity for *diagnostic* testing for Down's syndrome.

Two different types of diagnostic test are commonly used: **chorionic villus sampling** and amniocentesis. Chorionic villus sampling can be done from around week 11 of pregnancy and involves a small needle being inserted through the abdomen under local anaesthetic and into the womb with the help of ultrasound. A small piece of the placenta is then withdrawn and sent for testing. The test confirms the presence or absence of Down's sydrome by identifying abnormal chromosomes. However, the disadvantage of this test is that it can bring on a miscarriage in about 1 in 100 women, regardless of whether any abnormalities are diagnosed.

Amniocentesis is also an invasive test: a small amount of the amniotic fluid that surrounds the fetus in the womb is withdrawn using a needle around weeks 16–18 of pregnancy. The fetal cells are cultured and chromosomal abnormalities can be identified. This test is thought to carry a higher risk of miscarriage, approximately 1 in 50 (although this varies according to timing); again this risk applies whether the fetus does or does not have an abnormality.

The social implications of routine antenatal screening and testing

The 'tentative pregnancy'

Previous chapters have discussed the resurgence of biological determinism and genetic reductionism as explanatory paradigms for social issues such as aggressive behaviour and poor performance in intelligence tests. As Rothman (1988) argues, this creates a curious contradiction in relation to screening for disability. At the same time as the environmental causes of illness and disability (asbestos, drugs such as thalidomide, etc.) become more clearly understood, the biological determinist argument seems to be becoming more and more persuasive.

In relation to prenatal testing, Rothman argues that this has resulted in a situation where increased knowledge of the human genome has led to increased responsibility on mothers. She suggests that it is a curious scenario in which women are asked to 'choose' whether to bring a child with certain genetic predispositions into the world, but they are not given choices about the environment in which that child will live.

Extending this argument, Rothman describes how current antenatal screening and testing practices result in a paradoxical situation. We ask women to accept their pregnancies and take care of their babies until they get their test results, and then ask them to consider abortion up to 24 weeks dependent on these test results. She uses the notion of 'the tentative pregnancy' to cover the time up until the test results are received, arguing that women may not be able to consider themselves 'really' pregnant until the tests have shown the likelihood of a healthy baby. A secondary issue is that, if initial screening results are problematic, women are often asked to make choices about diagnostic testing, and potentially about termination of pregnancy, over a very short period of time.

The counter-argument to this, of course, is that the tests are designed to offer choice. On the basis of the knowledge gained from the screening and testing process, it is argued that a woman, or a couple, can make an informed decision as to whether or not they feel prepared or able to cope with the birth of a child with a disability. If they feel that they cannot, then abortion to prevent the birth of a disabled child is perhaps the most socially acceptable kind of abortion. Studies of attitudes towards abortion commonly find that individuals who are opposed to abortion on demand nevertheless approve of the use of abortion in these circumstances. However, the issue then becomes one of the status of the knowledge that antenatal testing provides and the boundaries of medical knowledge more generally. Research suggests that the reaction of most people to news of an abnormality is to try and establish how severe it is. Studies in Europe suggest that, on average, around one-third to one-half of people would hypothetically consider termination of an affected fetus, but that this figure varies widely with the perceived severity of the abnormality; for example, it is lower in muscular dystrophy than it is in cystic fibrosis (e.g. Denayer et al. 1992; Evers-Kiebooms et al. 1993). Unfortunately, this is not always the kind of knowledge that the tests can provide. Even within a single condition such as Down's syndrome, the spectrum of disability is quite large; while some people may be only mildly affected, others may be profoundly so. In other words, the technology cannot always provide the answers that people feel they would like to make a fully informed choice.

There is also a wider issue about the social acceptability of that choice and whether, in particular communities or societies, that choice has to be socially sanctioned. In this context, some regions in the UK have ceased to offer knowledge of fetal sex, which can be seen from ultrasound, because of a higher rate of abortion of female fetuses as a result. The withdrawal of this information illustrates that not all decisions that can be made on the basis of test results are seen to be acceptable, and which ones are will depend on social variables at that time. This point will be discussed in more detail later in this chapter.

Medicalization, routinization and informed choice

Antenatal testing and screening of the kind described above is only one component of the package of antenatal care that is routinely offered to pregnant women in Western societies. From the late twentieth century, many social scientists have turned a critical eye to this provision of antenatal care, arguing that it represents the 'medicalization' of pregnancy (e.g. Oakley 1984). Through this process, pregnancy is abstracted from its place as a social event and becomes primarily a medical one. In relation to this, Todd makes the following statement:

The prevailing view of patients is that they are, in varying degrees, ill. To the extent that they are sick, they have lost some control over their lives and normal routine activities, and this control is in part transferred to the doctor. Controversy exists over just how much control the medical profession should have over sick patients and how much control patients should retain over their treatment and thus their lives.

(Todd 1989: 4)

Todd goes on to discuss how this framework is particularly problematic for women in terms of reproductive processes. They are not, for the most part, ill, but are still required to enter the patient role for obstetric services. In this way, a biological or social process involving the patient as a person becomes a medical process focusing on medically framing and objectifying the issue to be addressed. Defining pregnancy as a medical problem makes medicine an agent of social control and, at the same time, makes women dependent on the medical profession.

In their study of the uptake of serum screening by pregnant women in a US context, Press and Browner (1997: 985) describe how serum screening was seen by these women as just another part of a wider package of antenatal care. This package as a whole was important, as one of their respondents put it, 'in order that things go right'. Implicit in this kind of statement is a maternal responsibility to cooperate with medical recommendations, an idea that another of their respondents described when she said: 'So I think if you don't get your prenatal care it's unfair to the baby'. Once testing is absorbed into this routine package of care, it is no longer an issue over which a conscious or deliberate choice has to be made.

This routinization of antenatal care more generally has other implications for screening and testing. As Green and Statham (1996) argue, tests that are routine are assumed to be necessary and appropriate. They draw on Richards and Green (1993), who suggest that the antenatal care offered to women in the UK is taken up almost universally because women want to do the best for their babies. However, this process of routinization, while making women more likely to accept screening, can present problems of its own. The identification of any abnormalities becomes doubly difficult, since they are likely to be unexpected. Green and Statham (1996: 143) use quotes from respondents to the Cambridge prenatal screening study to illustrate these difficulties. One respondent, who had had an abnormality detected, said: 'somehow, when you go for a routine scan for size, you can't believe that they'll find something so dreadful'. This illustrates nicely how the possible adverse consequences of a procedure that is seen as routine, and for a particular, limited purpose, may not be immediately evident.

Another, related issue is that pregnant women may have a different perspective on the screening process than health care professionals. For women, reassurance is an important element, while for obstetricians, the accurate identification of any abnormality is key. This possible conflict is illustrated by another respondent quoted by Green and Statham: 'seeing a doctor and he not saying there is anything wrong makes you feel better' (Statham 1994; cited in Green and Statham 1996: 143). The difficulty of being told that there is, in fact, something wrong in these circumstances is magnified by this conflict over the aim of screening.

Press and Browner (1997), in examining the acceptance of antenatal screening, draw on McKinlay's (1982) model of how a medical innovation becomes routinized to understand the widespread use of serum screening in a US setting. McKinlay asserts that, while there may be a prevailing image of medical innovations becoming accepted as standard only when careful evaluation has been carried out, this image does not reflect reality. Instead, promising reports and trials can lead to a situation where it comes to be seen as unacceptable to withhold a new technology from those clients who might benefit from it. Client enthusiasm for an innovation is often the last factor involved and is, in any case, influenced by professional enthusiasm. This model might equally be applied to the provision of screening in the UK, where, as Howe *et al.* (2000) argue, serum screening is now so firmly established that it is unlikely that it will ever be tested properly.

Thus far, the issue of informed consent for antenatal screening has been discussed only in the context of women's perceptions of antenatal screening as necessary to ensure the health of their baby. However, there is some research evidence to support the idea that not all women are aware that there is an active decision to be made, or that they are in fact consenting. Some critics have suggested that this is due to the way in which antenatal screening and testing are presented. Press and Browner (1997) describe how, in their research setting of a southern Californian health maintenance organization (HMO), women's understandings and decisions were shaped by institutional and provider support for testing. However, this issue was more complex than health professionals simply exercising a choice to advocate testing: the HMO in which they worked applied pressure, as it was concerned to avoid any further lawsuits where alphafetoprotein had not been tested and where subsequently problems had arisen with pregnancies. This perhaps sheds light on why nurses in the setting rarely explicitly drew attention to the fact that there was a choice to be made and, where they did, it was described as 'recommended'. Subsequently, 10 per cent of the women in the sample described how they had eventually agreed to be tested despite reservations. This, of course, raises questions as to what benefit the information gained from testing will provide for these women. For those sure that they do not wish to terminate a pregnancy in any circumstances, unfavourable test results have an ambiguous status. Theoretically, they provide women with an opportunity to 'prepare' for the birth of a child with a disability. However, they might also raise anxiety unnecessarily for the remainder of the pregnancy. Although many women in Press and

Browner's (1997) study saw the test generally as a good thing because it provided information, fewer acknowledged the potentially problematic nature of this information. The authors suggest that this viewpoint is rooted in a cultural view that information is always helpful, but is clearly problematic in a context where the only option to act on this information is, in the end, termination of pregnancy.

In a UK setting, the high uptake of antenatal screening for Down's syndrome has also led some researchers to question the adequacy of the information given to pregnant women and the process of informed consent. Smith *et al.* (1994) found that only 36 per cent of their sample of 353 women who had been offered serum screening understood that a negative result would not guarantee that everything was alright with the pregnancy. In addition, only 32 per cent understood that most women with positive results would go on to have a normal baby.

So far in this chapter, there has been no consideration of those women who, despite the influencing factors described above, do refuse antenatal screening and testing procedures. Markens *et al.* (1999) describe how it has sometimes been assumed that those women who do refuse testing are rejecting the wider idea of the medicalization of pregnancy, choosing to define their pregnancies in their own terms rather than biomedical terms. Their research among 'refusers' of serum screening in a US context found that, rather than rejecting technological intervention outright, these women often drew on the logic of the biomedical paradigm to reject screening. They did this by stressing that the procedure was not routine, it could be inaccurate and that it involved risks: one of these risks being ending up in possession of knowledge on the basis of which only an unsatisfactory decision (to terminate the pregnancy) could be made. In general, refusers linked the process of testing more specifically to abortion than those who accepted. Markens *et al.* argue that women may be more reluctant to have a test if explicit links to abortion are made, and more likely to accept when these tests are presented or perceived as routine.

Antenatal screening and testing and risk

The work of Markens *et al.* (1999) with women refusing antenatal testing gives one example of the different ways in which risk may be perceived. Although health care providers may focus on the risk of giving birth to a child with a disability, individual pregnant women may be more concerned with the risks that carrying out a particular test poses, either for their pregnancy or for their psychological well-being. In the Introduction to this book, we noted the growing emphasis placed on risk and risk prevention in recent years, both outside as well as inside health care. In fact, as Gabe (1995) notes, since the 1960s 'a veritable industry has developed concerned with risk, and particularly risk assessment'. He goes on to describe how risk assessment is often seen as a technical matter, which can be resolved by developing more accurate scientific information and by developing 'rational' means to make decisions about health risks. As a result of conceptualizing risk in this way, the focus of research has been on developing quantitative measures, to find out what the risks 'really are'.

Together with this emphasis on risk prevention, and related to it, there has been an increased focus on risk communication to the general public, in an attempt to bridge the gap between 'expert' and 'public' perceptions of risk. Gabe (1995) notes how work on lay perceptions of risk has increased over recent years, seeking to examine how 'acceptable' levels of risk are arrived at for individuals, for example in relation to smoking behaviour. He argues that this focus on the relationship between lay and expert knowledge reflects a broader concern among social theorists at the end of the twentieth century about the declining trust in expert authority in late modernity. In these societies, the judgements of experts may be accepted or rejected, as Giddens (1990) argues, on the basis of pragmatic calculations about the risks involved. Beck's (1992) notion of a 'risk society' is one in which new technologies reinforce the need for trust in expert authority on the one hand, but at the same time one which recognizes the ambiguous and uncertain nature of knowledge about risk, therefore undermining this trust. These issues are discussed in more detail in Chapter 7, in relation to genetically modified foods. However, they also have important implications for health care, as the work of Markens et al. (1999), and the following examples, illustrate.

Williams et al. (1995: 121), in describing the conceptualization of risk in the health field, state that 'like the fear of crime, public perceptions of risk often appear to bear no relationship to what some professional experts say about the "actual" probability of certain kinds of events taking place'. However, studies of health behaviour show that 'risky' behaviour is rarely explained by a lack of knowledge. Examining this issue in the context of HIV/AIDS, Grinyer (1995) draws attention to the view that, while only scientific knowledge officially merits the status of expertise, in terms of the context in which risk information is to be implemented, it is the public who are experts. They have lay expertise founded on their experience in a particular social world. In the case of new genetic technologies, this might, for example, include particular family circumstances in relation to a decision about antenatal screening. A family who already have a child with a disability, for example, may feel that any risk, however small, of a subsequent affected pregnancy is one that they cannot afford. On the other hand, a couple who have had great difficulty in conceiving may feel that any possible risk of miscarriage associated with testing is too great for them to take. Rejecting an 'official' version of risk, then, Grinyer argues, may best be viewed as a rejection of naïve assumption about an ideal world. In an ideal world, these kinds of complicating factors and uncertainties do not pre-exist, but in the real world they frequently do, and they have a very real effect.

Carter (1995) raises similar issues when he attempts to define risk by contrasting it with danger, arguing that whereas danger is an unambiguous state of peril, risk is an uncertainty, simultaneously pointing to the possibilities of security and insecurity. He goes on to describe how the information gained from risk assessment can be used in two ways. First, it can be used in a health promotion kind of framework, for whole populations. Second, it can be used to target 'at risk' individuals. Within the first framework, an individual (e.g. a smoker) has two choices: to become responsible for managing their own health or to become accountable for any sickness they may experience if they do not. Carter (1995: 138) goes on to argue that, while these programmes may allow identification of risk and the opportunity to act upon it, they 'cannot shield the individual from the cultural meanings which become attached to various behaviours'. Social, cultural and institutional processes all have a role to play in perceptions of health risks, as we have already seen in the case of antenatal screening procedures in terms of the ways in which these procedures are routinized and accepted. For those individuals who have refused antenatal screening and go on to give birth to a child with a disability, just as for the smoker who refuses nicotine replacement therapy and goes on to develop lung cancer, the cause of their personal tragedy may be seen to be pre-existing, and moral blame may result. This theme is explored in more detail later in this chapter, in relation to debates over disability and society.

Medical authority and uncertainty

The uncertainty of information gained from antenatal screening procedures in particular has important implications for individual assessments of risk and the decisions that are made on the basis of these. Uncertainty itself is also a key theme in the sociological analysis of antenatal screening. Ettore (1999) has coined the notion of genetic experts as 'genetic storytellers'. Her work examines the types of claims that experts construct in relation to antenatal screening, as well as the impact of these claims. Much is made of antenatal screening as a means to empowerment of pregnant women through knowledge, but Ettore argues that pregnant women are presented with 'manufactured uncertainty' (Giddens 1990), in the sense that they are given too much information about their risks and no real means of assessing them. Paradoxically, this giving of information can lead to an increased dependence on medical authority and medical recommendations to make sense of what they have been told. One of Ettore's interviewees acknowledges the difficulty of this issue by describing the influence of antenatal health professionals in terms of how 'their authority may be more respected than in other areas' (Ettore 1999: 553).

The issue of how much information is sufficient to act as a basis for medical decision making is a complex one and is discussed in more detail in the following chapter. Too little information is clearly unsatisfactory and, in extreme cases, can lead to individuals being unaware that they have made a decision at all. Too much information, however, is not necessarily empowering and can create confusion and dependency by default. In relation to antenatal screening and testing, these delicate issues are further complicated by the routinization of other aspects of antenatal care. Rothman (1988) goes beyond this to suggest that one of the reasons why antenatal screening has aroused so much concern is that it incorporates several historical strands that have always been contentious. These include the medicalization of reproduction and reproductive decision making, the availability of abortion and the remnants of eugenic thinking.

The right to reproduce?

Until now, we have largely focused on the context in which individual choices in relation to antenatal screening may be made, and the way in which it can be argued that this individual choice is undermined by circumstance. However, new genetic technologies are developing in an age in which, as Harris (1997) argues, we have an increased awareness of our rights. In this context, the question might also be posed as to what limits, if any, should be placed on our attempts to control the genetic make-up of our children?

The eugenics movement in the early twentieth century, and the compulsory sterilization acts of the 1920s and 1930s, called into question whether or not all individuals do have a right to reproduce. This question is also frequently debated in relation to disability and reproductive genetic counselling in families with known genetic disorders. On the one hand, Ettore (2000) describes how a mechanistic view of the body is privileged in reproductive genetics, and how the idea of genetic capital can be used to understand and determine whether or not a particular body should be seen as a reproductive resource. Those bodies that are not seen as suitable reproductive resources are, by implication, not seen as having the same right to reproduce as others. On the other hand, there is a common feminist argument, that for women to gain political, social and economic equality in our society, it is essential that they have the freedom to control their reproductive lives – that is, a right not to reproduce. These two examples illustrate how rights may be defined positively or negatively.

Typically, the idea of a right to reproduce has only been considered from the perspective of the parent. However, the other side of this argument, which is sometimes invoked, is the right of the child not to be born; in the USA, the first cases have been seen of lawsuits for 'wrongful birth'. More than 20 US states recognize an action for wrongful birth and some also allow legal action for 'wrongful life'.

This kind of lawsuit could, for example, be based on the liability of a genetic counsellor towards an infant with hereditary defects, on the grounds that he or she would not have been born at all if it were not for the counsellor's negligence. This negligence allegedly lies in the failure of the defendant adequately to advise the parents or to conduct properly the relevant testing and, therefore, prevent the child's birth. The action rests on the argument that, had the proper advice been given, the pregnancy would have been terminated. In other words, or in legal jargon, the plaintiff's 'defective life' constitutes a compensatable injury, in the same way that a disability as a result of someone else's careless driving, or an employer's failure to enact proper safety procedures, would. Although this kind of lawsuit would not currently be allowed under UK law, the notion it employs of a 'defective life' is one that is very much at the forefront of disability rights campaigns in this country.

Medical and social models of disability

As Shakespeare (1998) points out, prenatal testing fundamentally involves contested choices and rights. At the forefront of these are: a woman's right to choose; the civil rights of people with disabilities; the postulated rights of the unborn child; and the rights of the individual versus the rights of society.

Box 4.2: The rights of the unborn child

It is worth noting here that the rights of the unborn child are described as postulated, since both UK and US law do not currently give the fetus clear legal status until he or she is born alive. A fetus is recognized as an entity, whose status deserves some protection, but not as a legal person with rights. The extent of the protection that should be afforded to the fetus has been an issue of particular contention in the USA over recent years. Many US states have criminal and civil laws against prenatal drug abuse, and some of these allow compulsory detention and treatment of a pregnant woman in the interests of her developing fetus. They may also allow removal of the child from the mother once it is born. The enforcement of these laws, and the fact that those who have been detained disproportionately represent women from poorer and ethnic minority backgrounds, has sparked new debate on where the boundaries between maternal and fetal rights should lie.

Shakespeare also highlights the importance of considering the broader social and cultural context in which decisions around prenatal testing are taken. Although medical dialogue around genetics often promotes a discourse of prevention and cure of disease and disability, the disability rights movement is inclined to equate the new genetics with Nazi eugenics. In part, these opposing viewpoints come about because of the different way that disability is constructed in medical and social discourse.

The social model of disability distinguishes impairment (the medical condition of the body) from disability (discrimination and prejudice in society) (Oliver 1990). What this means is that the disability rights movement rejects the 'medical model' focus on impairment as the defining characteristic of life as a disabled person. Shakespeare (1998) describes how the disability movement itself argues that social barriers create disability and that the resulting difficulties of living as a disabled person are due to discrimination and prejudice, rather than impairment. This means that there is a further conflict between medical and social models of disability: medical models locate the problem with the individual, whereas social models locate it more widely in the attitudes and actions of society at large, in terms of the social and structural production of disadvantage.

By ignoring this dimension, then, the approach of medical science fails to distinguish between impairment (which is a biological construct) and disability (which is a social one). In addition, as Shakespeare (1998) suggests, there are many people, both from within the disability rights movement and outside it, who would contest the labelling of all genetic variation as a potential disease or disorder. By referring to these variations found in testing procedures as abnormalities, however, this view is reinforced.

Shakespeare (1999) goes on to develop this argument. While recognizing that clinicians and researchers do not espouse a clear-cut eugenic position, he suggests that there is an implicit 'narrative of tragedy' that surrounds discussion of disability. The obvious result of framing disability in this way is the implication that, where possible, it should be avoided. In this sense, antenatal screening itself is presented through a narrative of optimism – it is framed as a way to avoid the tragedy of the birth of a child with a disability, or to prevent the burden of a disabled child. This view is supported by what is known of the attitudes of obstetricians towards the termination of pregnancies as a result of antenatal testing. Farrant (1985) found that three-quarters of her sample of 323 obstetricians surveyed in 1980 required that women seeking chorionic villus sampling or amniocentesis should agree to a termination in the event of an abnormality being detected. Although there is some evidence that these attitudes have changed over the intervening years, Farrant's work serves as a powerful reminder of the social context in which apparently individual choices, both in relation to testing and termination of pregnancy, come to be made.

Part of the difficulty in reconciling social and medical models of disability lies in the way in which disability is defined. There is little clarity about what should be considered to count as disability, and even less over which disabilities are to be classified as severe. Nevertheless, as Shakespeare (1999) highlights, in rejecting a medical model of disability, those who espouse a social model need to be careful that they do not deny the real consequences of impairment, and that there is a recognition that different degrees of impairment can have different social consequences. There is a danger that the social model of disability can fail to take this into account.

Antenatal screening and eugenics

At the start of this chapter, it was suggested that, of all the applications of genetic technologies, it is antenatal screening and testing that have most often been equated with eugenics. Clearly, the processes in themselves are not straightforwardly eugenic in the accepted sense of the word. However, there is an important difference between eugenic intent and eugenic outcome. Some of the limitations of antenatal screening and testing in terms of individual choice have already been described in this chapter. In the final section, these limitations will be used to argue that the context in which these individual decisions are made can, even unwittingly, promote eugenic outcomes. Issues of routinization of screening, informed consent, the role of health care professionals and the social pressures around termination of pregnancy all have a role to play in this process.

In most cases, the identification of genetic abnormalities through antenatal screening and testing currently creates the possibility of genetic counselling, testing and termination, rather than cures or therapeutic interventions. However, as Press and Browner (1997) show, and as Shakespeare (1998) argues, it may still create the expectation that medical expertise will deliver a baby free from impairment or illness. In this way, Shakespeare suggests, the boundaries between health and disease are altered, so that what previously would have been thought of as a healthy fetus until shown otherwise becomes an at-risk fetus until testing has been carried out. This argument links back to Rothman's (1988) notion of 'the tentative pregnancy' and the idea that women may not consider themselves 'really' pregnant until these tests have been carried out.

Shakespeare (1998) also draws the distinction between *strong eugenics*, defined as population level improvement by control of reproduction via state intervention, and *weak eugenics*, defined as promoting the technologies of reproductive selection via non-coercive individual choices. Weak eugenics is what he suggests is happening at the moment, motivated by the medical judgement that disabled lives cause unacceptable suffering, and a wider social view of impairment as an unnecessary social cost.

Eventually, he argues, this adoption of weak eugenics might result in the kind of population level improvement that strong eugenics implies. This model illustrates how, whereas the intent of antenatal screening and testing may not be overtly eugenic, the sum total of the outcomes may be.

Policy development for antenatal screening

The delivery of antenatal screening, like most health care services, necessitates a compromise between the provision of an ideal service to relatively few individuals at high cost and a less ideal but more equitable service. The reason why it is seen as so important by social scientists is that, with the completion of the Human Genome Project, we will eventually have an increased ability to test prenatally not only for serious diseases, but also for relatively mild disease and late-onset disorders. We may also be able to identify elevated risks for common diseases such as heart disease and eventually non-disease characteristics such as height. Once we can test for these characteristics, there is a possibility that decisions to terminate pregnancies may be made on the basis of them. As these tests become available, there is a danger that existing policies, with all their variations and shortcomings, will be used as models for these new tests.

Pre-implantation diagnosis

One rapidly developing new technology for antenatal screening is pre-implantation diagnosis. This is a procedure that involves testing the early embryo after *in vitro* fertilization (IVF). One or two cells can be removed for testing, and embryos with genetic abnormalities can be identified and subsequently not implanted. The procedure is usually carried out for couples who are carriers of conditions such as cystic fibrosis, who may already have an affected child and feel unable to cope with another. In the UK, there are few licensed centres for performing the technique and screening for spontaneous genetic disorders such as Down's syndrome has only recently been approved in principle by the Human Fertilization and Embryology Authority, the body that regulates *in vitro* fertilization treatment in the UK (Ferriman 2001; Flinter 2001). However, centres elsewhere in Europe and the USA already offer this procedure, some of which use the procedure for sex selection of embryos unrelated to potential genetic disorders. Service development in the UK is currently highly regulated, with each new test to be provided by existing centres requiring a new licence application (Flinter 2001). However, the procedure is likely to become more common and, at the same time, the range of characteristics that can be tested for will become wider.

Using genetic information

Some decisions have already been made as to the acceptable uses of certain kinds of genetic information. Much has been made of the possibility of sex selection, but, as we have seen, some regions in the UK already withhold this information from prospective parents, for fears of how it will be used. This debate over the appropriate uses of information is at the heart of modern genetic testing dilemmas: if we offer people testing to give them information about their particular circumstances, then should we be prepared to accept whatever choice they might make on the basis of this information?

Box 4.3: Genetic testing for deafness

One example of the kind of situation that may occur is in genetic testing for deafness. Some forms of deafness have a hereditary component; surveys have shown that there is a group of deaf parents, sometimes referred to as 'culturally deaf', who would prefer to have deaf children. These culturally deaf individuals tend to be involved extensively with the deaf community, in terms of schools for the deaf, campaigning organizations, and so on. The reasons that they give for preferring to have a deaf child are that they are familiar with the social, educational and support networks within the deaf community, but not familiar with these in the hearing community. They also raise issues of communication and language development for a hearing child brought up in a deaf environment as potentially problematic. Within this group, a small proportion of these parents say that they would consider termination of pregnancy if a child was shown to be hearing (Middleton *et al.* 1998).

As stated at the outset of this chapter, antenatal screening and testing is generally conceptualized as a means to prevent the birth of a child with a disability. However, as the case of sex selection illustrates most clearly, there are potential scenarios in which it could be used to prevent the birth of what would generally be referred to as a 'normal' or 'healthy' baby. These scenarios become more complex when testing for disorders such as hereditary deafness is carried out within deaf families who may be strongly opposed to the construction of their particular disorder as a disabling factor. Scenarios like these may at the moment be relatively rare, but they will become more common with the ability to test for late-onset disorders and non-disease characteristics.

Using these kind of examples, however, illustrates how complex these issues are, and that the decisions that people might choose to make on the basis of genetic information are based on complex value systems and beliefs. It also illustrates the varying ways in which disability or abnormality may be defined by different societies, or groups within those societies. Fundamentally, though, it becomes clear that it is highly problematic to offer screening and testing and to ask people to make an informed choice on the basis of these test results, if we then tell them that their choice is unacceptable.

Summary points

- Although most antenatal screening procedures do not themselves use genetic technologies, they are commonly used as a basis for deciding who should be offered diagnostic genetic tests.

- Fears are often expressed about the eugenic possibilities of widespread antenatal screening and testing, since in most cases the only option to act on the information these procedures give is to terminate a pregnancy.

- Critics have argued that the use of these procedures means that pregnancies are now considered 'at risk' until proven otherwise, and that women may not 'really' consider themselves pregnant until satisfactory results have been received.

- The fact that these procedures are presented and perceived as part of routine antenatal care raises wider concerns about the medicalization of pregnancy and about informed choice. It has been suggested that while too little information is a bad thing, too much may paradoxically increase dependency on health care professionals.

- In considering the accusations of eugenics that have been levelled at antenatal screening and testing, we need to distinguish between eugenic intent and eugenic outcome. The context in which individual choices are made, in terms of attitudes of both health care professionals and wider societies to disability, affects these choices.

- Disability is constructed differently in medical and social discourse, and these constructions come into conflict in relation to antenatal screening and testing. There is little agreement about what counts as a disability or an abnormality, and this may vary widely according to social context. This variation needs to be taken into account in developing policy frameworks.

Further reading

Edwards, J., Hirsch, E., Franklin, S., Price, F. and Strathern, M. (1993) *Technologies of Procreation: Kinship in the Age of Assisted Conception.* Manchester: Manchester University Press.

Farrant, W. (1985) Who's for amniocentesis? The politics of prenatal screening, in H. Homans (ed.) *The Sexual Politics of Reproduction*. Aldershot: Gower.

Green, J.M., Statham, H. and Snowdon, C. (1994) *Pregnancy: A Testing Time*. Report of the Cambridge Prenatal Screening Study. Cambridge: Centre for Family Research, University of Cambridge.

Rapp, R. (2000) *Testing Women, Testing the Fetus: The Social Impact of Amniocentesis in America*. New York: Routledge.

Spallone, P. (1989) *Beyond Conception: The New Politics of Reproduction*. Basingstoke: Macmillan.

Stacey, M. (1996) The new genetics: a feminist view, in T. Marteau and M. Richards (eds) *The Troubled Helix: Social and Psychological Implications of the New Human Genetics*. Cambridge: Cambridge University Press.

5

GENETIC TESTING

Introduction

This chapter begins with a consideration of the different types of genetic testing and some of the specific difficulties that may be raised by these different types of test. Its focus is on testing individuals for disorders that evidence suggests may be present in their families. The differences between screening and testing are considered in the previous chapter; the implications of large-scale population screening are discussed in Chapter 6. This chapter then moves on to consider some of the more fundamental issues that arise from the general process of genetic testing, focusing on the following areas: confidentiality of genetic information; genetic testing and insurance; and autonomy and informed consent in genetic testing.

These issues will be considered in the context of the health care services that are intended to support genetic testing and, in particular, the process of genetic counselling. The chapter concludes with a discussion of the relevance of sociological and anthropological studies of family and kinship to genetic practice, considering how a knowledge of lay understandings of genetics may help us to comprehend the decisions individuals make in relation to genetic testing.

What is genetic testing?

As the British Medical Association (BMA) (1998) note, the single term 'genetic testing' encompasses a wide range of possible scenarios, in terms of the type of test, the disorder to be tested for and the stage at which this testing takes place. In general terms, however, genetic testing may be defined as follows:

Genetic testing is the analysis of a specific gene, its product or function, or other DNA or chromosome analysis, to detect or exclude an
alteration likely to be associated with a genetic disorder.

(Harper 1997: 8)

Within this broad framework, there are two main types of genetic
tests: **diagnostic** and **predictive**. Diagnostic testing is performed in a
symptomatic individual to aid in the diagnosis, treatment and management of the patient. There is broad agreement among clinicians and
commentators that the use of genetic techniques in ordinary diagnosis
(*after* a condition has begun to manifest itself) is generally thought to
offer few problems not raised by other kinds of diagnostic techniques.
Like other techniques, it offers the potential for identifying the most
effective and appropriate management of the condition. However, where
diagnostic genetic testing does differ from other forms of diagnosis is in
the implications it may have for other family members. The issues that
this raises of consent and confidentiality will be discussed in more detail
below.

In contrast, predictive testing raises many new issues, both in terms of
the delivery of health care services and in terms of the wider social
implications. Predictive testing may also be subdivided into two types
(Lenaghan 1998). **Presymptomatic** tests are carried out for genetic mutations associated with dominantly inherited conditions, where having
the mutation almost inevitably leads to the disease. One example of a
presymptomatic test currently in use is the test for Huntington's disease.
Predispositional tests are carried out for gene mutations that confer an
increased risk, but not a certainty, of developing a disease. Predispositional
tests are currently used to identify mutations in the BRCA1 and BRCA2
genes that are linked with breast and ovarian cancer. Potentially, these
kinds of test could also be used in cases where the link between the
genetic component and the risk of developing the disease is less clear –
for example, for multifactorial conditions such as heart disease. The
implications of testing for these more general genetic susceptibilities are
discussed in more detail in Chapter 6.

Most of the predictive genetic tests that are currently provided are
associated with reproduction, in the sense that they are used to provide
information about the likelihood of genetic disorders in future children.
However, as Lenaghan (1998) notes, predictive tests that provide people
with more information about their own chances of developing a disease
are becoming more common, and this leads her to raise a series of questions about how these tests should be used:

Which diseases should we test for and why?

Some of the diseases that can be identified through genetic testing are
untreatable, for example Huntington's disease. Although a negative result

may provide reassurance, a postitive result does not create the opportunity for medical intervention. There are two opposing viewpoints here: first, that we should carry out presymptomatic tests for diseases under the auspices of health care only if we can do something clinically about the disease when it is identified; and, second, that we should not deny individuals information about future events that they may wish to use in making life choices regarding reproduction, finance, and so on.

Box 5.1: Genetic testing and fatalism

In considering the consequences of providing information about the future, we need to think not only about those individuals who discover they will develop a disease for which nothing can be done, but also those who discover they have a predisposition for which preventative action could be taken. In the case of familial hypercholesterolaemia, there is some evidence to suggest that detecting a genetic predisposition can lead to a sense of fatalism. Rather than attempting to control the condition by modifying their lifestyles, individuals may see it as uncontrollable and unchangeable, because it is genetic (Senior *et al.* 1999). This fatalistic view has clear implications for preventative health care.

Should it make a difference whether the disease is common? Or serious?

The first of these questions is linked to public demand for health care and, more broadly, to the potential economic benefits of early identification and treatment of disease. In terms of the seriousness of the condition, it might be argued that individuals are more likely to want information on their genetic status where a serious condition is involved. However, the uptake rates for testing for Huntington's disease do not bear this out – currently, only around 10 per cent of those offered the test choose to take it. The fact that no treatment is available clearly has an impact on this figure, but it illustrates that there are no straightforward assumptions to be made about who will seek genetic testing and why.

These issues lead on to a third question:

If we decide that we will offer a test for a particular disease or condition, who is eligible?

Once a test is made available, some parameters may need to be set regarding who it is available to. One viewpoint here is that any available test should be given to an individual who asks for it. This is often the model that antenatal testing works on, although in some cases women will be asked to pay for a test that is not routinely offered to all clients. Although this scenario avoids imposing medical judgement on the availability of testing, it becomes problematic in relation to the predictive testing of children. Should children be tested as a result of their own, or their parent's, request? We will return to this question later in the chapter.

These questions, in turn, lead on to issues of confidentiality, consent and the right to genetic information.

Confidentiality

The British Medical Association (BMA 1998: 68) states that 'Patients have a right to expect that health professionals will not disclose any information which they learn during the course of their professional duties, unless the patient has given permission'. Contrary to popular belief, however, this duty of confidentiality is not absolute, and there are circumstances where it may be overridden. Most commonly, this is as the result of a legal requirement, but occasionally it is deemed necessary in the public interest, where the patient or others may be put at risk of serious harm if the information is not disclosed. The interpretation of this latter issue has important implications for genetic testing. Obviously, genetic information gained as a result of testing can be released with consent to third parties; those with an interest in this kind of information include employers, insurers and solicitors. However, as we have already noted, the difficulty with genetic information is the added dimension that genetic testing of one individual has relevance for other family members. Although other decisions to undergo medical testing or treatment are more purely personal, the very nature of genetic testing means that it is likely to have implications for others. As a result, this can present health professionals with a conflict between their duty, on the one hand, to maintain patient confidentiality, and their duty, on the other, to protect others from avoidable harm and suffering. The situation is further complicated by the viewpoint of some geneticists, who argue that, because of the nature of genetic testing, the patient is best conceptualized as the family, rather than the individual. From this viewpoint, maintaining individual confidentiality is less of a priority.

As these varying interpretations suggest, what this means in practice is that the level of confidentiality required for genetic information between families is not always consistent. The BMA believes that, while the doctor's duty of confidentiality is of fundamental importance, individuals should be encouraged to consider the implications of their actions for others, and uses the following two case studies to highlight the key issues involved.

Testing for a dominant disorder in an individual inevitably reveals information about the genetic status of other people related to that individual

An example of someone in these circumstances would be a woman who knows her maternal grandfather has Huntington's disease, but whose mother has no symptoms and has declined presymptomatic testing. If the daughter herself decides to undergo testing and the test proves positive, the daughter will know that her mother also carries the affected gene and has passed it on to her.

In this case, then, the daughter's decision to find out about her own genetic status could give her information about her mother which her mother does not know. The BMA's guidance in relation to this example is that, while ideally an agreement would be reached between mother and daughter in relation to the test, testing should not normally be refused on the grounds that it will provide information about a relative that the relative does not wish to know (BMA 1998).

An individual may discover from testing that other family members could be at risk of developing or passing on a serious genetic disorder

An example of someone in this position would be the mother of a son with Duchenne muscular dystrophy who has tested positive for carrier status. She knows that her sister is planning children and that information about her carrier status could be an important factor in her sister's reproductive decisions. If she does not share the information, her sister could give birth to an affected child and may feel she lacked the opportunity to make an informed decision on this basis. The BMA's guidance in relation to this example is that, while the information would clearly be relevant to others, this relevance does not justify disclosure without the individual's consent (BMA 1998).

This possible conflict between confidentiality and preventing harm is a difficult area and there is no general agreement. Like the BMA, the House of Commons Science and Technology Committee (1995) gives precedence to the duty of confidentiality, stating: 'If counselling cannot persuade someone to consent to sharing information with their relatives the individual's decision to withhold information should be paramount' (para. 228). This conclusion was reached on the grounds that failure to guarantee confidentiality would stop people from seeking testing that could be beneficial to their own health.

The Nuffield Council on Bioethics (1993), however, considering the same issues, concluded that in some cases warning others of potential serious harm was more important: 'In exceptional circumstances, health professionals might be justified in disclosing genetic information to other family members, despite an individual's desire for confidentiality' (p. 43).

Nevertheless, both reports emphasize the importance of trying to persuade the individual to disclose the information voluntarily, and the potential social consequences of being identified as having an abnormality or impairment of some kind. Disclosing information voluntarily, however, requires a certain level of family relations, and of communication lines within those relations, to work in practice. Genetic science is sometimes criticized for operating within a narrow notion of the family, which assumes straightforward blood linkages and positive family relationships within which lines of communication already exist. We will explore the potential problems associated with these assumptions in more detail at the end of this chapter.

Genetics and insurance

In considering the issue of confidentiality, as well as the potential harm that might result to an individual or their family as a result of genetic testing, the area of insurance is one of the most widely debated. In the USA, the results from genetic tests are widely used in assessing premiums for private health care insurance. In the UK, the government's Genetics and Insurance Committee, set up in 1999 by the Department of Health, initially agreed that the results of certain genetic tests could be used by companies when underwriting life insurance policies (http://www.doh.gov.uk/genetics/gaic.htm). These test results were to be used within the confines of a system of voluntary regulation based on a code of conduct drawn up by the Association of British Insurers (ABI). Under this agreement, the results of genetic tests for Huntington's disease were approved for use in October 2000, and the use of other tests was placed under review, including the tests for hereditary breast cancer and familial Alzheimer's disease.

These uses and potential uses of genetic information have led to concerns about who will have access to the information and why, although to some extent it may be argued that these concerns have developed after the event. Insurers have been using the results of other kinds of medical tests to assess premiums for many years. In the USA, the American Society for Human Genetics has adopted the position that there is no clear boundary between genetic and non-genetic tests (Thomson 1998). For individuals seeking health insurance, for example, information from genetic tests has the same status as other medical test results and may be used in calculating insurance premiums. Employers are another group who might wish to access genetic information, but in this case there is more legal protection. The Americans with Disabilities Act 1990 uses a wide ranging definition of the concept of disability, including individuals

who are 'regarded as having an impairment' (emphasis added) that substantially limits life activities. It seeks to ensure that those with disabilities, or who are so regarded, are not unfairly discriminated against in the
workplace or in their access to public services. In 2000, a specific amendment was introduced to prohibit discrimination in federal employment
based on genetic information. Under this amendment, information about
an individual's genetic tests or the tests of their family members, together
with information about family history, has protected status. The aim is
to ensure that individuals are employed on the basis of their current
ability to perform a job, rather than regarded as having an impairment
because of the possibility that they may one day develop a disease or
condition.

In the UK, the Disability Discrimination Act 1995 uses a less wide-
ranging definition of disability, applying only to those with a genetic
disorder who are currently classed as disabled. It makes no provision for
those who possess a genetic mutation that means that they may or will
develop a disorder in the future. As a result, the Disability Discrimination Act protects against employment discrimination, but only for those
who are displaying the effects of a genetic disorder. Although there is
little evidence that genetic information regarding future risks or possibilities is currently used by UK employers, the possibility remains open.
Discrimination in insurance in the UK is permitted if it is based on reliable
information such as a medical report or statistical data. The role of the
Genetics and Insurance Committee is not to investigate the arguments
for and against the use of genetic information in these circumstances,
but instead to establish whether the results of particular genetic tests are
sufficiently accurate for insurers to use when assessing an applicant.

Under the terms of their code of conduct, and their original agreement with the Genetics and Insurance Committee (GAIC), British insurers
could not insist that people take genetic tests. In addition, a certain
amount of life cover, originally set at £100,000 and intended to be
periodically reviewed, could be bought by an individual without them
revealing that they had taken a test. However, for larger amounts, if an
individual had taken an approved test and failed to disclose it, the policy
would be void. Despite the limitations of its scope, this agreement led to
widespread concern about the possible creation of a 'genetic underclass',
who would be unable to obtain insurance. Currently, approximately
99 per cent of the UK population who seek life insurance are provided
with cover. Ninety-five per cent are insured at a standard rate, with 4
per cent having to pay higher premiums. The remaining 1 per cent
are refused cover outright (Low et al. 1998). In line with this model, the
ABI was keen to stress that those testing positive were likely to be still
able to get insurance, but that this cover would be provided at higher
premiums.

However, the Fifth Report of the House of Commons Select Committee on Science and Technology, issued in April 2001, highlighted the

potential problems of the use of genetic test results by insurers, even within the limited terms delineated by the GAIC's process of approval (http://www.parliament.the-stationery-office.co.uk/pa/cm200001/cmselect/cmsctech/174/17402.htm). It recommended that insurers should publish clear explanations as to how genetic test results are used in calculating insurance premiums, and noted that there was no satisfactory means of monitoring and enforcing the ABI's code of conduct. The report also cast doubt on the reliability and validity of existing test results and recommended that the GAIC re-examine the decision to approve the use of the test for Huntington's disease by insurers. Most importantly, the report proposed a voluntary moratorium on the use of all positive genetic test results by insurers for a period of at least two years, including the proviso that, if insurers were unwilling to self-regulate in this way, government legislation should enforce a ban. This moratorium was supported by the Human Genetics Commission and, in May 2001, the ABI confirmed that they would comply with the moratorium, by extending the upper limit for insurance policies issued without disclosure of genetic information to £300,000. Above this level, only tests approved by the GAIC will be taken into account.

For insurers, the potential benefits of having access to genetic test results are obvious. They argue that tests will help them to assess risk more accurately and that asking for genetic information will prevent individuals who know they are at risk of developing a life-threatening illness from taking out huge insurance policies. This, in turn, is presented as a benefit for other clients, since the end result of paying out on large claims is a rise in the cost of cover for everyone else.

Although this argument appears relatively straightforward, it raises two major issues: first, there may be a conflict between genetic testing to ensure accurate and appropriate medical care for a condition, and having to pay inflated insurance premiums. This conflict could result in delays to diagnosis or treatment that are detrimental to an individual's health, and this in itself has economic implications.

Box 5.2: Biomedical research and genetic testing

Related to this point is the use of test results from biomedical research. Although test results from research have not to date been used in calculating insurance premiums, concerns have been voiced that the possibility might deter people from participating in research. The UK Forum for Genetics and Insurance, the Association of British Insurers and The British Society for Human Genetics have issued a joint statement confirming that research results will not be used in this way (Kmietowicz 2001a).

Second, all the tests that are currently used in the USA, or under consideration in the UK, do not have the same status. Some, for example the test for Huntington's disease, are diagnostic and are relatively accurate (although even here there is occasionally a 'grey area' in test results where it is likely but not certain that an individual will develop the disease). Others, such as the test for breast cancer, are predictive, so that carrying the BRCA1 or BRCA2 gene signifies only a strong predisposition to breast cancer, thought to be around 60–65 per cent. In these cases, individuals who are found to carry the mutation but do not develop the disease would be unfairly penalized.

More generally, it is argued that even individuals with the most common genetic disorders represent only a small fraction of the population at large, and that the economic case for disclosure of test results has been overstated by the insurance industry. As Morrison (1998) notes, only one in 20 life policies are actually claimed on death, and the proportion of claims related to genetics must be smaller still. From a social point of view, the creation of a genetic underclass is likely to have more far-reaching implications than a general rise in insurance premiums as the result of a relatively small number of large claims. This is particularly true in the USA, where there may be no available health care to those refused medical insurance. By contrast, it is sometimes argued that the existence of the National Health Service in the UK means that insurers do not need to be prohibited from using test results, because they will not undermine availability of and access to health care. However, some UK insurance companies have routinely asked clients for the results of genetic tests which have not yet been approved by the GAIC on accuracy grounds, for example early-onset Alzheimer's disease (Kmietowicz 2001b), and this was a key factor in the call for a moratorium. There is also research evidence that life insurers may not be operating a consistent policy in the way they treat genetic information. Low and co-workers' (1998) study of the evidence for discrimination on genetic grounds by UK insurers found that individuals who represented no increased risk (such as healthy carriers of recessive conditions) appeared to have had difficulties in obtaining insurance. They conclude that there is evidence of unjustified genetic discrimination by UK insurers, but that this does not follow a clear pattern and the reasons for discrimination are not straightforward. Some of the inconsistencies found may be a result of failure to understand the significance of genetic information, rather than a deliberate policy of discrimination.

Low et al. (1998) also highlight the fact that their study focuses on monogenetic conditions, where patterns of inheritance are relatively clear-cut. Predispositional testing, and testing for polygenic disorders, will yield much less precise information. Given the difficulties apparent in the insurance industry's handling of more straightforward information, the appropriate use of 'genetic probabilities' requires serious consideration.

However, as Warren (2001) points out, access to insurance is not perceived as a basic right in the UK and, therefore, questions about equity and justice are at odds with the way insurance is provided. Equally, it is unlikely that the welfare state will be extended to cover insurance provision. Nevertheless, the situation is complicated in the UK because of the link between life insurance and housing. Most UK housing is owner-occupied. Commonly, obtaining a mortgage requires a life insurance policy to be taken out by the applicant. If access to life insurance is affected through the use of genetic testing, then access to housing could also become problematic, and some commentators would argue that shelter is a basic human right.

Consent to testing

'There is general agreement in medicine that all procedures should be based on the free and informed consent of the individual tested. The fundamental basis for consent is respect for an individual's right to control what is done to his or her own body' (BMA 1998: 62–3). In common with other professional medical organizations, the BMA is also clear that it regards consent as a *process* of information giving and explanation that should facilitate an informed decision, rather than a one-off act such as signing a consent form. In terms of competence to give consent, an individual is presumed to possess the mental competence to make a decision unless it can be proved otherwise. What this means in practice is that an individual's decision may be viewed as rational, irrational or for no reason at all, but this does not mean that an individual can legally or morally be overridden (BMA 1998).

The principle of informed consent requires that, as well as the mental capacity to make a decision, an individual must also be in possession of sufficient accurate information. The decision must also be voluntary. Clearly, however, there is a possibility of conflict between respecting the individual's informed choices about his or her own health care and acting in what the doctor considers to be the patient's best interests. An individual may refuse genetic testing that would help to determine the most appropriate form of care to be provided, which might in the long term be seen as in their best interest. While recognizing this conflict, the BMA's advice to its members is that legally, 'testing . . . a competent adult without consent, or in the face of an informed refusal, could constitute battery' (BMA 1998: 64).

As we have noted, the principle of informed consent depends on the competence of the individual to make an informed decision. Where competence is judged to be lacking, health professionals must decide whether a particular test is necessary and in the best interests of the patient. One of the major criteria for determining competence concerns the comprehension of the information material to the decision, as well as comprehension of the likely consequences of deciding either way.

This latter point of comprehending the likely consequences is key to debates around testing. With the advent of presymptomatic testing, there is the real risk of consequent harm to the patient as a result of testing. These consequences may affect health, including depression and suicide in a Huntington's patient, social standing (e.g. stigmatization by the community) and potentially economic well-being (e.g. loss of employment or uninsurability). All of these issues need to be considered as part of the informed consent process when a person is considering participation in a genetic testing programme.

Box 5.3: Huntington's disease and the phenomenon of survivor guilt

In considering the implications of testing, concern is usually focused on those who receive results indicating that they are at risk of developing a particular disorder. Negative test results are largely assumed to be unproblematic. However, work with those at risk of Huntington's disease has shown that individuals who test negative may experience what has been termed 'survivor guilt', since they will not have to suffer what others in the family may have suffered. This guilt may be exacerbated by a belief that their negative test means that siblings are more likely to test positive, even though this is not the case (Huggins *et al.* 1992).

Informed consent and children

The question of what to do about children and young people who want to be tested for adult onset disorders raises particular problems. As Dickenson (1999) points out, existing case law allows young people under 18 years who are judged competent to consent for testing for adult onset disorders. However, some genetic units have a policy of not testing those under the age of 18 for diseases that will not manifest until adulthood. Although in the UK the Children Act 1989 provides for the possibility that a child's expressed wish may not serve his or her best interests, Dickenson argues that this is a paternalistic approach, and that autonomy and identity as a person only come through making choices which are enacted.

For other kinds of genetic testing, for example diagnostic testing, parental consent is deemed to be valid in much the same way as for any other kind of medical procedure. How these inconsistencies over different kinds of genetic testing are resolved is likely to depend on the severity of the disorders under discussion and the likely treatment options. However, there is increasing sociological evidence to suggest that children who have lived with illness or awareness of the possibility of illness have surprisingly high levels of understanding in relation to both medical procedures and their consequences (e.g. Alderson 1993).

Understanding genetic information

The principle of informed consent depending on comprehension of the information material to a decision raises a broader issue: Do people generally really comprehend genetic information? Although this issue is potentially problematic in relation to any technical medical procedure, it is sometimes argued that it is especially problematic in relation to genetic testing because of the complexity of both the technical procedure itself and the possible consequences. In addition, it raises a practical problem – how do we know whether an individual has an adequate understanding? Lay knowledge and attitudes to genetic testing have been the subject of a variety of studies over recent years; these studies have included actual clients of genetic services, members of a client's extended family and members of the general public as their subjects (Pilnick *et al*. 2000). In summarizing the results from one such study, Decruyenaere *et al*. (1992) draw a general conclusion that might equally be applied to the findings of many others: that the rate of technical advance in genetics contrasts sharply with the slow diffusion of information on this subject to the general population. This is true even of studies involving clients and their families (e.g. Suslak *et al*. 1985; Denayer *et al*. 1992). Taken as a whole, this body of research serves to illustrate that knowledge about genetics and genetic services is poor even among individuals who may be either at risk or thought to have special knowledge due to their kin relationship to an affected person (Pilnick *et al*. 2000).

Box 5.4: Genetic testing and risk status

In reviewing the findings of studies such as those discussed above, the lack of accurate information among those at risk of genetic disorders is often considered to be a particular problem. However, as the work of Evans *et al*. (1993) highlights, this may not always be the case. Using a questionnaire, Evans *et al*. examined the perceptions of risk in women with a family history of breast cancer. The questionnaire asked women about their perceptions of the risk of breast cancer in the general population, as well as their individual risk. As might be expected from previous work, less than half the sample were able to correctly identify their own life-time risk. However, there were a substantial number of women who significantly underestimated their own risk. As the authors suggest, for these women subsequent genetic counselling was likely to be a worrying or threatening experience, rather than a reassuring one.

Genetic testing and genetic counselling

As the studies discussed above serve to illustrate, the rapid advances in the field of human genetics have created an ever widening gap between those specialists involved with them and the general public who are the intended beneficiaries. Genetic counselling is seen as an important way of addressing this gap (Pilnick 2002). There is no one definition of genetic counselling that is universally accepted, but the following definition is widely quoted:

> An educational process that seeks to assist affected and/or at risk individuals to understand the nature of the genetic disorder, its transmission, and the options open to them in management and family planning.
>
> (Kelly 1986: 343)

In both the UK and the USA, genetic testing is largely offered in conjunction with genetic counselling. For some tests, such as the test for Huntington's disease in the UK, the test is not available without specific counselling beforehand. This counselling is usually carried out in the client's own home or in hospital outpatient clinics, and may involve clinical geneticists and/or genetic counsellors. Genetic counsellors are a relatively new addition to the health care professions. Initially, counsellors were often drawn from a nursing background, but now tend to be specialist Master's graduates in genetic counselling.

Despite the lack of a single accepted definition of genetic counselling activities, there are several principles underpinning the activity that have more widespread acceptance. Informed consent is one that has already been discussed, but non-directiveness and autonomy are also considered to be key.

Non-directiveness in genetic counselling

The concept of non-directive counselling, which originates from the writings of Carl Rogers on client-centred therapy, is well accepted in the genetics community. This concept is widely understood to mean that the role of the genetic counsellor should be that of information provider, rather than decision maker, and that information should be presented in a neutral and non-judgemental manner.

However, research has highlighted difficulties in practice with non-directive counselling, and the meaning of the term itself has also been contested. Definition of the term is critical, since it may be invoked to incorporate anything from solicited advice to persuasive coercion (Kessler 1997). Some commentators have suggested that the principle of non-directiveness has the potential to conflict with another principle that has become central to health care in recent years, that of individual autonomy.

Autonomy is a key tenet of bioethical approaches to medicine and is discussed in more detail in Chapter 9. Although upholding the principle of autonomy may be one way of guarding against accusations of medical dominance or paternalism, client autonomy may not be desirable to all those receiving a counselling service. An individual may decide that they would prefer a health professional to make a decision for them, based on their expert knowledge in the area. In this scenario, exercising autonomous choice would mean delegating the decision. This pattern of events is often the norm in other kinds of medical actions and is discussed in more detail below, but presents a particular problem for genetic counsellors. If a client wishes to abdicate his or her right to choice, how can the principle of non-directiveness be maintained?

Conflicts between the 'medical' and 'counselling' perspectives

An interesting issue, and one that is not often explicitly considered, is the way that the activities of health care professionals around an individual's decision to have a genetic test or not are framed as *counselling*. In practice, the work of genetic counsellors may encompass anything from facilitating decision making in relation to genetic testing through to diagnostic news delivery and subsequently giving information on available treatment or management options (Pilnick 2002). While counselling is the umbrella term used to describe all these activities, some are more easily reconciled than others with the client-led ethos to which genetic counsellors aspire. This client-led ethos, however, grows out of a counselling paradigm that is in sharp contrast to the typical organization of knowledge and interactional behaviour in medical encounters. In the 'traditional' kind of medical encounter, patients or clients present their problem and, after assessing this problem, the health professional typically proposes a course of action. In the psychotherapeutic model of counselling, it is the client who sets the agenda and who is encouraged to propose solutions to their own problems. This ambiguity of role for genetic counsellors may be a contributory factor to the difficulties of achieving the aim of non-directiveness in practice.

Difficulties in achieving client-led consultations

It has been argued (Clarke *et al.* 1996) that the ethos of genetic counselling ought to be one where the client sets the agenda; as a result, the first element of the counsellor's role is to listen. However, there is also plenty of evidence that this is not what occurs in practice (e.g. Michie *et al.* 1997). These findings have sometimes been interpreted as further evidence of medical dominance, or even more generally as counsellor incompetence.

However, sociological studies of the interactional processes that occur in genetic counselling suggest that the situation is more complex and that a variety of factors are at work.

In the first place, asking a client to set an agenda can be problematic, because to some extent it presupposes a knowledge of what is important or what will be taken to be relevant in that context. This scenario is illustrated by the following extract, taken from a consultation with a client with a family history of Huntington's disease, who has made inquiries about being tested himself.

> *Clinical geneticist*: . . . and you thought things through and you wanted to just find out a little bit more and look ahead and consider the pros and cons of, er, what the next step might be. Can I just ask? Have you got any extra questions that if you want to add to the obvious list?
>
> *Client*: Umm, not, not, that I think of the moment.
>
> (Pilnick 2002, transcription simplified)

This extract is taken from the very opening exchanges of a counselling session, where the geneticist is describing his understanding of what has brought the client to the clinic. There are two issues to note here. First, that the geneticist does explicitly invite the contribution of an agenda, or at least items for an agenda, from the client. The second is that the way that this invitation is framed not only requires some understanding on the part of the client as to issues that might be appropriate for discussion, but also which of these would be in addition to the 'obvious' list that the geneticist intends. What this illustrates is that encouraging or inviting a client to set an agenda will not always achieve the desired result.

Where client-led agendas are arrived at, however, these may lead to problems of their own. The following extract is taken from a consultation with a mother and daughter who have attended a genetic clinic together. There is a family history of breast cancer; although the mother has not developed breast cancer, one of her daughters has. Her other daughter, who is present, is considering testing for the genetic mutations associated with breast cancer.

> *Counsellor*: Even with the gene, then there's still only eighty percent . . .
>
> *Daughter*: That you'll ever develop it.
>
> *Counsellor*: Mmm.
>
> *Mother*: Yeah but . . . Well it's, say me mum passed it on to me.
>
> *Counsellor*: Yeah. It may be that it's skipped through you and gone to [daughter].
>
> *Mother*: Cos I mean the dad died of cancer so, what I'm trying to figure out is have I passed it on?
>
> (Pilnick 2002, simplified transcript)

In this case, although the daughter's agenda, as discussed at the beginning of the consultation, is to make a decision about testing, the mother's appears to be rather different. She has not herself developed breast cancer and, at the age of sixty, is unlikely to develop the hereditary form of the disease. In this section of the consultation, her agenda appears to be more concerned with establishing responsibility for the genetic disorder. What this extract highlights, then, is a rather more delicate issue: that allowing clients to set their own agenda may run the risk of excluding discussion of important issues or, as in this case, including those which are potentially less relevant to the decisions which are to be made. This consultation also illustrates the practical difficulties of taking the view that, in genetics, the family rather than the individual is the patient. Different family members may have different agendas in relation to counselling and testing and these may not be easily reconciled.

In addition, examining the actual process of counselling adds to the evidence suggesting that not everyone actually wants to make their own decision in these circumstances. Utterances of the kind 'what would you do in my situation' or 'what do most people do?' occur as a result. Responding to these kinds of utterances is particularly problematic for counsellors and links back to how broadly the concept of non-directiveness is to be interpreted. In broad terms, while coercion is clearly directive, statements such as 'In your situation, most people choose to do X' can also be interpreted as directive, since they implicitly offer the option to be like most people, or to depart from the norm. More broadly still, some commentators have argued that offering tests at all is directive, because it presupposes that people who have particular conditions will want to know about them.

Arguments over directiveness and autonomy are fundamentally linked to the difficulties of achieving informed consent to testing, and whether it is ever possible to understand fully the implications. Chapter 9 examines in more detail how these implications exist not only in an abstract philosophical sense but also in a social sense. As with other kinds of medical procedures, one of these implications is risk – not only of the procedure itself, or of the probability of being diagnosed with a genetic disorder, but also the risks to family relationships that may come with genetic knowledge.

Genetic testing and risk

As we saw in the previous chapter, there are two ways to apply information on risk assessment in relation to health care. In antenatal screening, it is applied generally, across the whole population of pregnant women. However, as Carter (1995) describes, the second way to apply expert knowledge is to identify individuals with a high probability of ill health and target them for specific interventions. Genetic testing falls into this category. Since individuals offered genetic testing often have no outward signs of illness, the categories 'healthy' and 'ill' become ambiguous for this group. It is possible for an individual who has a positive result in a predictive genetic test, such as the test for breast and ovarian cancer, to become other than healthy, without being definably ill. Within this kind of model as it applies to health care [other examples, Carter (1995), are HIV and cholesterol testing], the final step is usually the availability of a technology to modify an individual's identified harm. However, for genetic testing, in most cases any technological intervention is limited to counselling provision, and it is important to recognize the impact that this may have on individual perceptions of risk and subsequent decisions to test or not to test. The particular problem with trying to define a practically useful level of risk in relation to the application of genetic testing is that, for an individual, the only end result that is likely to count is whether they have an affected gene or not and, if so, whether anything can medically be done.

It is also important here to reconsider Grinyer's (1995) argument about the assumption inbuilt in expert assessment of risk – that decisions in relation to testing are made in an 'ideal world'. In an ideal world, for example, there might be clear lines of communication between family members and a clear understanding of biological relationships within the family unit. Evidently, this will not always be the case in reality, and particular family circumstances (wishing to conceal the paternity of a child, for example) will impact on how information about risk is perceived and the weight that it is given in the decision-making process. As these kinds of considerations illustrate, one of the key social implications of genetic knowledge is its impact upon families.

The use of family pedigrees in genetic testing

One issue that has not yet been considered in this chapter's focus on recent and novel applications of genetic science is the role that more established procedures continue to play alongside these developments. Nukaga and Cambrosio (1997) point out that, even in the age of the new genetics, enquiries into family stories of disease or illness routinely resort to the drawing of a family pedigree. This pedigree is constructed from an individual's knowledge of their family relationships and the occurrence of disease or illness within them. Nukaga and Cambrosio argue that, despite the pedigree's omnipresence and continued importance, it is rarely discussed in literature examining the new genetics, because it is considered unexciting, routine and unsophisticated, compared to activities such as genetic sequencing. They argue that the way in which genetic counselling is structured reinforces this decision – the first meeting with a client typically focuses on collecting family history information, and it is not until subsequent visits that the business of counselling proper is seen to begin. In this way, the taking of a family history is consigned to the realms of the factual and unproblematic. However, as the discussion of kinship that follows shows, this is far from the case. Nevertheless, despite the uncertainties and ambiguities that may be contained within them, through a process of history taking and transcribing, Nukaga and Cambrosio describe how 'family trees' become 'medical pedigrees', at the same time gaining legitimate status as clinical evidence. It is, then, important to reflect on the fact that the new genetics does not represent an entirely new medical reality, and that while genetic techniques themselves may increase in accuracy and sophistication, their effective use may rely on less advanced or precise procedures. The continued importance of family trees, and of lay concepts of family and kinship in drawing up these trees, means that this remains a key area for sociological and anthropological study in relation to the new genetics.

Family relations and kinship

By its very nature, a genetic disease or disorder affects not just individuals but families. It is clear, then, that cultural understandings about families, kinship and the nature of inheritance impact on the receipt of genetic information. However, as Richards (1996) points out, these understandings have not risen anew with the new genetics, and families have always discussed who a particular individual 'takes after', whether in appearance or behaviour. What is more important is that the term 'family' may mean very different things within different cultures and to different people within those cultures, and not all of these meanings will involve the kind of blood relationship with which genetics is concerned. Richards suggests the use of three terms – kinship, close family and household – to better define these meanings. Kin represents the wider family that we recognize, including aunts, uncles and grandparents. Close family are those kin with which we currently co-reside, or have done in the past – that is, parents, siblings, children. The relationship between members of a household can be more complicated – with changing family structures, divorce, remarriage, and so on, family members may become members of new households or cease to become members of existing ones.

Although the realities of individual family relationships may be highly variable, Richards (1996) argues that geneticists often infer biological relations from kin relations. Generally, this may give an accurate picture, but we cannot expect that genetic data will always fit with social relationships. In the same way, collecting family histories from clients, the means by which referral to specialist genetic services is often made, assumes a shared interpretation of family. In discussing family histories, however, clients may include non-blood relationships, or exclude blood relationships, on the basis of their own interpretations. Additionally, the reliance on family history as an aid to diagnosis can raise further problems. For those who have not maintained kin relationships beyond close family, information may be needed to complete a family history that cannot be obtained without renewing these relationships, and this renewal may be problematic and undesirable, even if it is possible.

As Richards (1996) describes, these different understandings of family relationships also impact upon different understandings about inheritance and may create a resistance to adopting Mendelian explanations of inheritance. For example, a child or sibling who looks most like an affected relative may be seen as at greatest risk of inheriting a disease, on the grounds that physical similarity shows that they have inherited the same genes, including the affected ones. Emotional closeness or distance to an affected relative may also be seen as a predictor of risk. Even where risk factors and probabilities are apparently understood, there may be problems. Richards draws on Wexler's (1979) assertion, that we find it hard to believe that chance has no memory, to illustrate this. For example, a couple with a recessive disorder who have already had one affected child may feel that next time they are likely to have an unaffected one, even though they understand on another level that the one-in-four probability exists independently for each pregnancy.

The importance of lay perspectives

Acknowledging these lay theories about the transmission of genetic disease is important because, as in other areas of health care, lay knowledge has an impact on the way individuals respond to the available health care services. In terms of genetic testing and service delivery, this knowledge reflects not only kinship relations and understanding of kinship systems, but also personal experience and familial histories of disease and beliefs about the aetiology of disease. In this way, it can affect both who sees themselves at risk of genetic disorder and how that risk is constructed. Parsons and Atkinson (1992), in examining lay constructions of genetic risk, found fundamental differences between medical and lay understandings of the statistical issues involved. These differences led the authors to express concerns over the potentially far-reaching consequences for reproductive behaviour. Parsons and Clarke (1993) found similar differences between lay and health professionals' perspectives, especially regarding the thresholds used to distinguish high and low risk. Several of their sample did not retain their risk in any kind of numerical form at all. Instead, they had translated it into a descriptive category that resolved it into greater certainty for themselves, for example 'not so bad'.

This transformation of risk factors into something with a personal meaning for an individual illustrates the practical differences between the way in which medical information may be handled by health professionals and their clients. In Bosk's (1992) study of paediatric genetic counselling services in the USA, he reflected on the potential conflict between counsellor and client perspectives. He argued that, while counsellors give explanations in terms of abstract biological processes, 'parent understandings are very specific and personal. They are fashioned out of highly situated understandings for this particular pregnancy, this particular family, this particular person' (Bosk 1992: 48).

To give meanings to these abstract explanations, then, it may be *necessary* to transform them into something more personal and specific. In their work with those at risk of Huntington's disease, Cox and McKellin (1999) describe the effects of an awareness of risk or an affected family member on the way individuals perceive their own status. Although this knowledge does not alter the abstract calculation of risk, it can fundamentally alter the lived experience of risk, for example whether it is seen as 'not so bad'.

As these latter sections of this chapter have tried to illustrate, then, the focus for social scientists should not only be on the social consequences of genetic testing, or on ethical principles such as autonomy and confidentiality. Understandings of genetics and genetic knowledge are also primarily a social product. As a result, genetic testing and the provision of health care services around testing needs to take these understandings into account. Respecifying the research agenda in this way also raises questions as to the weight that should be given to the ethical principles of autonomy, non-directiveness, and so on. Despite the recognition of genetic counselling as a process where counsellor and client understandings meet, it has rarely been studied as such. Although there is a growing body of research into genetic service provision, it is largely concerned with outcome measures such as recall, impact on reproductive decision making or client satisfaction (Pilnick 2002). Examining the processes involved in the delivery of genetic services, and the understandings that clients bring to these services, moves the focus of debate firmly from philosophical to social scientific issues.

Summary points

- The term 'genetic testing' encompasses several types of test. A test may be diagnostic or predictive. Predictive tests may be presymptomatic or predispositional. Predispositional tests can only provide information about the likelihood of developing a particular disorder.

- There are many different views about which tests we should offer and to whom. Some commentators believe that any test that is possible should be available if it is required. Others believe that availability ought to depend on factors such as the severity of the disorder, its prevalence in the population and whether there is any medical treatment available for its management.

- Issues of confidentiality and informed consent are particularly important for genetic testing. Genetic information has implications for other family members, and also potentially for employers and insurers. However, research suggests that comprehension of genetic information by those in contact with genetic services is generally poor.

- Genetic counselling is a major means through which genetic information is communicated to at-risk individuals. Although its principles of non-directiveness, client autonomy and client-led agendas may be ethically desirable, in practice they are difficult to achieve and can create difficulties of their own.

- Cultural understandings of family and kinship, and of the nature of risk, impact on the receipt of genetic information. To comprehend how people make sense of the information they are given and how they utilize genetic services, we need to take these understandings into account.

Further reading

Chapple, A. and May, C. (1996) Genetic knowledge and family relationships: two case studies, *Health and Social Care in the Community*, 4(3): 166–71.

Chapple, A., Campion, P. and May, C. (1997) Clinical terminology: anxiety and confusion amongst families undergoing genetic counselling, *Patient Education and Counseling*, 32: 81–91.

Finch, J. and Mason, J. (1992) *Negotiating Family Responsibilities*. London: Routledge.

Hallowell, N. (1999a) Doing the right thing: genetic risk and responsibility, *Sociology of Health and Illness*, 21(5): 597–621.

Hallowell, N. (1999b) Advising on the management of genetic risk: offering choice or prescribing action?, *Health, Risk and Society*, 1(3): 267–80.

Parsons, E. and Atkinson, P. (1992) Lay constructions of genetic risk, *Sociology of Health and Illness*, 14: 437–55.

Pilnick, A. and Dingwall, R. (2001) Research directions in genetic counselling: a review of the literature, *Patient Education and Counseling*, 44: 95–105.

Strathern, M. (1992) *After Nature: English Kinship in the Late Twentieth Century*. Cambridge: Cambridge University Press.

6

THE HUMAN GENOME PROJECT, GENE THERAPY AND PHARMACOGENETICS

Introduction

This chapter gives a broad overview of some of the predicted developments for medicine as a result of the advance in new genetic technologies. It begins with a brief discussion of the Human Genome Project, its aims and its likely impact on medicine and medical practice in the near future. Following a broad consideration of the social and ethical issues that are raised as a result, and in particular the debate over patenting and intellectual property rights, it then moves on to look more specifically at some of the key areas of advance.

Gene therapy has been one of the most eagerly awaited medical applications of genetic science, as well as one of the most high profile. This chapter examines the aims of gene therapy, some of its successes and failures to date, and gives an account of the key sociological concerns arising from the process.

Pharmacogenetics is perhaps the area in which we are most likely to see significant advances in health care in the short term. The potential benefits and problems arising from these advances will be considered, from the point of view of patients, health care professionals and the pharmaceutical industry. The development of pharmacogenetic science, however, is dependent on large-scale biological sample collection, which raises particular issues of its own. This chapter draws on the Icelandic experience of collecting this kind of database to explore the potential issues in a UK and US context.

The Human Genome Project

The overarching aim of the Human Genome Project is to identify all of the approximately 30,000 genes in human DNA. It is an international collaboration that began formally in 1990 and was originally planned to last 15 years. However, the project has advanced more quickly than was initially predicted and the expected completion date is now estimated as 2003.

The stated goals of the project are as follows:

- To identify all the genes in human DNA.
- To determine the sequences of the three billion chemical bases that make up human DNA.
- To store this information in databases.
- To develop faster, more efficient sequencing technologies.
- To develop tools for data analysis.

Additionally, between 3 and 5 per cent of the US public funding for the project has been set aside annually to address the ethical, legal and social issues that arise from the project (Human Genome Project Information: http://www.ornl/gov/hgmis).

The US arm of the project is coordinated by the US Department of Energy and the National Institutes of Health. In the UK, the major collaborator is the Sanger Centre, which is funded by the Wellcome Trust (http://www.wellcome.ac.uk) and the Medical Research Council. Free public access to the human genome sequence has been a key feature of the research from the outset and regular updates are published on the World-Wide Web (http://www.sanger.ac.uk). This policy has been criticized, however, for allowing private biotechnology companies to benefit from the results of publicly funded research while retaining the results of their own research, which builds on these public discoveries.

On 26 June 2000, the programme announced a working draft of 90 per cent of the human genome. To achieve this, five-fold sequencing coverage was used – each part of the sequence was read five times to minimize any room for error. In 2001, a working draft of the full genome was announced. The ultimate goal is 99 per cent completion at ten-fold coverage by 2003.

Applications of genome research

Current and potential applications of findings from the Human Genome Project are diverse in range and scale. They include applications to medicine, risk assessment, forensic science and agriculture. In the area of medicine, the particular benefits envisaged are as follows:

- improved diagnosis of disease;
- earlier detection of genetic predispositions to disease;

- rational drug design;
- gene therapy and control systems for drugs;
- pharmacogenomics and 'custom medicines'.
  (Human Genome Project Information: http://www.ornl.gov/hgmis/ project/benefits.html)

As a result of these benefits, it is argued that we are at the dawn of a new era of molecular medicine. Whereas traditional medical practice is characterized by the treatment of symptoms, molecular medicine will enable us to focus on the fundamental causes of disease. Diagnostic tests will be more specific and hence more accurate, and drug treatments can be designed to be more effective and have less unwanted side-effects.

However, as Cardon and Watkins (2000) suggest, the hyperbole surrounding the Human Genome Project may more accurately reflect the scale of the undertaking, as opposed to its immediate impact. A consensus sequence of the kind that currently exists will enable classification of gene or protein families, which may help to predict function and enhance our understanding of the ways in which genes are organized and controlled. Despite these advances, there is unlikely to be a significant impact on medicine and medical practice in the short term. In fact, Cardon and Watkins (2000) suggest that the greatest benefit for medicine will be derived from sequence *differences* rather than consensus. It is these differences that will be important if the goal of personalized medicine is to be achieved, or if predictions are to be made about an individual's risk of developing a particular disorder. The discovery of new disease genes will potentially enhance our understanding of the aetiology of disease and, in turn, lead to new avenues for drug research and development.

Box 6.1: Investigating differences: single nucleotide polymorphisms (SNPs)

DNA polymorphisms are common variations of DNA sequences. If a **single nucleotide polymorphism** can be identified that is inherited along with a particular disease, it may be linked to a gene conferring susceptibility to that disease. This approach is used to 'map' susceptibility genes for 'complex' or multifactorial disorders. However, replicating the results of this research can be difficult – many samples are required and different sets of susceptibility genes may operate in different populations (Mathew 2001).

As we have already seen, research in this area is funded both publicly and privately, with a growing number of privately owned biotechnology companies involved. For all researchers working in this area, however, there are issues regarding who, if anyone, owns the genetic information produced as a result of this research. This debate over patenting and intellectual property rights affects not only those working on the human genome, but also those who work in plant and animal genetics.

Intellectual property rights

For a researcher or company to 'own' a product of research, it must first be patented. In the USA, patents are determined by the Patent and Trademark Office (USPTO). Patent applications are judged on four criteria; in terms of genetics, inventors must:

1 Identify novel genetic sequences.
2 Specify the sequence's product.
3 Specify how the product functions in nature (i.e. its use).
4 Enable a person skilled in the field to use the sequence for its stated purpose.
   (Human Genome Project Information: http://www.ornl.gov/hgmis/elsi/patents.html).

In the UK and Europe, patenting is governed by the European Union Directive on the Legal Protection of Biotechnological Inventions 1998 (http://www.european-patent-office.org/epo/pubs/oj99/2_99/2_109.pdf). Under the terms of this Directive, inventions which are new, which involve an inventive step and which potentially have industrial applications may be patented even if they contain biological material or a process through which biological material is produced, processed or used. However, the human body, and the simple discovery of one of its elements, including the sequence of a gene, does not in itself constitute a patentable product.

As a result of these criteria, the 'raw products' of nature are generally not patentable. Plant and animal varieties, for example, are specifically excluded from the EU Directive. Patent applications are usually made when DNA products have been isolated, modified or have undergone some other kind of biochemical process to produce a substance not found in nature. However, the regulations do not preclude the patenting of genetic information in all circumstances. A human gene or protein can meet the criteria to be considered an invention if it has been isolated or produced by a technical process and if an industrial application for the sequence or partial sequence has been disclosed.

The time taken to issue a patent varies. In the USA it is generally a three-year process, while in Europe it takes approximately 18 months. In the USA, patents are valid for 17 years from the issue date, but the patent holder is required to allow use of the product or discovery to others in exchange for a fee. In the UK, patents are normally valid for 20 years, although this may be extended in certain circumstances.

To date, over three million genome-related patent applications have been filed. The USPTO has issued some patents for gene fragments, which has sparked some controversy. Scientists have argued that broad patents should not be granted in the early stages of human genome research to applicants who have not characterized genes or determined their functions and uses. Genetic tests developed to screen for particular genes or genetic mutations in humans, for example, are usually patented and licensed by the owners of the disease gene patent.

Box 6.2: Gene patenting

Human Genome Sciences (HGS), in Maryland, USA holds approximately 100 patents. Controversially, it holds a patent on a gene called CCR5 that is thought to play a role in allowing the HIV virus to enter human cells. But HGS is not responsible for this finding, which has come from the research of others. However, they already hold the patent.

As a result of these fears and criticisms, since December 1999 the USPTO has invoked more restrictive guidelines around the patenting of genes and gene fragments, using the criterion of usefulness. The new rules call for demonstration of 'specific and substantial utility that is credible' (Human Genome Project Information 2000).

In terms of international law, the World Trade Organization's trade-related intellectual property rights agreement (TRIPs) will be the most decisive factor. Under the terms of the 1994 agreement, patents are available for all inventions, whether products or processes, as long as they contain a new, inventive step and have industrial application. Plants and animals themselves cannot be patented, although plant varieties can be protected (http://www.wto.org/english/tratop_e/trips_e.htm).

The debate over intellectual property rights

Research scientists in public institutions argue that science will advance more rapidly if there is free access to cumulative knowledge. Intellectual property law, however, rests on the assumption that, without an end benefit in the form of licensing rights over a product or discovery, no-one will be prepared to invest in research and development. Those who defend it argue that the likely alternative is secrecy, since this is the most effective way to prevent competitors from using a discovery. The current system has an incentive to disclosure because of the licensing fees that are involved.

More specifically, the arguments for and against gene patenting can be summarized as follows:

The potential positive impact of patenting

1 Research and research productivity will increase. The cumulative basis of knowledge that will be available to all researchers (albeit at a cost) will push forward the boundaries of research and avoid wasteful duplication.
2 Patents will give all researchers access to new discoveries and the need for trade secrecy will decrease.
3 Patents will attract investors to research and development by ensuring a return on their investment, since the end product of the research will be protected. This argument is sometimes extended to suggest that genetic research is our best hope for winning the battle against currently untreatable diseases, but that its success depends on attracting private investment.
4 Researchers can be individually rewarded for their discoveries and the money accrued through successful patenting could, in turn, further their research.

The potential negative impact of patenting

1 Research may be inhibited because of the costs to third parties of using patented materials. If a number of different patents in relation to the same area of research are held by different companies, further research in the area could become extremely costly. As a result of this cost, the available resources may be underused.
2 Patent holding by private companies may lead to a monopoly, as in the case of genetic testing markets. For example, a US biopharmaceutical company, Myriad Genetics, holds US and international patents on a method for diagnosing a predisposition for breast and ovarian cancer using the BRCA1 and BRCA2 genes that confer susceptibility, and has sought a monopoly on testing. Where there is a monopoly on a product, companies can command a higher price for use of it. The potential end result of this process is genetic tests that are out of the price range of some individuals or health care providers; this has already been an issue for the NHS in the provision of testing for breast cancer. It can be argued that the outcome will be a negative impact on the health of individuals that will maintain or widen existing health care inequalities.
3 Research and development of new products can be a lengthy process and patent applications remain secret until a patent has been granted. Companies may begin work on a product and later discover that a new patent has been granted during the course of their research. This would at best lead to unexpected licensing costs, and at worst could lead to penalties for infringement of patent.

4 There is inequity in the patenting system. The system potentially re-
wards those who make routine discoveries of partial or uncharacter-
ized DNA sequences and penalizes those who determine the actual
practical application of a discovery or product. Since patents are often
broadly written, a patent holder might control all future diagnostic
or therapeutic developments or inventions in a particular area. More
narrowly defined patents would go some way towards overcoming this
objection.

Obviously, it is biotechnology companies who have been at the forefront of the case for patenting DNA, since they have the most to gain
from a commercial point of view. Opposition has come from a variety of
sources, including patient groups and professional associations. Alongside these specific arguments run the more broad themes of concern as
to whether what is really being patented here is part of nature. The
British Society for Human Genetics is strongly against patents on human
gene sequences, believing that parts of the human body should not
be patentable. Although not totally against the idea of patenting, their
view is that only specific constructs containing human gene sequences
that have particular utility are properly patentable, and only then if
these are novel, non-obvious and useful (British Society for Human
Genetics: http://www.bham.ac.uk/BSHG/patent_cg.htm). The Wellcome
Trust supports the idea that basic sequence data should not be patented,
and that any patent involving a gene should describe the function of
the gene and its use, particularly with regard to health care (http://
www.wellcome.ac.uk/en/genome/patenting.html).

There are also objections from many religious leaders, opposing
what they see as the patenting of life. In 1995, almost 200 religious
leaders issued a statement opposing gene patenting, in an attempt to
put pressure on politicians to reform patent law. As Cole Turner (1995)
notes, the press interpreted this statement as a conflict of 'religion vs
science'.

The concern over possible conflict between public and private information is also relevant here. If information is held in public databases,
there may be adverse consequences for private companies; if it is held in
private databases, it may be adverse for research. Most gene isolation to
date has been carried out by public sector institutions such as universities, using funding from governments and charitable organizations, and
has been helped by a free interchange of materials and information.

Gene patenting and 'biopiracy'

The term 'biopiracy' is used to describe the process through which large
corporations exploit the knowledge and biological resources of third
world communities. The corporations stand to make large profits, while
the communities go unrewarded. Khor (1996) describes how transnational

corporations are using the genetic materials of the medicinal plants and food crops of third world communities as a starting point for the manufacture of pharmaceutical and agricultural products. He suggests that this 'gene rush' has become a twenty-first century version of the 'gold rush' in the scramble for profit. However, backed by citizens' groups, these communities are beginning to protest at the awarding of patent rights to companies, arguing that it is the communities who have been responsible for identifying and evolving the use of plants for food, medicine, and so on. This knowledge and innovation is discarded in the patenting process. Legal petitions have been filed and test cases have been brought.

Box 6.3: Challenges to patenting

In February 1995, the European Patent Office withdrew key parts of a patent granted to Plant Genetic Systems, a Belgian company, and Biogen Inc., a US company, for genetically engineered herbicide-resistant plants. The patent was for plant cells made resistant to herbicide and originally covered not only the gene added to the plants (which was taken from a bacterium), but also all plant and plant cells containing the gene. The challenge was brought by Greenpeace and the ruling from the Patent Office's Appeal Board stated that although a patent may apply to genetically engineered genes and plant cells, it may not cover a whole plant, its seeds and any future generations of plants grown from the cells. This case is interesting for the limits it apparently sets on patenting in Europe: genetically engineered cells and genes may be patented but plants and seeds may not (Khor 1996).

The action of biopiracy is not a new one, although the ethical issues have only recently been taken seriously. In the nineteenth century, the British explorer Henry Wickham took rubber plant seeds from the Amazon, as a result destroying the region's once prosperous rubber-based economy (Faiola 1999). As some commentators have suggested, there is a paradox at work here: through expressing moral objections that prevent 'nature' being patented, indigenous communities are denied a way of protecting their knowledge. Critics argue that these patent laws have been designed primarily to protect the products of wealthy developed nations.

At the 1992 Earth Summit, 150 countries signed a biodiversity convention that says nations should be rewarded for the use of their resources with a share of the profits. In this way it is argued, 'biopiracy' could become 'bioprospecting'. Some countries are trying to turn this convention into law; in some Amazon states, for example, foreign researchers are required to sign contracts to pay royalties on any income derived from local plants. Voluntary profit sharing is another proposed solution that is also being carried out, for example the California-based Shaman Pharmaceuticals, which allots a share of its research budget and of any eventual profits to community groups in the host country (Faiola 1999).

Having considered some of the social and ethical issues arising from genome research itself, this chapter now turns to focus on specific health care applications of this research. Gene therapy and pharmacogenetics are the two areas that will be considered in detail.

Gene therapy

Gene therapy may be defined as an approach to treat, cure or ultimately prevent disease by changing the way in which a person's genes are expressed. It can be targeted to **somatic cells** (ordinary cells in the human body) or **germ cells** (egg and sperm cells). There is an important distinction between the two. In somatic cell gene therapy, any change that is introduced will change the individual's genome, but this will not be passed on to their children. By contrast, germline gene therapy aims to pass on any changes that are introduced to the next generation. Clearly, the implications of germline gene therapy are far-reaching and have sparked much discussion about ethics, desirability and the potential for unintended consequences. However, this area is not under active investigation in humans.

As the Human Genome Project Information website is at pains to stress, gene therapy is at the moment still very much in its experimental stages. Although gene therapy has received much publicity, plenty of it adverse in nature, there are many factors that have prevented researchers from developing successful gene therapy techniques. Part of the difficulty is linked to the rapidly changing state of knowledge in this area. Although a working draft of the human genome has been sequenced, we are still far from knowing the function of most human genes. Additionally, genes may have more than one function. Trying to alter genes without fully understanding their functions could have disastrous consequences. Finally, as in other areas of genetic science, the scope for dealing with polygenetic disorders, and those diseases caused by interactions between genes and the environment, is small.

There are also more immediate practical problems facing gene therapy. Most obviously, it requires experimentation on human volunteers. Although patient groups themselves have been some of the most vociferous advocates of gene therapy, there have been several high-profile cases in which gene therapy has failed and has sometimes resulted in fatalities.

> **Box 6.4: Fatality as a result of gene therapy**
>
> In 1999, an 18-year-old American, Jesse Gelsinger, died as a result of his involvement in gene therapy experiments at the University of Pennsylvania. He was undergoing treatment for a liver disorder that prevented the liver from effectively processing toxins produced by the breakdown of proteins. He died of multiple organ failure, apparently brought on by a severe immune reaction to the corrective genes that he received. The case was particularly controversial because the disorder under investigation is not in itself usually fatal and can be managed with prescribed drugs and dietary modifications. Mr Gelsinger was thought to be the first person who had died directly as a result of gene therapy, and the US Food and Drug Administration ordered a temporary closure of the gene therapy experiments at the University of Pennsylvania as a result.

The second practical difficulty is how a new or altered gene can be inserted into a patient's body. Delivery of therapeutic genes to a patient's cells is carried out using vehicles called 'vectors'. The most common vectors are viruses, chosen because they have naturally evolved a way of entering human cells and delivering their genes as part of their disease-causing mechanism. In gene therapy, this biological process is turned on its head: the disease-causing genes in a virus are replaced by therapeutic ones. However, this modification does not solve problems of potential toxicity and the presence of the virus in a patient's body may still trigger a response by the immune system. There are also difficulties with targeting the new genetic material to the appropriate site. As a result, researchers are experimenting with other methods of delivery such as lipid complexes.

Despite the controversy over gene therapy, there have also been some high-profile successes. French researchers, for example, have successfully used gene therapy to treat two babies with severe combined immunodeficiency (SCID). Since their immune systems do not function normally, sufferers from the disorder are usually required to live within tightly controlled sterile areas and eventually undergo bone marrow transplantation (Dobson 2000). Gene therapy in this case involved providing a normal copy of the defective gene that causes SCID, so enabling the normal growth and development of the immune system. The success of this project, which was announced shortly after the death of the US patient, has been seen as an important milestone for gene therapy. Researchers in the field of gene therapy have argued that, as with other avenues of medical research, it is not possible to protect research subjects from all possible harm without denying them potential benefits. Stockdale (1999) describes the way in which the development and use of somatic gene cell therapy for the treatment of disease has often been assumed to be relatively unproblematic. However, he cautions that gene therapy is not 'readily assimilated to any easily understood model of therapeutic action and poses considerable problems for understanding' (Stockdale 1999: 581). This lack of understanding of the difficulties involved, among professionals as well as patient groups, has contributed to the aura of a miracle technology, although the reality is a far more ordinary story of an ongoing and, as yet, often unsuccessful research programme.

Sociological perspectives on gene therapy

Although the highly technical research carried out in this area may seem very far removed from the early work of Francis Galton and his family pedigrees, for example, from a sociological perspective some parallels can be drawn. Just as Galton was keen to attribute undesirable characteristics such as feeble mindedness to heredity, Martin (1999) describes how, in the area of modern genetics, the introduction of powerful new technologies is closely linked to the construction of new accounts about the origins of disease. In terms of these accounts, some less common conditions are the results of genetic defects, whereas other, more common, conditions are seen as having a significant genetic component. In this context, altering an individual's genes becomes a legitimate medical intervention to be viewed in the same way as taking prescription drugs or undergoing surgery to correct a 'defective' body part. Martin also argues that this kind of model of the 'genetic body' underlies the distinction between the ways in which somatic and germline gene therapy are viewed. Somatic cell gene therapy can be conceptualized as a discrete intervention, and the distancing of the scientific community from germline therapy works also to distance them from any ideas of eugenics that may be bound up with the alteration of future generations.

In addition, Stockdale (1999), drawing on work with cystic fibrosis patient groups and physicians, argues that the problems of conceptualizing gene therapy as a discrete invention has unfortunate consequences for patient groups, giving them a false sense of hope. Focusing on gene therapy runs the risk of excluding discussion of other issues that have an impact on the lives of people living daily with the realities of a serious illness. Likewise, viewing gene therapy as a 'cure' means that other support services may come to have a lower priority and, as one of Stockdale's respondents notes, the hope of *future* gene therapy 'just doesn't lessen the realities of the struggle we all face' (p. 592). The potential benefits of future discoveries need to be set in this day-to-day context.

Pharmacogenetics and pharmacogenomics

If it were not for the great variability among individuals medicine might as well be a science and not an art.
(Sir William Osler, in *The Principles and Practice of Medicine*, 1892)

Pharmacogenetics is the study of how genetic variability alters people's response to drug therapy. It uses the variations in human genetic make-up to predict how individuals will metabolize and respond to drugs. It can help to address the problem of why some patients respond well to drugs and others do not, or why some patients require higher or lower doses of a particular drug (Snedden 2000).

In describing research in this area, the term 'pharmacogenomics' is also used. Pharmacogenomics is a more recent term concerned with the discovery of new drug response genes and the development of new molecules to target these genes. As a result, pharmacogenomic research has two main components: it involves both developing drugs that will target a particular disease and tailoring them to take into account a person's genetic make-up to avoid side-effects (Snedden 2000). Since this is a rather technical difference, the two terms are often used interchangeably in the literature.

Potential benefits of pharmacogenetics

The long-term practical benefit of pharmacogenetics is that, in the future, prescribing medicines for common conditions such as diabetes, osteoporosis and asthma could be based as much on a person's genetic profile as on their symptoms. Major pharmaceutical companies are investing heavily in techniques to allow drugs to be tailored to different genetic profiles to improve efficacy and minimize side-effects.

Evidently, the Human Genome Project is linked very closely to developments in pharmacogenetics. Although the sequencing of the full draft has progressed rapidly, unravelling the function of each gene will take much longer. However, as the function of each gene is uncovered, pharmaceutical companies will be able to use this information in drug development and aim to produce more effective medicines with fewer side-effects.

Minimizing side-effects from prescribed medicines may seem like a limited goal, but in fact adverse drug reactions are an inherent part of modern medicine, and also a large-scale problem. Adverse drug reactions are the fourth largest cause of death in the USA, with a meta-analysis of published work in this area estimating that 106,000 patients die and 2.2 million are injured each year as a direct result of drug therapy (Lazarou *et al.* 1998). In the UK, it has been suggested that 1 in 15 hospital admissions can be attributed to adverse drug reactions. These adverse reactions are often unpredictable, and the importance of the Human Genome Project lies in the fact that much variation in drug response appears to be inherited (Wolf *et al.* 2000). Put simply, the reason why some groups of people have adverse reactions to particular drugs is likely to have a genetic basis, and so those people who are likely to suffer adverse reactions could be identified in advance, and given lower doses or alternative treatment. Although clinical trials to evaluate the safety and efficacy of new drugs involve large numbers of patients, it is often not until a drug is in general use that the true prevalence of adverse drug reactions is identified. Pharmacogenetics potentially provides a solution to this problem.

More specifically, Wolf *et al.* (2000) describe four predicted developments as a result of pharmacogenetic research:

1 Establishing prescribing guidelines in situations where the metabolism of a drug varies widely as a result of genetic factors. Where appropriate, this prescribing advice could relate the recommended dose of a drug to a patient's genotype.

Box 6.5: Pharmacogenetics and drug dosage

Dosage tailoring could be particularly useful for drugs that have a small therapeutic window, such as warfarin. Warfarin is an effective and commonly used anticoagulant (preventing blood clotting), but patients who metabolize warfarin slowly can be at risk of severe bleeding as a result of minor cuts and bruising. Identifying slow metabolizers by genotype would enable doses to be tailored to avoid this.

---

2 Establishing and recording personal pharmacogenetic profiles for individuals that could be consulted before any treatment decisions are made.

Box 6.6: Initiating appropriate treatment from the outset

In the case of childhood leukaemia, two of the most commonly used drugs, methotrexate and mercaptopurine, have hugely varying response profiles. At least nine genetic subgroups have been identified and, in some cases, protocols are already used to identify non-responders. This knowledge has increased cure response rates considerably, particularly in the case of mercaptopurine. Since early treatment is crucial in leukaemia, it also means that non-responders to mercaptopurine can begin treatment immediately with an alternative, rather than having first to discover that it is not effective.

---

3 Reducing the need for hospitalization as a result of drug therapy. As well as reducing the care needed as a direct result of adverse drug reactions, there would also be a less direct benefit. There are some drugs,

for example warfarin, with which treatment is often initiated as a hospital inpatient because of the *risk* of an adverse reaction. Pharmacogenetic advances could help in identifying whether this risk is relevant to a particular patient, or whether treatment might safely be started at home.

4 Developing new drugs for patients with specific genotypes. This is sometimes called 'drug stratification'.

As a result of these advances, it is claimed that the distribution of medicines could be rationalized, in the sense that they would be given to those most likely to respond and benefit from them. Scarce health care resources, it is argued, would be distributed on a rational basis rather than on the current basis of geography or ability to pay. However, this rationalization of distribution does nothing to promote equality in health care. Instead, it provides a scientific basis for inequality, which will continue to exist.

Ethnicity and varying responses to treatment

Another contentious area related to patient benefit is that of race or ethnicity. In the study of genetic variation that pharmacogenetics demands, one area of inquiry has been to focus on genetic variations in different ethnic groups, to determine whether this might provide an explanation for observed differences in response to, for example, drug treatment for high blood pressure. It is sometimes suggested that this avenue of research offers an opportunity to move away from ethnic and racial stereotypes, by focusing attention solely on observable biological difference. However, the relationship between genetics and race or ethnicity has historically often been an unhappy one, and recent studies such as *The Bell Curve* (described in more detail in Chapter 3) have reinforced fears of discrimination in relation to new genetic advances. Simplistic genetic notions of race have been undermined by the discovery that there is more variation *within* different ethnic group populations than *between* them. However, an alternative potential outcome of this focus on genetic differences between ethnic groups is that the concept of race will come to be redefined through genetics, with the identification of distinct and discrete groups within populations who can in some way be biologically defined as 'other' to the norm.

Pharmacogenetics and pharmaceutical companies

It is the potential benefits that pharmacogenomics offers for patients that have been most widely discussed, but a pharmacogenomic approach also has benefits for pharmaceutical companies. Most obviously, there is the possibility of cost decreases in drug development for the pharmaceutical industry. Drug research and development is an extremely lengthy and costly business; it can currently cost around £220 million and 15 years to get a drug to market. However, it is also an uncertain business: between 80 and 90 per cent of drugs never make it beyond clinical trials and on to the market because of the serious side-effects they produce (Sneddon 1999). Pharmacogenetic developments, then, could make this process faster and more efficient. Clinical trials, in particular, which are sometimes literally a process of trial and error, could be designed more efficiently. They could also allow pharmaceutical companies to revive drugs that have failed in the past, either because of low response rates or bad side-effects. For these already existing drugs, it may be possible to identify genetic factors for response and so target or avoid particular sections of the population on the basis of genetics.

Although the benefits are clear, these advances also have a potential downside for the pharmaceutical industry. This downside is that there would be smaller markets for drugs once they were developed. Rather than one drug for diabetes that works better for some people than others, 'drug stratification' means that there would potentially be several drugs targeted at specific sub-groups within the diabetic population. This would lead to a loss of economies of scale for drug companies. There are also potentially legal implications regarding the liability of companies. A company marketing a drug that showed adverse drug reactions in some of the patients given it could face litigation if genetic tests were available to determine the likelihood of reaction and they were not used.

The status of pharmacogenetic knowledge

As we have seen in previous chapters, over recent years the relationship between science and medical practice has been the subject of much sociological study. Elston (1997: 2) draws attention to the 'vast array of institutions and practices in modern society that articulate the application of scientific method to the study and management of human health'. She goes on to describe how

> human disease genetics is . . . a field in which laboratory science and clinical practice are particularly close. Because of the controversy that surrounds the field and because few applications have become routinised, sociologists of medicine cannot treat the technologies as given and sociologists of science cannot remain in the laboratory.
>
> (Elston 1997: 6)

This relationship has important implications for the study of pharmacogenetics. Since much pharmacogenetic development is still at the laboratory stage, its development continues to run alongside its entrance into health care. In this sense, while there might appear to be great scientific promise from a pharmacogenetic approach, its large-scale technological applications are for the most part untested, in a social sense as well as a scientific one. Whether they will come to be accepted as a routine part of health care depends not only on their technical efficacy, but also on how they are perceived and constructed by those who use them and who they are used on. The routinization of antenatal screening, discussed in Chapter 4, provides one example of the many factors that may influence this process. Perhaps more than any other area of the new genetics, pharmacogenetics highlights the need for sociological approaches to consider the ways in which science, technology and society are co-constituted, and the resulting effect on the way concepts of health and illness are used and applied to individuals. This is particularly true of pharmacogenetic applications aimed at preventative health care.

Pharmacogenetics and preventative health care

More generally, genetic profiling is also opening the door to a greater understanding of individual susceptibility to common disorders and how this might be addressed with new drugs. This is a complex area, since most disorders are not caused by a single gene. However, the success in identifying the genes responsible for some monogenic disorders has led to an increased interest in investigating the genetic component of complex diseases. This process of establishing whether and to what extent a disease has a genetic component is sometimes referred to as 'genetic epidemiology'(Kaprio 2000). The size of the genetic component in relation to environmental factors is also an area for study within genetic epidemiology, but, in practice, what is encompassed by the term 'environmental factors' can vary widely. As with the search for genes that are involved in particular human behaviours or traits, much of this research uses family studies as a basis for identifying individuals who are at increased risk of a particular disorder, attempting to establish whether this shared risk has an environmental or genetic basis. However, the benefits of the genetic epidemiology programme are less contentious. Potentially, it offers the possibility of increased preventative care: by identifying a gene which confers susceptibility to heart disease, for example, the idea is that advice on diet and lifestyle could be given to that person to prevent the disease occurring in the first place. In the case of genes such as BRCA1 and BRCA2, which are already known to be associated with breast cancer, the aim is to clarify the relationship between these genes and other risk factors. As a result, better estimations of the risk of developing breast cancer could be given to individuals, and these individuals could use this knowledge to better inform, for example, a decision to undergo prophylactic mastectomy.

Pharmacogenetics and environmental medicine

Although genetic epidemiologists are interested in the relative size of genetic effects in relation to environmental effects, there has also been

specific interest in the potential use of pharmacogenetics in environmental medicine. Just as there are genetic variations in an individual's
response to drugs, so individuals vary in their response to environmental
factors, such as chemicals and viruses.

As our knowledge of this area expands, it is possible that, just as
people could be screened for a genetic risk of coronary heart disease,
they could also be routinely screened and given an 'environmental risk
factor' rating (Snedden 2000). Although this may offer the individual
opportunities for limiting or preventing their exposure to risk factors,
there would of course be attendant consequences for employment, such
as rejection for particular jobs. As Snedden describes, this scenario raises
a number of ethical questions. Two of these in particular are crucial to
the debate over this kind of screening. First, who is responsible for any
risk that is discovered? Is it the responsibility of the individual or of the
employer? And, second, what will happen if people choose not to be
screened? Could employment be refused on these grounds? As a response to these concerns, the Nuffield Council on Bioethics (1993: 3) has
laid down several guidelines. These state that:

> Genetic screening of employees for increased occupational risks ought
> only to be contemplated where:
> (a) there is strong evidence of a clear connection between the work-
>   ing environment and the development of the condition for which
>   genetic testing can be conducted.
> (b) the condition in question is one which seriously endangers the
>   health of the employee or is one in which an affected employee
>   is likely to present a serious danger to third parties.
> (c) the condition is one for which the dangers cannot be elim-
>   inated or significantly reduced by reasonable measures taken
>   by the employer to modify or respond to the environmental
>   risks.

This last point is particularly important, since it implies that employers
should not use genetic screening as a means to abdicate their responsibilities in respect of health and safety. Under the terms of the guidelines,
it would not be acceptable to employ a group of people who could 'safely'
be put at risk because of their genetic resistance instead of enacting standard health and safety procedures.

Thus far, the discussion has focused mainly on the potential advantages
of these new genetic technologies from a biological or pharmacological
point of view. However, it is not only biologists and pharmacologists
who are interested in examining different genetically based responses
to factors across large populations. For sociologists, there is potentially
interest in studying the link between a particular genotype and socioeconomic factors such as behaviour and lifestyle. These kinds of large-scale
research programmes pose specific problems, but that does not mean
that they are a distant reality. In the UK, plans are already underway for

a large-scale biological sample collection, and in Iceland there is already an operational database.

Plans for major DNA collection in the UK

In 1998, the Medical Research Council received £12 million to support national DNA collection. This money has been used to establish a series of regional DNA banks as well as a proposal to create a single, vast new resource – the UK Population Biomedical Collection, a joint initiative with the Wellcome Trust and the Department of Health (Kaye and Martin 2000) (http://www.wellcome.ac.uk/en/1/biovenpop.html).

The collection will focus on understanding the interactions between genes, environment and lifestyle, and will focus particularly on diseases of later life such as cancer and heart disease. Envisaged to contain DNA from up to 500,000 people aged between 45 and 64 years, it will link this genetic information to personal medical records, family histories and lifestyle and environmental histories through general practices. Conceived as a longitudinal study, it will span many years and require ongoing data collection. Recruitment will be coordinated by regional centres. Initially, the collection will be used to study cardiovascular disease, cancers and respiratory and metabolic disorders, together with later onset neurological and psychiatric disorders (Berger 2001).

Despite the existing commitment to this research, there are still several ethical and policy questions to be resolved. These include access to personal medical information and, importantly, how the research will be overseen. Kaye and Martin (2000) suggest that, since the precedent for this kind of large-scale sample collection is in Iceland, where a similar huge database is already under collection, evaluation of the Icelandic experience highlights the key issues facing the UK or other countries planning similar endeavours. In Iceland, DNA samples have been collected by a commercial biotechnology company, deCODE genetics, from a large number of people with common diseases (for example, heart disease), and genetic linkage and association studies are being carried out. In the longer term, these individual DNA profiles will be integrated with the medical records of almost every Icelandic citizen and with publicly held genealogies. (Since Iceland has had a relatively static population, with little immigration and emigration, and because there is a relatively small gene pool on the island, family histories are more accessible, traceable and verifiable than in many other countries.) The linkage of these databases will allow deCODE to carry out genetic epidemiological research.

As Kaye and Martin (2000) describe, the proposal to construct the database was widely debated in parliament, the media and the community. Opposition came not only within Iceland but also internationally, with particular concern over the speed of the initiative and lack of

---

Box 6.7: Obtaining consent for biological samples

The initial proposal in Iceland was that individuals' medical records would be held in the database and linked to genealogies and DNA samples without the use of consent. After public pressure, this was subsequently changed to an opt-out system. This lack of consent was probably the most contentious issue around the database, since it was seen as a breach of Icelandic law and, in particular, of the Icelandic Patients' Rights Act. A specially approved act of parliament, the Icelandic Health Sector Database Act 1998, requires that the Data Protection Commission (DPC) and two new government appointed bodies are involved in planning and supervising the database. The DPC has powers of investigation and can have free access to what is on the database or premises at any time. These bodies will report back to the minister of health who has the power to revoke deCODE's license at any time. However, the database was not fully operational until 2001, so these systems have not yet had time to be properly tested.

---

consultation. In addition, there were recurring concerns over consent, security of data and commercial ownership of research findings.

Lessons from Iceland for the UK

One key issue is that explicit prior consent will be sought in the UK, although this consent will have to be general and allow use of samples for a wide range of purposes. It will also include agreement to periodic follow-up. A second issue is that the data collected will not be exclusively licensed to a single private company, although there will be an interface with pharmaceutical and biotechnology companies (Berger 2001). In terms of regulating the databases, Kaye and Martin (2000) contrast the Icelandic and UK systems. Medical research in the UK is primarily governed by guidelines from the Department of Health, the Medical Research Centre and the General Medical Council. In contrast to Iceland, where the Patients' Rights Act controls medical research on humans, there is no corresponding law in the UK and regulation of medical research has largely been left to the medical profession (although Britain does have legislation controlling medical research in animals).

There are currently no guidelines from these bodies relating specifically to population collections. The World Medical Association and the World Health Organization have announced that they will be drafting guidelines. However, these will be international and critics – Kaye and Martin (2000) among them – argue that they are unlikely to be sufficiently

specific and sensitive to the UK context for them to work comprehens-
ively. They also raise questions about the role of research ethics committees in the UK. These committees play the central role in the regulation of
medical research, and all research proposals that involve human subjects
must be approved by them. However, they are localized and not necessarily consistent: even in one city there may be different committees
based at different hospitals and they may have different requirements. A
further limitation is that they grant approval or otherwise before the
start of a project, but rarely ask for reports or intervene once a project
is underway, since they do not have powers of enforcement. The Data
Protection Commission in the UK keeps a register of all those that process
personal data, but operates mostly through issuing codes of practice, and
enforcement of its powers tends to occur only when these codes have
been breached and complaints have been made.

Potential problems with large-scale biological sample collections

The kind of research described requires large population collections of
biological samples: to control for natural variation, a minimum of around
500,000 individuals is needed. The broad focus of research presents problems of its own, since each sample is likely to be stored for long periods
and used many times in an attempt to establish correlations and controls. This has important implications not only for consent, but also for
patient confidentiality and privacy, and potentially for human rights.

Informed consent

Critics argue that any meaningful notion of informed consent is un-
achievable in this kind of research programme, given all the possible uses
to which a sample may be put. Even where consent is obtained as broadly
as possible, researchers may subsequently wish to use the sample in ways
that were unanticipated at the time the sample was collected.

More fundamentally, Hilary Rose (quoted in Spallone and Wilkie 2000)
argues that people make sophisticated judgements when they give their
consent to donation of biological samples for research, or consent to take
part in clinical trials. As part of this process, people make judgements
about the use of the research and the professionals they deal with. Seen
in this way, informed consent is not just about understanding the technical issues or risk assessments associated with a particular project. To
participate, people need to agree with the goals of the research and the
goals of the institutions involved, and they need to have trust in those
carrying out the research.

Rose goes on to describe how these factors may become particularly
problematic where medical information will be used for commercial gain

by drug companies. As a result, the idea of reciprocal altruism that under-pins other biological sample donation, for example blood donation, needs to be revisited in the context of commercialization.

Returning to the issue of trust raised by Rose, it can be argued that this is likely to be particularly pertinent, at least in the short term. In the wake of high-profile medical scandals in the UK, such as events at the Bristol Royal Infirmary, the trial and conviction of Harold Shipman for murdering his patients and the discovery of organs from corpses retained without consent at Alder Hey Children's Hospital, public trust in the medical profession has been seriously eroded. More particularly, ques-tions have been asked about the conduct of medical research and the processes involved in obtaining informed consent.

Informed consent and risk communication

In the previous two chapters, we have considered the way in which risk information may be used in health care either at the population level or at the level of the 'at risk' individual. Part of the difficulty with implementing pharmacogenetic programmes is that any practical use of the information they provide falls somewhere between the two. Large-scale biological sample collection will identify at risk individuals, but anonymization of samples may prevent this information being used on anything other than a general level. Even where this information can be provided directly to the individual concerned, in many cases the extent of the risk, or the consequences of it, will not be specifiable in advance of the sample testing process. Since the outcomes are to an extent inde-terminable, the potential risks of participating in this kind of project may also be hard to define. Therefore, what is already an uncertain area becomes even more so.

Patient confidentiality and privacy

This is the second key issue raised by large-scale sample collection. If samples are anonymized, this will limit the use to which they can be put; for example, it will rule out subsequent socioeconomic analysis of correlations with behaviour and lifestyle. However, if samples are not anonymized, then those individuals participating in research may not have full control over the use of their genetic information.

Confidentiality of information is a particularly sensitive issue in rela-tion to genetics. Insurance companies, as we have seen in the previous chapter, are one obvious group of organizations who would have inter-est in a person's genetic profile. Other groups might include public health authorities, the criminal justice system and relatives of the person, and defensible responses to requests by these bodies will need to be de-veloped (Lowrance 2001). However, pharmacogenetics research programmes bring a new dimension to this issue, since they could result in the more frequent routine screening of generally healthy people who neither have any symptoms nor any family history to suggest a genetic disorder.

A further group of people with a likely interest in this kind of information are employers. Discrimination here is likely to be less widespread because of existing legislation in both the USA and UK designed to protect people with disabilities. However, this protection depends on how disability is defined; the limitations of legislation in dealing with predispositional test results in particular are discussed in Chapter 5.

Protecting anonymity

Spallone and Wilkie (2000) describe the dilemmas involved in protecting anonymity, noting the potential conflict between maximizing both patient confidentiality and research possibilities. Data collected for large-scale research projects can be made anonymous, if all information capable of identifying the individual to whom the data relates is removed and destroyed. Although this may seem an ethically desirable solution, its drawback is that further information can then never be added. This limits the long-term use of any sample collection and may prevent the identification of long-term effects of, or correlations between, particular genetic information. An alternative solution is to encode the data, so that they are anonymous to the research team and the key is held elsewhere. The presence of a key, however, means that if necessary findings could be linked. This would allow updating for longitudinal studies. In relation to the UK database, Kaye and Martin (2000) ask what sanctions will be taken if security of the database is broken and how third-party and commercial access will be regulated. They suggest that, in many countries, including the UK, a legislative approach has been ignored in favour of administrative, professional guidelines and contend that government inactivity could be seen as supporting a *laissez-faire* market-driven approach. Since research institutions themselves face potential conflicts of interest in developing guidelines, they recommend that policy making is best handled by legislative action that would establish standards and require public and private institutions to adopt appropriate policies and review mechanisms.

Currently, anonymous information collected from medical information can be used by third parties for commercial gain without consent from the individual from whom the sample comes. As Spallone and Wilkie (2000) note, the fact that this was challenged in the High Court and the challenge was initially upheld (although subsequently overturned on appeal), illustrates that the terms of medical and scientific research, and the way in which they are viewed by the public, are changing. In the debate around the implications of new genetic technologies, privacy and confidentiality are often upheld as the key issues, because of the potential for discrimination that may result when they are breached. It is important to remember, however, that these two issues are important for all kinds of medical information, and that policies intended to ensure genetic privacy will also need to address the privacy of health-related information in general.

Human rights

Issues of consent, confidentiality and privacy in turn relate to human rights issues and, in particular, to addressing the question of how this information, once collected, will be used. Human rights legislation circumscribes the application of new technologies that otherwise might encourage discriminatory or stigmatizing practices.

 ◦ A question that arises here is the potential of knowledge being used to ration treatment, as well as to develop it, and there have been high-profile cases of the use of genetic knowledge in this way.◦

Box 6.8: Genetic knowledge and treatment rationing

The apoE gene has been linked with early onset of Alzheimer's disease. However, one of the variants of this gene (apoE4), which is linked with early onset, is also linked with being less likely to respond to the drugs currently available to treat Alzheimer's. Since these drugs are very expensive, this information could be used to ration treatment. However, having the early onset variant does not mean that a patient will not respond, just that they are less likely to than a patient without this variant. In this case, then, people could be denied treatment on the basis of probability.

Alzheimer's disease is one specific example where this knowledge could be used, but there is a much broader concern that underlies the practical uses of this knowledge. What happens if genetic non-responders become by default an untreatable class? How will the NHS goal of access to health care for all be affected? In response to this concern, some scientists have put forward the counter-argument: that by focusing on susceptibility genes, which all individuals are likely to have in one form or another, the stigma of genetic testing will be changed and more people will benefit from early identification and appropriate treatment or prevention.

The limitations of a purely scientific viewpoint

Thus far, consideration has been given to some of the social and ethical problems surrounding the implementation of pharmacogenomic and pharmacogenetic research. However, for sociologists, there are more fundamental issues concerning the models of health, disease and human behaviour that these programmes assume. Taking a purely scientific perspective on this rests upon a rational model of how the world works. However, as the placebo effect in clinical trials clearly illustrates, response to treatment is not always so simply characterized. As Spallone and Wilkie (2000) suggest, the social world is more complex than biological reality. One of the best examples of this in relation to genetics is the different understandings of kinship and biological relatedness held by the public and summarized in Richard's (1996) discussion, which is considered in Chapter 5. To assume that these understandings represent any kind of straightforward biological reality is potentially over-simplistic and erroneous.

As we have seen, the claims that are made for medicine and health as a result of these research programmes also rely to some extent on reconceptualizing diseases or disorders as being genetic in some way. As a result, the idea of a genetic disease becomes reconstructed to mean not just those things which are demonstrably and directly heritable, but also those things, like cancer, which have among other things a genetic component.

Once again, the long-term implications of genetic reductionism need to be considered, so that pharmacogenomics does not encourage us to understand medical events purely in terms of genetics rather than as within a social and environmental context. Environmental factors, gender and diet, can all impact on the way a patient responds to a drug and to their general state of health. A new issue raised by pharmacogenetics is what the psychological effects of being classed as a 'genetic non-responder' might be and how this might affect patient outcome. As the case of Alzheimer's disease shows, issues of rationing and inequity will also need to be addressed. Furthermore, while those people who are 'genetically right' for the drugs that pharmaceutical companies want to sell will be advantaged, this advantage may not fit with the overall goals for improving a nation's health in particular areas.

There is also the potential for a shift from a public health emphasis, in terms of disorders like high cholesterol and susceptibility to heart disease, into an individual model of personal 'defects'. This shift downplays the importance of the social factors implicated in causing disease, for example income, diet and access to facilities.

One final issue that has not yet been addressed in this context is the clinical autonomy of doctors. Clinical autonomy is a much valued and protected principle in medicine, but it is probable that clinicians will see this as being eroded if prescribing becomes a mechanized process of carrying out genetic tests to find an appropriate drug and then supplying it. The resistance to disease management programmes on both sides of the Atlantic offers some indication of the likely response by the medical profession (Pilnick *et al.* 2001).

In summary, then, the Human Genome Project and the research that builds on its findings offers many new possibilities for health care. The widespread use of some of these, for example gene therapy, is likely to be in the medium to long term. Pharmacogenetic developments, on the other hand, are likely to come about sooner and to affect a wider population. The new benefits that these developments might bring, however, need to be considered alongside the new social and ethical issues that they raise.

Summary points

- Information from the Human Genome Project has many implications for health care, enabling a greater focus on the fundamental causes of disease. However, it is unlikely to have a marked effect on medicine and medical practice in the short term.

- Work on the Human Genome Project has highlighted issues of who, if anyone, is entitled to 'own' genetic information. The consequences of gene patenting for the cost of health care are potentially significant, as the case of breast cancer testing already shows. The impact of 'biopiracy' on developing world resources is a growing concern.

- Gene therapy is one of the most widely heralded possibilities of the new genetics. Success so far has been mixed, and it has been argued that a focus on gene therapy contributes to the 'geneticization' of individuals with a genetic disorder, and shifts the focus away from the day-to-day realities of living with an inherited condition.

- Pharmacogenetics is where short-term advances in medical care are most likely to be seen. However, although drug therapy may be rationalized as a result, there is also a risk of creating an untreatable 'genetic underclass'.

- Large-scale biological sample collections of the kind needed for these research programmes raise particular issues of informed consent and confidentiality. The new benefits that may arise from these programmes need to be considered alongside these issues.

Further reading

Kevles, D. and Hood, L. (1992) *The Code of Codes: Scientific and Social Issues in the Human Genome Project*. Cambridge, MA: Harvard University Press.
Lindpainter, L. (1999) Genetics in drug discovery and development: challenge and promise of individualizing treatment in common complex diseases, *British Medical Bulletin*, 55(2): 471–91.
Nelkin, D. and Tancredi, L. (1989) *Dangerous Diagnostics: The Social Power of Biological Information*. New York: Basic Books.
Thompson, L. (1994) *Correcting the Code: Inventing the Genetic Cure for the Human Body*. New York: Simon & Schuster.

7

GENETICALLY MODIFIED FOODS

Introduction

This chapter is concerned with the release of genetically modified (GM) organisms in plants used as foodstuffs. Following an explanation of what is meant by the term **'genetic engineering'**, the proposed advantages and disadvantages of GM food are considered from a social perspective. Reactions to GM food in both the USA and UK will then be examined, in terms of the sociological debates around risk, trust and the social significance of food.

In the UK, the release of genetically modified organisms in plants used as foodstuffs has arguably been the most visible and the most contentious result of new genetic technologies. Genetically modified foods have been both heralded as a solution to world hunger and perceived as a catastrophic threat to the environment.

How are GM foods made?

Genetically modified foods are the products of plants that have been genetically engineered. Genetic engineering may be defined as the transfer of parts of the genetic material from one cell to another, or the introduction of changes into the genetic material. Through this process, new characteristics can be introduced into a cell. This transfer can take place between different types of cell, for example from animal to plant or from micro-organism to plant.

What plant genetic engineers have done may in some ways be viewed as an extension of the plant breeding programmes that have always taken place. In these programmes, different varieties of plant have been crossed with the hope of producing an end result with a particular desirable characteristic, for example high crop yield, hardiness or resistance to pests. However, this has often been a process of trial and error, and may result in the transference of undesirable characteristics at the same time. The major difference with genetic engineering is that it removes much of the uncertainty from this process: if a gene that carries pest resistance can be isolated and introduced into a new plant, then breeders can be much more sure it will display this property. The possibilities are also greater, since genetic material not just from other plants, but from other sources, can potentially be used.

The debate over GM foods has been constructed very much in oppositional terms: participants are either 'pro' or 'anti' GM. On the pro side, scientists are seen as determined to capitalize on their discoveries. Potential social benefits occur as a by-product of further advancing the boundaries of science. On the anti side, the general public has often been constructed as the hapless consumer whose views are not being heard. Not only are they against the use of technology in this way, but choice is denied to them through the lack of legislation and the alleged unsatisfactory labelling of GM products. However, to construct the debate in these opposing and simplistic terms is not helpful. As with many technological developments, a fundamental issue for discussion is not the technologies themselves but the uses to which these are put. These uses need to be considered in the light of wider debates over trust, risk and choice. Nevertheless, before considering these secondary issues, it is helpful to consider the main arguments put forward for and against GM food.

Proposed advantages of GM food

The main argument in defence of GM foods is the one described at the outset of this chapter and may be seen as a kind of 'normalization', drawing on processes that have long been practised and accepted in all agricultural societies. Scientists have argued that the production of GM crops is best viewed not as a new or separate phenomenon, but as an extension to traditional breeding programmes. As Jones (1999) points out, this kind of biotechnology has been exploited for centuries, through processes of crossing and artificial selection, and the end result of these 'natural' processes is also a plant with new combinations of genes. These processes have also led to the geographical redistribution of genes, so that plants once native to a particular continent may be more widely grown. The soya bean, for example, was native to Asia but is now grown throughout the Americas.

This framing of GM technologies as an extension to a natural process works to minimize the perceived threat of the potentially new and strange. However, GM crops are not only presented as substantially the same as the products of normal agricultural practice, but also more beneficial.

These greater benefits come about because of the greater control over the end product that technology provides. Specific and selected genes can be introduced to a plant, rather than the random assortment that results from traditional cross-breeding.

Specificity

This specificity has the potential to confer further advantages. Individual genes can be added to confer desirable properties without substantial alteration of the original plant. This kind of process may be used to improve herbicide tolerance or insect resistance (thus reducing the need for chemical sprays), to improve growth in dry or otherwise adverse conditions, or to improve the nutritional value of crop plants. Maize, for example, is the most important source of protein in many parts of the world, but it does not contain all the proteins essential to humans. Through genetic engineering, these missing proteins could potentially be added.

Box 7.1: 'Golden rice'

One application of genetic modification with particular import-ance for the developing world is 'golden rice'. 'Golden rice' is rice that has been genetically engineered to produce a large quantity of a precursor of vitamin A, betacarotene. Vitamin A deficiency is a particular problem in areas of Asia where rice forms the staple diet, and can cause blindness or even death. By boosting the vitamin A content of rice, this deficiency could be targeted.

An ability to target specific characteristics accurately also means that individual genes can be 'switched off'; for example, the gene that controls ripening or softening in fruit (Jones 1999). This has been successfully carried out in tomatoes, which can then be stored for longer, transported more successfully and are better for producing tomato paste or puree since less ripe fruit contains more natural thickeners. Other undesirable properties of food products, such as the toxins in kidney beans, would be potential targets for this process.

Transgenic modification

Genes from organisms other than plants can also be introduced: these are sometimes called foreign genes or transgenes. These may be used to confer desirable agricultural properties on the plant, as in the example of nitrogen fixing. Plants need nitrogen to thrive and some leguminous plants (e.g. beans and peas) are able to obtain the nitrogen they require from the air by cooperating with nitrogen-fixing bacteria. However, cereal plants also require nitrogen, but do not have this ability; to encourage their growth, nitrogen-based fertilizers are often used. These fertilizers are costly and can cause pollution. The bacterial genes that are responsible for extracting nitrogen efficiently from the air have already been isolated and cloned. The next step in this process will be to try and transfer these to plants such as wheat or rice. However, genes may not be added solely to improve the agricultural properties of particular plants, but could also be used to make these plants produce renewable sources of key substances such as antibodies, drugs or biological factors.

Consumer choice

The selection processes described potentially lead to more efficient agricultural practice, greater crop yields and less wastage. It is argued that these efficiency savings would, in turn, lead to cheaper food for the consumer. GM technology also provides the possibility of engineering food crops specifically in line with consumer requirements – for example, flavour, texture and taste. However, these qualities are the product of multiple rather than single genes and are, therefore, more difficult to manipulate.

Benefits for the developing world

The increased efficiency of agricultural practice which technology potentially offers may not only be beneficial to the individual consumer, but also to societies and economies at large. The ability to grow specially engineered crops in otherwise hostile conditions, for example where there is a shortage of water, could obviously be beneficial to communities living in parts of the world where drought is common. The possibility of better crop yields is important at a time when, despite a slowdown in the rate of growth, the world population is continuing to increase overall. The increase in the last 50 years or so has been due principally to the increase in population in developing countries. The population in the developing world is increasing at approximately three times the rate of that in the developed world (Russo and Cove 1998).

There are almost three times as many people in developing countries as in the developed world, yet they have similar amounts of arable land. However, the quality of this land is different. Degradation of cropland through the use of inappropriate agricultural techniques and overuse of scarce resources is a problem, particularly in Africa. In developing countries, on average, there is about one-third as much food per person. It is estimated that 18 per cent of the world's population do not have enough food and that six million children under the age of five die each year of malnutrition in developing countries (Hawkes 2000). The possibility of greater crop yields from the same amount of land is clearly one potential way of alleviating this problem. A more viable agricultural programme would also lead to increased employment in rural areas.

Disadvantages of GM food

Despite the dialogue of normalization of GM procedures, one of the key concerns expressed over the use of these technologies is that they represent scientists 'playing God'. In other words, genetic modification of food means science doing what nature will not, by breaching the natural barriers between species. As a result, the relationship between humans and nature will potentially be deliberately distorted. As Gofton and Haimes (1999) note, this argument might equally be applied to all new uses of genetic technology, for example genetic testing and antenatal screening. However, for reasons that will be considered later in this chapter, it has been most vociferously applied, in the UK at least, to GM foods. The 'Frankenfoods' headlines that began to appear frequently in the press from 1997 encapsulate these concerns succinctly. The following examples are taken from UK daily papers, and illustrate the common portrayal of GM food as unnatural:

Fast food giants bin mutant grub. (*Daily Star*, 19 February 1999)

'Frankenstein food' faces supermaket ban. (*The Daily Telegraph*, 26 January 1997)

'Frankenstein' drives demand for organics. (*The Guardian*, 21 February 1999)

In particular, the reference to Mary Shelley's story of Frankenstein conveys not only an air of menace but also a subtext that these products are not fully under the control of their creators and are likely to have unforeseen consequences. The headline from *The Guardian* illustrates another dimension – that the 'unnaturalness' of GM foods is often contrasted with the 'naturalness' of other products, particularly organic ones.

Consequences for the environment

Opponents of GM food argue that any unforeseen consequences of GM crops are likely to be most catastrophic for the environment. Biodiversity may be threatened, and characteristics introduced as desirable into one plant may naturally spread to others where they are far less so. The spread of herbicide resistance, for example, which is desirable in crop plants, could spread through cross-pollination to weeds, creating 'superweeds'. Insect resistance may have an effect on non-target insects, with implications for the food chain and the ecosystem as a whole. In a laboratory, organisms can be isolated and effects can be monitored individually. However, GM crops growing 'naturally' cannot be isolated and, since the organisms in an ecosystem are interdependent, altering one component is likely to have effects on all the others, which may not be entirely predictable.

Consequences for health

Unforeseen consequences for human health are also a possibility through eating food products made from GM crops. Butler et al. (1999) describe how genetic technologies will produce foreign proteins that have never before been in the food chain. These could potentially be consumed in large amounts by those at the top of the food chain (i.e. humans) and, while there may be no short-term effects, it is impossible to know what the long-term effects might be. Just as it is possible to remove toxins or other undesirable substances through genetic modification, so it is possible to introduce them.

Box 7.2: Panics over the safety of GM food

Arpad Pusztai, a scientist at the Rowett Research Institute in the UK, announced in a television interview in April 1998 that his experiments showed intestinal changes in rats that he claimed were caused by eating genetically modified potatoes. He said that he would not eat modified foods himself and that it was 'very, very unfair to use our fellow citizens as guineapigs' (*The Lancet* 1999: 1811). In the media furore that followed, Pusztai had the use of his laboratory withdrawn, but this did not prevent widespread public alarm. An investigation by the Royal Society concluded that Pusztai's evidence was flawed, although Pusztai and colleagues countered that their work was incomplete. On 21 May 1999, the UK government proposed a research programme to investigate the possible health risks of GM food.

Consequences for the developing world

In the face of claims that GM technology will provide a solution to world hunger, critics argue that hunger is not a problem of food production, but a problem of social injustice. Food distribution, rather than food production, is the primary issue, and this is a result of the balance of power. Although biotechnology may be able to increase productivity, this will not necessarily have any impact on food shortages on its own, if patterns of distribution remain the same. In addition, biotechnology companies are profit motivated, and while some of their innovations have obvious potential, these come at a price. An example is the so-called terminator gene that can be inserted into GM crops, meaning that after one season the plant cannot be propagated from itself and new seeds must be purchased for each planting. From an environmental point of view, this has the benefit of reducing the chances of gene leakage to other plants, but it also has clear commercial implications. This type of commercial ploy could easily outweigh the potential benefits. As Leeder (2000) suggests, the end result may be to increase debt to multinationals and to increase the north–south wealth disparity.

Patenting

Biotechnology companies are market-led and need to protect the recovery of their research and development costs through sales of their products. As in the pharmaceutical industry, this has led to what is called 'key' patenting: patenting basic compounds or inventions on which products are built, which then requires everyone who uses them subsequently to pay a fee. A report issued in 2000 by the Academies of Sciences of seven different countries, including the USA, the UK and some from the developing world (e.g. India), suggests that broadly written patents on GM food technology may prevent it being used where it is most needed (http://www.nas.edu). The report also urges companies to ensure that the benefits are more widely available. Issues of patenting, and of the 'ownership' of naturally occurring entities such as plants and their products, are discussed in more detail in Chapter 6.

We noted at the beginning of this chapter that constructing the debate over GM foods as a pro and anti debate is potentially counterproductive. A brief review of the proposed advantages and disadvantages demonstrates that the key factor in many of the contested issues is the way in which technologies might be used and how they will be controlled, rather than the technologies themselves, and we will return to this theme later in the chapter. In fact, there is little objective evidence about the impact, particularly in the longer term, of GM crops and GM foods. For example, there is little evidence available to confirm whether modified genes inserted in one plant can be 'accidentally' transferred to other plants through cross-breeding. Nor is there any widely accepted proof of the threat to health, particularly in the long term; it appears to be the threat to the environment that is considerably greater. It should be noted that this threat is disputed by the agricultural industry, with risk analyses to date having produced mixed results. However, it is also this threat that is potentially the most difficult to regulate.

The regulation of GM foods

Genetically modified crops and food products are currently tested by a process of 'substantial equivalence' – that is, they are compared to conventional foods by toxicity, nutritional qualities and other characteristics. If these characteristics are found to be 'substantially equivalent', then the product is allowed on to the market. The onus is on the biotechnology company responsible for the product to demonstrate that it meets these criteria. In the UK, the Advisory Committee on Novel Foods and Processes, under the umbrella of the Novel Foods Division of the Food Standards Agency, is responsible for this process (http://www.foodstandards.gov.uk). However, there is also a recognized need to assess the potential risks of unpredictable occurrences. Regulatory authorities predict the properties of new proteins, for example, by analysing their structure in comparison with known proteins. What is more difficult is the assessment of the potential presence of undesirable products such as toxins. There is also the more widespread problem of extrapolating the results of tests in animals to humans (Butler *et al.* 1999).

The Advisory Committee on Novel Foods and Processes (ACNFP) began life as the Advisory Committee on Irradiated and Novel Foods in 1982. Its name was changed in 1988 to reflect more accurately the work which it began to do. Current UK food law requires companies to refer novel foods and food processes to the committee once they have conducted their own safety evaluations. The ACNFP consists of 15 scientists with expertise in different areas and is one of a number of committees that advise the government with regard to food and report to the Food Standards Agency (others include the Committee on Toxicity and the Food Advisory Committee). The remit of the Committee is:

> to advise Health and Agriculture Ministers of Great Britain and the Heads of the Departments of Health and Social Services and Agriculture for Northern Ireland on any matters relating to the irradiation of food or to the manufacture of novel foods or foods produced by novel processes having regard where appropriate to the views of relevant expert bodies.
>
> (Moseley 1999: 26)

Final decisions on food safety are based on the concept that there should be *reasonable certainty* that no harm will result from its consumption. This concept applies equally to food products derived from GM processes and ingredients and to those that are not.

European regulation

In the European Union, the safety of GM food is controlled by Regulation EC No. 258/97, which is specifically concerned with novel foods and novel food ingredients. Introduced in May 1997, this regulation mandates a pre-market safety assessment for all novel foods. Before a food can be approved, it must satisfy three criteria:

- It must not present a danger to the consumer.
- It must not mislead the consumer.
- It must not differ from foods for which it is an intended replacement to an extent that normal consumption would be nutritionally disadvantageous to the consumer (Moseley 1999).

Regulation in the USA

The US government agency responsible for legislation in this area, the Food and Drug Administration (FDA), has not changed its stance since 1992. In January 1999, they announced: 'FDA has not found it necessary to conduct comprehensive reviews of foods derived from bioengineered plants . . . consistent with its 1992 policy' (*The Lancet* 1999: 1811). Under this policy, genetically modified crops receive no more consideration for possible health risks than any other new crop plant. The population of the USA, where up to 60 per cent of processed foods have genetically modified ingredients, seem as yet unconcerned.

Critics of the regulation process

Critics suggest that testing GM foods by substantial equivalence is necessary, but not on its own sufficient to establish public health safety. There have been calls to use the disparity on reaction to GM foods between consumers in the USA and in Europe as a kind of natural experiment, to establish the long-term effects on health and the environment (Leeder 2000). However, these effects may not be apparent for many years. There have also been calls to treat GM products in the same way that new drug or medicinal products are treated, requiring them to undergo an extended period of testing first in animals, and then in human volunteers, before allowing them on to the market.

Just as the regulatory responses have been different in the UK and USA, so has the response from the public. These differences can be analysed in terms of the wider sociological debate on trust.

Trust

In the UK and Europe, as we have seen, media coverage of GM foods has been intense and often sensational (Leeder 2000). However, this has not been the case in the USA. Analysts have suggested that this disparity in reaction may have its foundation in other food scares that have occurred recently in the UK and, to a lesser extent, in Europe. Of particular relevance is the BSE (bovine spongiform encephalopathy) outbreak in cattle, responsible for human variant CJD (Creuzfeldt Jacob disease) in humans. This has led to a public lack of trust in food production generally, and a reluctance to believe assurances from scientists that technologies are safe, when these same assurances were given with BSE. Critics and consumer groups have become sceptical of the reliability of safety assessment procedures and the judgement of expert committees. BSE was caused in the UK by a change in the processing of animal feed when the feed industry was deregulated. These circumstances also destroyed public trust in commercially driven enterprises, since companies were perceived to have acted irresponsibly. In the case of BSE, the public was told that food safety could be left in the hands of the producers, but cost-cutting in animal feed which led to cows being fed infected materials from dead animals undermined that safety. Since GM technologies are also profit driven, the same fears are present, but the presumption of trust that existed before BSE has now been destroyed.

Two quotes from Shaw's (1999) study of the way 'experts' on food construct public concerns about food highlight these issues. The first is from a member of an organic food pressure group, who says:

> there has been a sea change in public attitudes towards food safety and food quality collectively as a result of the food scares . . . the public are asking a series of questions that they were never asking before. 'Where has my food come from?' 'How did they produce it?' 'Did they look after safety and quality aspects?'
>
> (Shaw 1999: para. 7.2)

This view that recent food scares have caused a change in public attitudes to food and food production can then be extrapolated to explain the public reaction to GM foods. Another of Shaw's informants, a food retailer, describes this as a public interest in the *integrity* of food:

> People want to know questions about where it is from, where has it been produced . . . I think there's just an enormous curiosity about all aspects of food from that point of view, its origins, its integrity, that we just didn't have before BSE, before salmonella and listeria . . . Certainly genetic modification, that goes back to the integrity of the food.
>
> (Shaw 1999: para. 8.1)

Discourses of integrity and trust, then, are fundamental to understanding the way in which GM foods have been received by the public in the UK. A growing lack of trust in scientists and regulatory bodies has been matched by an increasing confidence in pressure groups such as Greenpeace and Friends of the Earth. Since these groups do not have a commercial agenda, and since the commercial agenda of farmers is seen as a causative factor in the BSE scare in particular, they are increasingly seen as sources of unbiased and impartial information. University scientists have also suffered from this lack of trust, although perhaps to a lesser extent. With the increasing commercialization of university science, they are less likely to be seen as dispassionate and detached in relation to their research.

In the USA, there has been no comparable food scare in recent years and so issues surrounding the production of food have been less widely debated in public. Some commentators have suggested that the lack of public response to the introduction of GM foods in the USA also reflects a different underlying attitude to food production. Consumers in the USA may be more accepting of the industrialization of food production more generally, since agricultural businesses are conducted on a much larger scale. In this context, genetic modification is just one more component of this process. In the UK, farming is often perceived as a smaller scale and 'natural' activity, hence the concern when this perception of 'naturalness' is undermined.

The deficit model of public understanding

Governments and scientists often counter public concerns with the argument that public opposition is based on a lack of understanding of the technology involved. According to this viewpoint, the acceptability of GM foods will increase through education and the dissemination of accurate and objective information. From a sociological point of view, this deficit model is fundamentally flawed, since it fails to take into account issues of trust. Parallels may be drawn here with the debate over compliance with medical treatment that began in the 1970s (see Stimson 1974). Whereas previously it had been assumed that those patients who failed to comply with doctor's orders had failed to understand or recall them, research began to show that people often made deliberate decisions not to comply with medical advice. These decisions might be made on the basis of a lack of confidence in the doctor's opinion. They might also be made as a result of comparing the perceived benefits of compliance with the costs. This kind of lay cost–benefit analysis also has implications for GM foods. Public acceptance may have more to do with the perceived benefits of GM food for the consumer; benefits for food producers in terms of efficiency and productivity may be clear, but these will not necessarily benefit the consumer. Issues of choice are also important here: when tomato puree made with GM tomatoes was introduced, it was clearly labelled, and consumers could make a conscious choice whether or not to purchase it. However, the introduction of genetically modified soya into manufactured products without labelling, since it was not separated at source from non-modified soya by its US producers, caused widespread concern. An initial unwillingness to segregate the two crops led to the subsequent rejection of these products in the UK. This feeds into a wider argument – that every adult is free to put his or her own life in danger, but the deployment of GM technologies potentially removes that choice. Increased food labelling will give individuals the right to decide whether or not they want to purchase GM products. However, those consumers who choose not to will still be affected by potential environmental consequences. This argument, of course, does not only apply in this scenario – many individuals, for example, are against the use of nuclear power but are still potentially put at risk by the siting of power stations.

Discourses of risk

Sociological approaches to risk can also increase our understanding of the response to GM foods. Whereas scientists acting in a professional capacity may scale levels of risk objectively, risk perception among the general public is a more complex issue. Sociological approaches to risk start from the assumption that 'risks are socially constructed or framed and collectively perceived' (Gabe 1995: 8–9). As a result, risk is a subjective perception rather than an objective phenomenon, and does not have a straightforward relationship with 'expert' knowledge. Risk has become a key theme for sociologists in the analysis of modern societies. Gofton and Haimes describe the way in which virtually all approaches to genetic modification have foregrounded the possible risks, stating that:

> there is understandably an attraction towards 'risk' as the key analytical concept – how to establish its importance as part of the debates on biotechnologies; how to define it; how to predict, calculate and measure it; how to identify the appropriate expertises towards the different types of risk that will arise; what regulatory forms will enable the control of risk and so on.
>
> (Gofton and Haimes 1999: para. 1.5)

Beck (1992) argues that we live in a 'risk society', where the calculation of risk operates as a control mechanism on the development of capitalism. On a fundamental level, of course, it might be argued that risk is involved in any activity, and that the important question is whether irresponsible risks are being taken. However, this viewpoint ignores the socially constructed nature of risk. Nevertheless, the debate highlights the importance of acknowledging limits to scientific certainty. As Hadden (1979: 111) points out, 'Accurate assessment of risk often requires information that is simply not available or that is ambiguous. This ambiguity creates "areas of judgment", points at which experts can legitimately differ'. In other words, it does not create certainty. Perhaps then, as a *Nature* editorial states, the best that scientific research can do is to place acceptable limits on uncertainty (*Nature* 1999).

The confirmation of scientific discoveries

In Chapter 3, we considered the idea that a scientific 'discovery' can only become a fact when it is supported and legitimized by the scientific community. The confirmation of experimental results is a key part of this process. Collins (1992: 19) argues that replication is 'the scientifically institutionalised counterpoint of the stability of perception'. However, as Atkinson *et al.* (1997) note in discussing Collins' work, despite its central place in scientific orthodoxy, the confirmation of experimental reality is not necessarily straightforward in practice. Replication is a complex process, but it has little reward attached for those who do it. Instead, replicating results serves to confirm the esteem of those who made the discovery in the first place. In any case, failure to replicate results will not necessarily be seen as disproving the original findings (as in the case of the monarch butterfly, discussed in Box 7.3), but may instead be attributed to a failure to reproduce the original experimental conditions, for example. The perceived credibility of individuals and their institutions also has a role to play in this process. As a result, Latour and Woolgar (1979) argue that negotiations on what counts as proof are no more or less disorderly than in law or politics, and that what becomes accepted as scientific reality is the consequence of this process rather than the cause.

Moral panics

Since the risks of GM foods are still so highly contested, it is also useful to examine reactions in the UK in the light of the concept of 'moral panics'. Goode and Ben Yehuda (1994) identify five elements of a moral panic.

1 *Concern*. A moral panic is characterized by a heightened level of concern, which is measurable through concrete means. In terms of GM foods, this would apply to the explosion of media commentary, combined with the many opinion polls demonstrating widespread public concern (e.g. Frewer and Shepherd 1995; Bredahl 1999).
2 *Hostility*. There is an increased level of hostility towards the group or category regarded as engaging in 'deviant' behaviour. In this context, hostility has manifested itself in the accusations that scientists are playing God and the expressed lack of trust in the official reassurances of safety.
3 *Consensus*. A moral panic requires substantial agreement that the threat is real and serious. This is perhaps best illustrated by the Puzstai affair, where, despite the fact that his work was subsequently discredited by a body of eminent scientists, Puzstai's view held sway in the public domain. As a result of the ensuing debate, the government acted on this widespread concern by announcing a research programme into the effects of GM foods on health.
4 *Disproportionality*. This is arguably the key criterion for identifying a moral panic. Goode and Ben Yehuda describe this as a sense on the part of members of society that the threat or danger posed by a particular phenomenon is more substantial than a realistic assessment would allow. However, they also conclude that it can be the most difficult characteristic to assess. In the case of GM foods, there is little substantial evidence on the realistic potential impact, and it is difficult

to make short-term assessments of long-term consequences. Nevertheless, the media reporting of 'Frankenfoods', with the attendant suggestion that they are out of the control of their creators, is one example of this kind of response. The focus on the findings of one scientist, as opposed to the many who subsequently scrutinized his work and found no cause for alarm, is another.

Box 7.3: The monarch butterfly

The case of the monarch butterfly is another potential example of disproportionality of response, as well as the process of confirmation of experimental results, in relation to GM foods. Following the publication of an article in *Nature* (Losey *et al.* 1999) suggesting the toxicity of pollen from GM corn to the monarch butterfly, there were widespread calls to halt research and predictions of ecological disaster. Researchers dusted corn pollen onto the leaves of milkweed, a plant that grows around corn fields and is the main source of food for the caterpillars of the monarch butterfly. The results showed that high pollen levels were toxic to the caterpillars. However, the research was conducted in a laboratory setting and subsequent studies gave conflicting results. The original research was also criticized for the levels of pollen it exposed caterpillars to, and it was argued that these were far in excess of levels of natural exposure. Despite the inconclusive nature of the research, it is still widely cited as evidence of the danger of GM foods.

---

⑤ *Volatility.* Moral panics tend to errupt fairly suddenly and to be relatively short-lived. They may then become routinized or institutionalized, in the form of legislation, social movement organization, and so on. A further review of the media headlines shows that the most vociferous of these appeared over a relatively short time-scale. *The Guardian* and *The Observer*, for example, carried only two stories between them on GM foods between July and December 1998. Between January and June 1999, this figure rose sharply to 97, with most of these stories appearing in just one month, February. July to December 1999 saw 54 stories, with a further fall to 28 in the first half of 2000. The specific reporting of the Puzstai affair followed a similar pattern over a shorter time-scale, and died down in the UK press when the UK government proposed its research programme.

Conceptualizing the reaction to GM foods as a moral panic is more useful in understanding it than resorting to the straightforward deficit model more generally applied to the public understanding of science.

Goode and Ben Yehuda's (1994) criteria for describing the reaction to a particular phenomenon or scenario as a moral panic illustrate that there is a complex interplay of factors that work together to arouse and maintain public concern.

The relationship between science, power and controversy

This complex interplay of factors and the way that they work together is also explored by Nelkin (1979). She notes that the development of science and technology remained largely unquestioned during the rapid economic growth after the Second World War. Since then, however, belief in technological progress has been tempered by an awareness of the problems it may bring, and this awareness has been heightened by unpredicted and high-profile incidents with disastrous consequences (for example, those involving nuclear power). The 1960s and 1970s saw the rise of political action directed against science and technology, alongside a demand for greater accountability and public participation in decision making. Nelkin argues that there are several different concerns that may be expressed by protests against science and technology: equity, fear of risk, freedom of choice and the infringement of science on traditional values and beliefs. One of the reasons why GM food has been a major cause for protest, in the UK at least, is that it may be seen to raise all these concerns. This is partly because it has a clearly discernible potential impact, not only at the individual level of consumption, but also at the environmental level. However, as Nelkin (1979) reminds us, we should bear in mind that many protests may be less against science and technology themselves than against the power relationships associated with them, and against the use of scientific rationality to mask political choices. As controversies develop, scientists' expertise is used to fortify political positions, with the authority that their expertise brings. In cases of technical ambiguity, political criteria for regulation can prevail, whereas scientific consensus narrows policy options (Hadden 1979; Nelkin 1979). These themes are evident in the anti-GM movement, in terms of the concerns that are voiced over the effect on agriculture in developing countries, and over the disputed evidence in relation to the Pusztai affair and the trial sites for GM crops. In this light, it is interesting to consider more carefully why there has been no equivalent moral panic over the medical application of new genetic technologies.

Medicine *vs* food

In exploring this apparent discrepancy, sociologists have made distinctions between the way in which food and medicine are culturally constructed and perceived. Gofton and Haimes (1999) suggest that medicine is constructed and perceived as a professional and separate arena, where experts are entitled to hold privileged and superior knowledge. The doctor–patient relationship has at its heart an asymmetry of power and knowledge. Food, on the other hand, is constructed and perceived as a mundane and everyday arena, where professional status and opinion is not privileged and does not hold sway. Risk may be an allowable consequence if an individual is seriously ill, but it may not be acceptable when attached to the basic and everyday act of eating.

Conrad (1999a) argues that there are three reasons why biotechnology has been accepted in medicine, yet resisted in food. First, medical applications of new genetic technologies affect the internal and individual environment, not the external one. Second, they reinforce the idea that disease is a discrete and easily identifiable commodity, which, having been located, can be isolated and treated. This leads to the third reason, that the body is depicted as a machine with parts that can be replaced if they do not function correctly, so 'bad' genes can be found and replaced.

In considering these arguments, it is important not to draw too marked a distinction between food and medicine. Both have an important impact on health. As Gofton and Haimes (1999) comment, the BSE/CJD scare may be seen as much as a health scare as a food scare. Nevertheless, the particular place that food occupies in society is an important issue for analysis.

Understanding the social significance of food

Increasingly, food is produced by outside 'experts'. In industrialized societies, the average person has no contact with food production. This may encourage suspicion, or as Shaw's (1999) work suggests, concerns over the 'integrity' of food. It may also account for the rise in popularity of organic foods, in the sense that, in the face of previous food scares and conflicting claims over the safety of GM technology, a return to the past is seen as the safest option.

Another factor, often overlooked as a result of the prevalence of the 'deficit model', is that food choices are morally accountable. This accountability is heightened when food is being chosen for others, for example by mothers for children. Choices and risks that may be perceived as acceptable for an individual may be seen as unacceptable if this choice is being made on behalf of another. As Murphy et al. (1999) note, adults themselves may be passive rather than active choosers, in the sense that it may only be when something disturbs their assumptions (for example, a food scare) that their decisions become overt.

A sociological approach to food choice also highlights that the notion of choice in itself can be problematic, as choice rarely comes without constraints. Caplan et al. (1999) argue that, although it is often assumed that people are free to choose what they eat in the contemporary West, such an individualistic view fails to take account of social and cultural constraints on eating. These include money, time, ethical and religious beliefs, as well as the choices of other family or household members. To understand more about food choice, then, we need to focus, as Henson *et al.* (1999) suggest, not only on *what* people select to eat but on *how* they select it: how these decisions are arrived at and the factors that influence them. ☺

Understanding the importance of these factors highlights the over-simplistic nature of the deficit model of understanding. Food choice is a complex area and is not determined solely by individual preference. The work of Macintyre *et al.* (1999) on the impact of publicity of both the risks of BSE and of a high fat diet clearly illustrates that respondents had high levels of knowledge about what was considered to be healthy or dangerous. However, they made different choices in relation to this knowledge, in the context of both their immediate social networks and of their understandings of food and information production systems.

On the one hand, then, for the debate over GM foods to move forward, the social significance of food needs to be more widely recognized by scientists. On the other hand, as Murcott (1999) cautions, the sociology of food itself needs to move on. Although the body of research that currently exists helps us to understand how people choose to eat what they do, Murcott argues that we need to broaden the scope of this research to look at what goes on in the food science laboratory as well as in the supermarket or the kitchen.

Summary points

- The debate over GM foods has largely been conducted in oppositional terms, focusing on issues of health, consumer choice, consequences for the environment and consequences for the developing world. However, this oppositional construction runs the risk of over-simplifying complex issues.

- From a sociological point of view, a lack of public trust in food production in the UK is a key factor in understanding hostile attitudes. Assurances of safety have been given in the past in relation to beef consumption and the subsequent disconfirmation of these assurances has led to a lack of confidence in 'expert' assessment.

- Differing attitudes to GM food in the USA may reflect the lack of comparable food scares across the Atlantic, as well as different attitudes to the industrialization of food production. These differences illustrate once again that the 'deficit model' of public understanding cannot satisfactorily explain the ways in which new genetic technologies have been received, highlighting the importance of social context in determining risk perception.

- The differences between the ways in which medical and agricultural applications of genetics have been received reflects the different ways in which food and medicine are culturally constructed and perceived. Eating is an everyday occurrence, where we are all 'experts', and where risk is less acceptable. Medicine, on the other hand, is a specialist arena.

- To move the debate over GM foods forwards, more attention should be focused on the social significance of food and on the contexts within which people make their food choices.

Further reading

Almas, R. (1999) Food trust, ethics and safety in risk society, *Sociological Research Online*, 4(3) (http://www.socresonline.org.uk/socresonline/4/3/almas.html).

Beardsworth, A. (1990) Trans science and moral panics: understanding food scares, *British Food Journal*, 92: 11–16.

Beardsworth, A. and Keil, T. (1997) *Sociology on the Menu*. London: Routledge.

Frewer, L., Howard, C. and Shepherd, R. (1996) Public concerns in the United Kingdom about general and specific applications of genetic engineering, *Science, Technology and Human Values*, 22: 98–124.

Irwin, A. and Wynne, B. (eds) (1996) *Misunderstanding Science? The Public Reconstruction of Science and Technology*. Cambridge: Cambridge University Press.

Lupton, D. (1996) *Food, the Body and the Self*. London: Sage.

8

CLONING

Introduction

This chapter begins with a description of the process of cloning and a summary of the main aims that lie behind the pursuit of cloning research. It then moves on to look at two potential applications of cloning: **reproductive cloning** and **therapeutic cloning**. Some of the differences between the applications of these technologies, as well as the differences in the way they have been perceived and received, will be explored. The regulatory framework surrounding cloning, and the way in which this has changed since the late 1990s, will be outlined. The final section of the chapter will focus on public responses to cloning, exploring the role of narratives and the media in informing these responses.

What is a clone?

The process of genetic engineering, as described in more detail in Chapter 7, allows the transfer of genetic material to occur between different living things. Through this process, the characteristics of the organism to which the material has been transferred can be changed to create new, advantageous characteristics. Genetically modified food is one application of this process, but there are many other applications and potential applications of the technology in the areas of food production, medicine and agriculture. Cloning is perhaps best viewed as a particular kind of genetic engineering and, although it is often thought of as a new development, animal cloning experiments have been part of science since the 1950s.

The word **clone** is used in many different contexts in biological research, but in its strictest sense it refers to a precise *genetic* copy of a molecule, cell, plant or animal (National Bioethics Advisory Committee

1998). In some of these contexts, cloning refers to technologies that have been long established and practised, for example the selective breeding of crop plants in agriculture through the practice of taking cuttings. To distinguish these different practices, what is covered in this chapter is more correctly described as nuclear transplantation cloning.

Nuclear transplantation cloning

In very basic terms, nuclear transplantation cloning occurs when the complete genetic material of one organism is transferred into a fertilized egg of another.

There are four key steps to this process:

1 The **nucleus** of an egg is removed, leaving it with no genes at all.
2 A new cell is placed under the outer membrane of the egg.
3 Electricity is used to 'open' the egg and the cell, so that the contents of the cell, including the genetic material, can enter the nucleus of the egg.
4 The electric current has a similar effect on the egg to fertilization – it 'jump starts' it into developing.

One of the key points about nuclear transplantation cloning is that the end result is an organism that has only one genetic parent. By contrast, sexual reproduction occurs through the mixing of genetic material from two parents. However, strictly speaking, the product of nuclear transplantation cloning is not *absolutely* identical to its genetic parent, since small amounts of **mitochondrial DNA** from the egg donor will remain in the donor egg when the nucleus is removed.

Although cloning experiments had been going on throughout the second half of the twentieth century, early experiments were only successful when the genetic material transferred was from an early embryo. Animals are made up of many different types of cell (e.g. brain, heart, liver), which, in any one organism, contain the same genetic information but which develop differently from **stem cells**. Embryo cells, however, are sometimes described as less differentiated than adult cells, meaning that they have not yet completed this process of differential development from stem cells. It was not until the 1990s that there was the first successful attempt to carry out this procedure using adult genetic material from an already differentiated cell. An adult udder cell was used, and this attempt produced the sheep known as Dolly.

Dolly was born on 5 June 1996 in Scotland, but her birth was not announced until 27 February 1997 (see Wilmut *et al.* 1997). She was the product of a decade long research programme (and 277 attempts) that aimed to develop animals that could produce drugs for human use. The cloning of Dolly was a landmark in the development of new genetic technology and captured the imagination of people worldwide. The possibilities that cloning technology appeared to offer were simultaneously incredible and terrifying. Perhaps, unsurprisingly, the possibility most frequently debated as a result of Dolly's birth was that of human cloning. However, the broader significance of the development in terms of the relationship between science and society was also raised. As Harris (1997) argues, in many ways the birth of Dolly has come to be seen as illustrative of the responsibilities of science and scientists to the communities in which they live.

Why pursue cloning research?

The suggested goals of cloning encompass direct benefits to medicine and the biotechnology industry, as well as the more general goal of the advancement of science.

The principal justification for cloning is that it opens new perspectives for therapeutic medicine. In terms of animal cloning, the major benefits can be broken down more specifically as follows, drawing on the National Bioethics Advisory Committee's (1998) statement of the goals of cloning research.

1. To generate groups of genetically identical animals for research purposes. This would have the advantage of eliminating the genetic variation that can lead to experimental variation and so create problems in generalizing research results.
2. To rapidly propagate desirable animal stocks. The major application here may be animals with particular advantageous characteristics, for example milk yield, but cloning technologies have also been seen as a way of preserving near extinct species such as the gaur.

Box 8.1: Cloning extinct species

The gaur is a rare type of wild ox, nearing extinction. In 2001, a cloned gaur was created by fusing skin cells from a gaur that died in 1993 with cow eggs stripped of their nuclei. This is the same process that was used to create Dolly the sheep, but in this case the DNA of one species was inserted into the eggs of another. Unfortunately, Noah, as the gaur was named, died after just 48 hours. Initial suspicions were that his immune system was compromised, but it later became apparent that he had succumbed to a common bacterial infection. However, the death rate of cloned animals in general is approximately twice as high as in those conceived through sexual reproduction, meaning that there are questions over its utility for this purpose.

3 To improve the generation and propagation of **transgenic** livestock. The most straightforward application here is the production of proteins (e.g. growth hormones). As a result of genetic engineering, these proteins can be produced in, for example, a sheep's milk, from where they can be easily extracted and purified. In this way, an animal could become a continuous producer of medicine for its lifetime, and further producers could be cloned from the original. This principle potentially applies to many other substances that are needed in the treatment of human diseases and disorders, for example the production of Factor VIII to enable blood clotting in haemophiliacs. This line of research also has implications for the production of donor organs in transgenic animals: a human gene could be introduced into animal cell lines, and cells expressing the transgene could be used as a source of donor material.

Box 8.2: Xenotransplantation

While using transgenic animals (animals with 'foreign' genes) for transplantation purposes is seen as an important development, in the wake of the BSE and human variant CJD crisis, the possibility of introducing diseases into the population through cross-species transplantation, or **xenotransplantation**, is seen as very real. Some pig viruses, for example, can be transmitted across species and the possibility of hitherto unknown infectious diseases cannot be discounted. For these reasons, xenotransplantation is unlikely to solve the problem of the shortage of organs for transplantation in the near future (White 2001).

---

4 To produce specific targeted genetic alterations in animals for research purposes. These alterations could be useful in medical research, by creating accurate models of human genetic disease on which new therapies could be tested or disease processes better understood.
5 To improve knowledge of biological processes – how cells age, for example, or what goes wrong in cells to produce particular diseases.

Many of the advantages listed above represent important advances for medical science and, as with other areas of genetic development, it has been argued that they represent a difference of degree rather than kind over processes that are currently used and accepted. The principle of generating groups of genetically identical animals for research purposes, for example, is something that is already used in medical research: laboratory animals are often selectively bred to be as similar as possible in their biological response to a particular stimulus. Cloning would allow this process to be carried out more accurately. In the same way, animal breeders already attempt to propagate desirable animal stock through selective breeding, and cloning would potentially offer a more efficient short-cut to the same result.

Despite these apparent advantages, critics have suggested that we need to be sure of the long-term consequences before proceeding too quickly with this kind of research agenda. In particular, uncertainty surrounding the long-term implications of cloning for health remains. There is some evidence to suggest that Dolly has suffered from premature ageing and studies of subsequently cloned animals have shown a high mortality rate either in late gestation or shortly after birth. These complications illustrate that the technology is still at a relatively early stage of development.

Box 8.3: Dolly and ageing

Much of the debate over the long-term health implications of cloning has its origin in the report that Dolly the sheep showed signs of having aged prematurely. Telomeres are structures on the tips of chromosomes that become shorter with age; analysis of Dolly's telomeres found that their length was consistent with the fact that she had been derived from the cell of a 6-year-old ewe, rather than her own chronological age (Shiels et al. 1999). Although these findings have not in themselves been contested, other researchers have argued that the link between telomeres and ageing is not so well established for any firm conclusions to be drawn from this discovery.

Although there have been objections to the development of animal cloning, it is in the area of human cloning that debate has tended to crystallize.

Human cloning

In terms of human cloning, there are two key areas where benefits are predicted. These different applications of cloning technology are commonly referred to as 'therapeutic cloning' and 'reproductive cloning'. Therapeutic cloning is seen to have particular benefits in the field of organ and tissue transplantation. Many human diseases can now in theory be treated by organ transplantation. However, the most common reason for failure when organs are transplanted is rejection, where the body recognizes the donor organ as foreign and begins to fight it. Nuclear replacement cloning could overcome this by providing a potential source of organs or tissues that would not be rejected as foreign because they would be genetically identical to the transplant recipient. It would also overcome the possibility of introducing new diseases into humans through using transgenic animals as donors. We will consider therapeutic cloning in more detail later in this chapter.

Reproductive cloning

In the chapter on antenatal screening, the idea that individuals have a right to reproduce was introduced. Assisted reproduction technologies are already widely used in medicine and involve a variety of parental and biological situations: who is the donor and who is the recipient, for example. To take the following as an illustration, *in vitro* fertilization (IVF) may use sperm from the prospective father or may use it from an anonymous donor. It may involve an egg from the prospective mother or again from an anonymous donor. In cases where both individuals in a couple are infertile, IVF can still be carried out using a surrogate mother and donor sperm. In this latter scenario, it could be argued that cloning would be a preferable option, since it would use one member of the couple's genetic material to produce a biologically related child. Again, some people would argue that the use of cloning in such circumstances would represent a difference of degree rather than kind from IVF. The end result is a child genetically related to only one half of a couple, but this is also the result of many commonly used IVF procedures.

Moral debates over reproductive cloning

Much of the debate over cloning in this context has been conducted through moral argument – that is, whether it is *morally* right or wrong to allow or prohibit cloning. Advocates of cloning for human reproductive purposes often draw on the principle of the right to reproduce, suggesting that it is morally indefensible to deny a woman the right to have the child she seeks.

Critics of cloning commonly draw on the philosopher Emmanuel Kant's principle of human dignity (e.g. Kahn 1997). This principle states that an individual should never be thought of as a means, but always as an end. Using this principle, it is argued that cloning should not be used as a *means* for people who in effect want to continue their blood line. Although a desire to be a parent may be seen as socially valid, adoption would achieve this end. Propagating one's genes, on the other hand, is not seen as socially valid.

This argument, while it may be morally persuasive on the surface, is not as straightforward as it might appear. Those people who are able to have children through unassisted sexual reproduction may do so for a variety of reasons, one of which may be a desire to continue their blood line, and others of which we may find even less palatable than this.

However, we do not intervene in these cases. Additionally, as Harris (1997) argues, the wholesale application of this principle to many other areas of medicine is problematic. He gives the example of blood donation, where the donor is used as a means to an end for the beneficiary. Using this abstract principle as a practical guide to action highlights some of the problems of a traditionally bioethical, moral approach to medical practice.

The major problem with taking this kind of moral approach to cloning is that it does not give sufficient consideration to the broader social context in which decisions are made. In Chapter 9, the way in which the key principles of bioethics often conflict with each other is discussed. In addition, sociologists have argued that the making of policy is more complex than applying rules or principles. Abstract principles and rules cannot dictate policy, because they do not contain enough specific information. As Light and McGee (1998) argue, principles may provide a moral background for policy and practice, but policy must be informed by empirical data and relevant specific information. By contrast, they suggest that a sociological approach to ethical dilemmas in medicine takes the dilemma out of its clinical setting. It asks who the stakeholders in the issue are, and who has the power to decide that there is a moral issue in the first place and what the 'right' thing to do is in any set of circumstances. Moral issues are not just there to be debated, but are socially constructed. These criticisms of bioethics from a sociological point of view are considered in more detail in Chapter 9.

Taking an abstract moral approach, then, runs the risk of oversimplifying the debate over new genetic technologies. People's desire for cloned offspring, for example, might be far more complex than a desire to propagate their own genes. One such scenario might be where one or both members of a couple who are biologically able to reproduce unassisted have a genetic disorder that they do not want to pass on. Cloning could provide an opportunity to ensure this. At the moment, the only way to achieve this is through pre-implantation diagnosis, where very early embryos are tested and only those found to be free of the genes for the disorder in question are implanted into the uterus. The process results in any affected embryos being discarded. Cloning also potentially offers opportunities to gay individuals who wish to procreate without using DNA from a member of the opposite sex. Cloning technologies could also be used to make existing IVF techniques more effective – for example, increasing the number of embryos for potential implantation and therefore increasing the likelihood of successful conception.

Common misunderstandings about cloning

Cloning does not produce identical copies of the same individual person. It only produces identical copies of the same genotype. So to clone George W. Bush, for example, would not be to clone multiple presidents of the USA. This misunderstanding relates back to the prevailing popularity of genetic determinism as a perspective – the idea that genes are responsible for all aspects of human behaviour. Clones would only be as alike as identical twins are alike, so while there may be strong physical similarities, they would not be an identical *person*. In any case, identical twins usually share the same time and culture, whereas clones would not necessarily share even that.

The metaphor of the identical twin is often used to explain the results of the process of cloning. Using this metaphor poses the question: Do artificial clones raise any difficulties not raised by the phenomenon of 'natural' twins? Certainly, it has been assumed that they do. The European Parliament passed a motion in 1997 stating that, with regard to the new ethical problems raised by cloning and 'the alarm caused' by Dolly, it held the view that each individual has a right to his or her own genetic identity (http://europa.eu.int/abc/doc/off/bull/en/9703/p103061.htm).

It is unclear, however, what happens to this right in the case of identical twins. Nevertheless, by comparison with children who are produced through unassisted sexual reproduction, there is a biological difference for cloned offspring. A cloned child would have only one genetic parent, whereas identical twins have two. Although this does not raise a particular moral problem, it is of interest to social scientists in terms of the potential impact that this might have on family and kinship structures. However, in considering this impact we need to remember that the model of the nuclear two-parent family is outdated and no longer represents the norm for many sections of our society. One of the criticisms of genetic science from a sociological point of view is that it tends to operate with a very simplistic and straightforward model of family, as discussed in Chapter 5 in relation to the sharing of genetic test results. In reality, however, an increasing number of children are raised by lone parents and may not have contact with their other biological parent. For those children born as a result of IVF using sperm or eggs from anonymous donors, the identity of one of their biological parents will never be known. In this context, a more appropriate question in relation to cloning may be whether not knowing your father is on a par with knowing that you do not genetically have a father.

Cloning and privacy

Cloning does raise issues regarding privacy that are not raised by IVF. Some critics have argued that the privacy rights of a clone would be at issue in the USA, since, under the Fifth Amendment, there is protection of 'a person's right to regulate the disclosure of information about himself'. This potentially causes a problem because, for a clone, a great deal of genetic information may already be known from his or her genetic parent. In this way it is suggested that a clone would in a very literal way live his or her life in the shadow of another individual. Holm (1998) describes this 'life in the shadow' as a potential partial re-enactment of someone else's life. Less dramatically, there is a very real issue of the implications cloning brings to genetic screening and testing. For example, whereas an individual with a biological parent who tests positive for a genetic disorder such as Huntington's disease will know that they are potentially at risk, a cloned individual could be diagnosed by default, in the absence of seeking that information for themselves or choosing to pass it on.

Summarizing objections to reproductive cloning

As Wilkie and Graham (1998) describe, the overwhelming initial reaction to the idea of cloning in the media was negative. This negativity was shared by both professional bodies and lay individuals. As an example, the World Health Organization's initial statement on cloning (issued on 11 March 1997) was as follows:

> WHO considers the use of cloning for the replication of human individuals to be ethically unacceptable as it would violate some of the basic principles which govern medically assisted procreation. These include respect for the dignity of the human being.

This statement represents a fairly typical instant reaction to Dolly. However, over the intervening years, attitudes have begun to change. By May 1997, following a report by a working group on cloning set up by WHO, the organization was raising concerns that much of the opposition to human cloning stemmed from 'science fiction accounts', and that legislators and policy makers were acting from a position of 'moral panic' rather than appropriate deliberation (Butler 1997). The British Medical Association, for instance, while still opposed to reproductive cloning, now discusses cloning as a possibility that should be openly debated and for which we should develop appropriate policy frameworks (http://www.bma.org.uk/ethics/nsf/webpagesvw/cloningbriefing).

This change in attitude is due in part to debates over where the burden of proof should lie in relation to new genetic technologies. For some commentators, this is related to our general presumption in favour of individual liberty, and the idea that any prohibition on this should be the exception rather than the norm. Following this line of thought, proponents of cloning argue that the fact that something is repulsive to someone as an individual should not be sufficient grounds to ban it. It might be argued, for example, that abortion is an example of a medical procedure that is repulsive, at least for the 'pro-life' element of the debate over termination of pregnancy. However, both US and UK laws recognize that there are circumstances in which abortion may be the most appropriate outcome for a particular individual.

Aside from the fundamental objection that cloning is morally wrong, the second major argument that has been advanced is that it is unnatural, in the sense that it represents artificial interference with nature. Clearly, cloning does represent an interference with natural processes, but the weakness of this argument lies in the fact that very many modern medical technologies could have the same accusation levelled against them. There is nothing 'natural' about blood transfusions, or organ transplants, or the use of life-support systems, for example. This argument is particularly problematic in relation to commonly used IVF technologies, which could undoubtedly be categorized as artificial interference, but have become widely accepted. As a participant in the Wellcome Trust public consultation exercise on human cloning puts it, 'When the first little girl was born from IVF, it was like, oh my god . . . But we've all grown up with the idea and it's not so terrible' (Wellcome Trust 1998: 32). What this line of thought illustrates is the possibility that some of the objections to cloning might be more accurately characterized as objections to an unfamiliar technology with potentially far-reaching consequences, rather than to the actual process itself.

As the attitude of the World Health Organization demonstrates, there appears to have been a gradual shift in the way that cloning has been perceived by scientific and medical groups. In particular, views on therapeutic cloning, to be discussed later in this chapter, have tended to be much less hostile and have served to reopen the debate over cloning more widely. Moving from an initial reaction of moral revulsion, a more commonly expressed idea now is that we need to consider cloning in the same way as any other new technology. In other words, we need to assess its safety and efficiency and the potential for harm it might bring, rather than engaging in an abstract moral debate. Although the moral debate is unlikely to disappear, if the potential benefits of cloning become more widely accepted, then there will be less of a moral issue.

This change in attitude, however, assumes that cloning is a practical as well as a possible technology. Dolly was the eventual result of many failed pregnancies and some deformed births. Any moral concept of harm needs also to be extended to the process of cloning itself, as well as to the possible psychological consequences of existing as a clone. In the light of the uncertainty over the premature ageing of Dolly, there are unanswered questions about the possibility of serious genetic malformations and the attendant consequences of these. The subsequent successful cloning of other mammals highlights the potential applications of the process, but Dolly serves to remind us that what is under debate here is a highly inefficient reproductive technology, compared to other methods of assisted conception that are currently available.

Sociological perspectives on cloning

From a sociological viewpoint conceptualizing the issues around cloning as a moral debate is not the only problematic approach. As always with the field of genetics, there is also a problem in seeing this only as an issue of individual choices to clone or not to clone. For example, there is a potentially eugenic outcome as a result of the sum of these choices that may privilege particular genotypes over others. In this sense, cloning potentially offers eugenicists more control over populations than any previous technology. However, in this context, it should probably be seen alongside prenatal testing and pre-implantation diagnosis as one of several technologies that allows prospective parents to exercise choice over the genome of their offspring, and all of these may equally be accused of encouraging objectification. For sociologists of science, there are questions around why cloning research has been so actively pursued, frequently with little success, and it has been argued that cloning represents the ultimate scientific power – creating life in the laboratory. There is also the problem of the resurgent popularity of the genetic determinist viewpoint, and the possible attendant expectation that clones would display particular characteristics as a result of a particular genetic make-up. Interestingly, it should be noted that some biologists have drawn on genetic determinist arguments in *objecting* to human cloning. These objections are made on the grounds that cloning is an evolutionary dead end, since we can only replicate what exists and not improve it.

Therapeutic cloning

Therapeutic cloning may be defined as the medical and scientific applications of cloning technology that do not result in the production of genetically identical fetuses or babies. Instead, cultures of cells could be cloned and used for treating human disease. Examples of the potential use of therapeutic cloning would be the multiple production of particular bodily cells and tissues that could then be used for transplantation. Two of the most common suggested uses of this multiple production of cells are to provide donor brain tissue for those with Alzheimer's disease, and to provide skin grafts for those who have suffered from severe burns or injury. Therapeutic cloning has already been carried out successfully in mice; here cells are removed and cultured and then transplanted back. However, the possibility also exists that particular cell types could be cultured from human embryo cells. Although many people find the idea of using human cloning to produce individuals for use solely as organ donors morally unacceptable, they are often less hostile to the idea of this kind of mass production of bodily cells for therapeutic transplantation.

Two quotes from the Wellcome Trust's report on public perspectives on human cloning illustrate these views nicely. One respondent described her views as follows: 'for selective parts I have no problems (skin, organs). Otherwise, let nature be nature' (Wellcome Trust 1998: 24). In her response, this respondent makes a distinction between interfering with whole individuals and interfering with their constituent parts. This distinction appears to be important for many people, arguably because it makes the process of cloning more identifiable as a discrete medical intervention of the type that already commonly occurs in modern medicine. A second respondent's views on the same topic illustrate the clearer possibility of practical benefits that is often associated with therapeutic cloning: 'After reading about the two children who'd been badly burnt in a house fire, the idea of producing skin for skin grafts seemed a good idea' (Wellcome Trust 1998: 24).

However, not all respondents to the Wellcome Trust exercise expressed positive views towards therapeutic cloning. For some, what underpinned their views was the debate that is crucial for all new genetic technologies, and in understanding the sometimes unhappy history of genetic knowledge: how do we make a distinction between things that work for the individual good and things that work for the good of society? One respondent encapsulated this debate as follows: 'If it enabled ageing to be slowed down then no – how can this planet sustain such an over-population?' (Wellcome Trust 1998: 24).

This kind of question is rarely debated in relation to new genetic technologies and the positive impact it is hoped they will have on health care. The predicted outcome of this positive impact is clearly that more people will be born free of, or survive longer after treatment for, genetic diseases. However, an ability to enable or prolong life in this way has huge implications for health and social welfare systems and for sustainability more generally. Unfortunately, these are difficult and sensitive issues to debate, because of their links to a potentially eugenic agenda.

However, despite these objections, in general terms, reactions to therapeutic cloning have been far less universally hostile. On the whole, it appears that therapeutic cloning is seen as less frightening, less potentially harmful and with more obvious and immediate benefits. It is important to remember, though, that just as with reproductive cloning, not all activity that would come under this heading would necessarily have any direct therapeutic benefit immediately. However, research is likely to increase our fundamental biological knowledge about cell and tissue growth and disease.

Regulatory framework

Because of the fears that cloning has created, the regulatory framework surrounding the technologies involved has come under intense scrutiny. Although the benefits and disadvantages of other new genetic technologies have often been debated alongside their development and introduction into food or health care, immediate reactions to cloning sought to prevent its development. However, this reaction was strongest in relation to human cloning and, as might be expected, there are different regulatory frameworks governing human and animal cloning.

For animals, the House of Commons Science and Technology Committee, which issued its report in March 1997, acknowledged public concerns in the UK but also recognized potential benefits. The BMA concurred with this view. As a result, the recommendations here concern taking steps to prevent any misuse of developments rather than an outright ban on cloning research (House of Commons Science and Technology Committee 1997).

For humans, the legislation that covers cloning in the UK is the Human Fertilization and Embryology Act 1990. Historically, the Act has its beginnings in the birth of Louise Brown, the first 'test tube' baby, after which Britain set up a voluntary system of regulating IVF clinics. Then, in the early 1980s, a committee chaired by moral philosopher Mary Warnock was set up. The report's main focus was on embryo research, but as part of this it addressed human cloning. The recommendation from the report was that human cloning should be prohibited, and provisions for this were subsequently included in the Human Fertilization and Embryology Act of 1990. As part of the Act, the Human Fertilization and Embryology Authority (HFEA) was created.

Under the terms of the Act, no human embryo can be created outside the body – and no eggs or sperm can be kept outside the body – without a licence from the HFEA. In effect, this means that the prohibition of cloning in the UK rests on licence rather than law, although the HFEA have made it clear that it will not issue licences for human cloning. Nevertheless, there have been frequent calls to amend the legislation to give a straightforward legal ban, and this scenario looks increasingly likely. Enforcement of the 1990 Act rests with the HFEA as well, since it is a statutory body. The Act does allow the creation of human embryos for the purposes of research, but they must not be implanted in a woman and they must not be kept for more than 14 days. As a result, fetal tissue has already been widely used in medical research. (This is an area in which UK law differs from international law, where the use of fetal tissue in research is often prohibited.) However, the regulations governing this research in the UK are very specific. Research on embryos is permitted only:

Box 8.4: Regulating developing technologies

In actual fact, the precise legal wording of the 1990 Act does not encompass the procedure that made Dolly because, at the time, the method by which Dolly was produced was not considered to be possible. This highlights a consistent problem in genetics: that regulation when technologies are already possible is often too late, but trying to anticipate discoveries can also create problems of its own.

- when all relevant animal research has been done, and then only:
- to discover advances in the treatment of infertility;
- to increase knowledge about congenital disease or malformation;
- to develop more effective means of contraception
(http:// www.hmso.gov.uk/acts/acts1990/ukpga_19900037_en_1.htm).

Legislative responses spurred by the birth of Dolly and the apparent possibilities of human cloning also occurred subsequently. In its resolution of 12 March 1997, the European Parliament also stated that cloning of human beings 'cannot under any circumstances be justified or tolerated by any society, because it is a serious violation of fundamental human rights . . .' (http://europa.eu.int/abc/doc/off/bull/en/9703/p103061.htm).

In the USA, where there was no existing legislation to prevent cloning, the then President Clinton responded quickly. In 1997, he issued a moratorium on using federal money to pursue research into human cloning. However, this did not prevent the private sector from carrying out research in this area; many of the reports of progress in human cloning come from the USA, although their accuracy is often disputed. The National Bioethics Advisory Committee was asked to report. Although they upheld the need for an immediate ban on grounds of safety (arguing that this should also extend to privately funded research), they highlighted the need to review this legislation frequently. Their suggestion was that it should be reviewed every three to five years as the technology developed. As a result, human reproductive cloning is now the subject of the Human Cloning Prohibition Act (1997). Privately funded biomedical research into cloning itself and human embryonic stem cell research has been permitted, but on 31 July 2001 the US House of Representatives voted for a ban on all cloning of human embryos (and, subsequently, any creation of new embryonic stem cell lines for research purposes). To become law, the bill must first pass through Senate, but the strong support of President Bush for a ban means that legal prohibition looks likely.

In the UK, however, while the ban on human reproductive cloning remains, steps have been taken to relax the legislation around therapeutic cloning. In June 1999, the UK government set up an advisory group to consider possible therapeutic benefits and, in 2001, proposed a change in law to allow the use of embryonic stem cells for research outside the areas of infertility and reproduction permitted by the HFEA Act 1990 (Mayor 2001a). This followed a report from the Nuffield Council on Bioethics that made the case for human stem cell research, with the aim of developing therapies for diseases such as Parkinson's and conditions such as stroke (Nuffield Council on Bioethics 2000). Tissues and organs develop from stem cells, so stem cells provide a source from which specialized cell lines can be generated and replicated. However, the Council took the view that, since sufficient embryos were already donated for research from IVF treatments, there was no need to allow the creation of additional embryos specifically for this purpose. It also followed a report from the Department of Health, which argued that research using embryos should be permitted, including embryos created by cell nuclear replacement. However, if embryos are to be specially created, as UK law allows, then the HFEA must be satisfied that there are no other means of meeting the stated research objectives. This difference in legislation between the USA and UK has led some commentators to suggest that there will be a 'brain drain' of stem cell researchers leaving the USA for the UK as a result.

Nevertheless, as with any regulatory framework, questions arise as to whether these controls are adequate and how illegal research will practically be prevented. In the UK in particular, there is a current climate of public lack of trust in regulators – and a feeling that 'if it can be done, it will be done'. In a US context, Berg and Singer (1998) argue for sensible and flexible guidelines to be overseen by a regulatory body, rather than a legislative approach that is cumbersome, time-consuming and discourages research and public engagement. These issues of the advantages and disadvantages inherent in different regulatory approaches are considered in more detail in Chapter 10.

Media and public attitudes to cloning

Together with the development of research into the process of cloning itself, there is a growing body of sociological research that shows how public attitudes towards cloning, alongside other new genetic technologies, are influenced by media coverage. Research illustrates how that media coverage, in turn, draws on science fiction literature, images and metaphors. It is argued that, because of where these images come from, the metaphors and comparisons used in the discourse about new genetic technologies, and particularly about cloning, largely have negative connotations and so both reflect and stoke public fears.

Examples are the common use of terms such as 'Frankenstein food', as discussed in Chapter 7, and frequent references to the science fiction literature such as *Brave New World* (Huxley 1932) and *The Boys from Brazil* (Levin 1976). In assessing this process, Nerlich *et al.* (1999) describe how the framing of problems and issues in society often depends on metaphors. Metaphors enable us to understand one thing in terms of another and so can be used to express commonly held feelings that are difficult to articulate. In the same kind of way, they argue, just the title of a cultural reference can invoke a whole story or script, and give a whole interpretative frame to the problem. In this way, the term 'Frankenstein food' invokes the mad scientist who creates a human monster (and whose story ends in disaster and lack of control). In terms of cloning, referring to *The Boys from Brazil* stokes and reinforces the

O

Box 8.5: *The Boys From Brazil*

Ira Levin's (1976) novel tells the story (parts of which are loosely factually based) of Dr Josef Mengele, a medical doctor known as the 'angel of death' in the German concentration camps during the Second World War. He conducted 'medical experiments', often involving brutal torture, on concentration camp inmates, and was particularly fascinated with identical twins and the role that biology and environment played in their development. After the war, many high-ranking Nazis escaped to South America, including Mengele. Levin's novel is set in South America and focuses on the fictional attempt by Mengele to resurrect Hitler for the twenty-first century, using a piece of tissue taken from under Hitler's rib with his permission while he was still alive. Volunteer women are used as 'vessels' to carry 94 clones, who are then sent for adoption. However, like Hitler, they are placed in families with an elderly father, who must subsequently be killed to recreate the circumstances of Hitler's own childhood. Interestingly, this process emphasizes the role of nurture in the nature–nurture debate, by assuming that identical genetic material must be coupled with an identical environment to produce an identical personality. The large number of clones originally created also suggests the limitations of the 'carbon-copy' theory. Nevertheless, the book, and subsequent film, are a frequent reference point for those anxious about the consequences of human cloning.

commonly held fear that cloning could and will be used to produce carbon-copies of individuals such as Adolf Hitler for evil intent.

Science fiction and science fact has often been fused in the media and that, of course, has an important effect on public attitudes to genetic science. Studies such as the Wellcome Trust (1998) report demonstrate clearly how popular culture is used to help express public attitude. They also demonstrate the circularity of this process, in terms of how media reports of new genetic technologies influence public perceptions.

Wilkie and Graham (1998), in discussing media portrayals of Dolly the sheep, describe the contrasting discourses of concern and promise that underpinned this coverage. Analysing these discourses, they argue that there is little tradition in Britain of scientists speaking directly to the media about their research and that, as a result, research aims are often misunderstood or misinterpreted because no information is provided as to *why* research has been carried out. Obviously, this can result in inaccurate and damaging speculation. In terms of press accounts, they suggest that it is scientists rather than the press who are portrayed as enjoying power without responsibility. Equally, and relatedly, the scientific community in Britain failed to address, or be prepared for, the cultural implications of Dolly's birth. In explaining the media reaction to Dolly, Wilkie and Graham draw on Mazur's (1981) hypothesis, that the rise in reaction against a scientific technology appears to coincide with a rise in quantity of media coverage, suggesting that media attention tends to elicit a conservative public bias.

More fundamentally, Nelkin and Lindee (1998) describe how the cloning of Dolly was used to evoke seemingly far-fetched scenarios that expressed prevailing social and political tensions – for example, the creation of perfect people or the redundancy of men in the reproductive process. These scenarios also highlighted growing tensions over the commercial control of biotechnology and fears over the commodification of the body. Nelkin and Lindee make the important point that popular interpretations and speculations of science are often dismissed on the basis of ignorance, but to dismiss these is also to dismiss the broader social meanings attached to these speculations. In this sense, reactions to cloning can perhaps best be understood as representing wider fears of the power of science and of what it means to be human.

Summary points

- Cloning is a particular kind of genetic engineering, used to produce an organism genetically identical to its parent. Although cloning is often thought of as a new technology, it has been part of science since the 1950s.

- Dolly the sheep was a landmark in the development of new genetic technology, both biologically and socially. She was cloned using adult genetic material, which had previously been thought impossible, and her birth has come to be seen as illustrative of both the incredible and terrifying possibilities that science offers.

- The principal justification for cloning is that it opens new perspectives for therapeutic medicine, particularly in relation to transgenic animals. However, it is the prospect of human cloning that has been most widely debated.

- There are two types of human cloning: reproductive cloning and therapeutic cloning. The debate over reproductive cloning has largely been conducted in a moral arena, focusing on whether it is *morally* right or wrong. Conducting the debate on this level fails to give sufficient attention to the social context in which decisions are made. It has been argued, for example, that reproductive cloning represents only a difference in degree from existing IVF procedures. However, there is a danger in seeing cloning only as an issue of individual choices.

- Therapeutic cloning does not produce genetically identical fetuses, but cultures of cells or tissues that can be used for transplantation. Public reaction to this use of the technology has been less hostile and regulatory frameworks have been less prohibitive, perhaps because this is more easily conceptualized as a discrete medical intervention with immediate practical benefits.

- Media coverage of cloning has drawn extensively on science fiction images and metaphors. These metaphors enable the public to understand complex ideas, but also impact on attitudes to the new genetics. Dismissing popular interpretations, however, risks dismissing the broader social meanings that are attached to these interpretations.

Further reading

Bodmer, W. and Weatherall, D. (1998) Life after Dolly, *Science and Public Affairs*, Summer, pp. 15–17.

Dawkins, R. (1998) What's wrong with cloning?, in M. Nussbaum and C. Sunstein (eds) *Clones and Clones: Facts and Fantasies about Human Cloning*. New York: W.W. Norton.

Nelkin, D. and Lindee, M.S. (1995) *The DNA Mystique: The Gene as a Cultural Icon*. New York: W.H. Freeman.

Posner, E.A. and Posner, R.A. (1998) The demand for human cloning, in M. Nussbaum and C. Sunstein (eds) *Clones and Clones: Facts and Fantasies about Human Cloning*. New York: W.W. Norton.

Turney, J. (1998) *Frankenstein's Footsteps: Science, Genetics and Popular Culture*. New York: Yale University Press.

Wilmut, I., Schnieke, A.E., McWhin, J., Kind, A.J. and Campbell, K.H.S. (1997) Viable offspring derived from fetal and adult mammalian cells, *Nature*, 385: 810–13.

9

BIOETHICS
Robert Dingwall

Introduction

This chapter looks at some ethical issues raised by the new genetics and their implications for the way we make individual and social choices about how, when, where and by whom these technologies should be used. It also looks at the social construction of the dominant approach in bioethics and asks whether its apparently impersonal philosophical principles actually institutionalize a particular ideology of citizenship. We begin, however, by looking at elements of ethical theory and the way they generate commonly used principles for making moral judgements about actions.

Ethical theory

Historically, there have been two main approaches to ethical questions. *Consequentialist* approaches focus on the outcomes of actions. Did the action achieve a morally desirable goal, whatever might be said about the processes involved? *Deontological* approaches treat people as having certain inherent rights to protection from abuse, regardless of the merits of the outcome. These might include rights to privacy, to respect or to self-determination, all of which are enforceable even if this compromises some socially desirable result. You just should not treat people that way, whatever good you hope to achieve.

The most influential contemporary approach in bioethics combines elements from these two sources (Beauchamp and Walters 1999; Beauchamp and Childress 2001). It can be expressed as four principles: non-maleficence, beneficence, autonomy and justice. The first pair are consequentialist and the second pair are deontological. Although these principles are often treated as a simple checklist, their interpretation is actually quite complex. What do they mean?

–Non-maleficence

For an action to be considered ethical, it must not harm anybody affected by it. Different bioethicists differ in how widely they define harm and who or what they include in the category of beings that must not be damaged. Some bioethicists concentrate on physical harms, while others include possible social harms. These might include being embarrassed by the public disclosure of private medical information, such as the fact that you have suffered from a sexually transmitted disease or had a pregnancy termination. The release of medical information might also lead to financial exclusion if banks, insurers or loan companies discovered you were a poor health risk. Bioethicists vary in their views about whether non-maleficence is limited to other humans or whether it may also encompass some or all of the animal or plant kingdoms (Singer 1990). Some argue that we should treat other primates as though they had the same rights as ourselves (Cavalieiri and Singer 1993). Others think that we can only have a right to non-maleficence because we accept this as a duty towards others. Since animals, even Great Apes, and plants cannot act in a non-maleficent fashion towards us, they cannot claim a right to be so treated or, at least, their claim to protection is less than another human's might be. We may be entitled to value the welfare of animals and plants below our own and to use them for our own purposes, provided that the benefit to us is reasonably proportional to the harm done to them (arguments on both sides can be found in Regan and Singer 1989).

– Beneficence

An action should achieve some positive good rather than simply being carried out for its own sake. It is not, for example, sufficient to carry out research on human subjects merely to increase scientific knowledge. There must be a clear potential benefit either to those taking part or to others similarly situated in the future. There is room to debate what constitutes a benefit, whether the benefit is proportional to the risks, how we weigh possible future gains against present hazards, and so on. As with non-maleficence, there is also an argument about the extent of our obligations to act beneficially when our actions affect non-human entities. Are we justified in sacrificing animals to the pursuit of knowledge for its own sake or for the benefit of humankind rather than for their own species?

– Autonomy

Human beings in full possession of their faculties should be allowed to determine their own fate. Other people should not take decisions for them or restrict their decision making. This principle is often used to criticize medical paternalism, where doctors limit the information and choices offered to patients in the belief that they, as experts, know better than the patients what actions are in their best interests. It also underlies the notion of informed consent, that people have a right to be aware of all the risks and benefits attached to a course of action and to decide on their own whether to accept them. Bioethics often struggles to deal with the definition of 'full possession of their faculties'. Does autonomy apply to people with mental health problems? Does autonomy apply to people with Alzheimer's disease? Does autonomy apply to children? Who counts as a child for this purpose? A related issue is the position of people whose rights to self-determination may be compromised, like prisoners. Can a convicted prisoner freely decide whether to take part in a risky medical experiment?

Justice

People who are equal in relevant respects should be treated equally. Although this seems to be equally important in ethical analysis, when justice and autonomy conflict, autonomy almost always wins. Part of this reflects the difficulty of defining 'relevant respects' and 'equal treatment'. The principle is intended to be one of non-discrimination on medically relevant criteria. However, this leaves open the possibility of discrimination on social criteria, which amounts to the same thing. For example, in the USA, it may not be acceptable to discriminate between people in need of health care on the grounds of race. However, it is entirely acceptable to discriminate on the grounds of income, which has a similar effect. There is a comparable difficulty in deciding what is a medically relevant criterion. In the UK, some cardiac surgeons have refused to give coronary artery grafts on smokers the same priority as non-smokers. Is this discrimination against an autonomous patient choice or on the basis of the different risk–benefit ratio of the intervention and a desire to focus resources on those most likely to benefit for longest? Similarly, should age be disregarded as a criterion in allocating organs for transplant, focusing purely on the prospective recipient's current health status, or should preference be given to the youngest recipient at a given health status on the basis that they are likely to survive longest post-transplant? What does justice require?

We shall demonstrate the application of these principles to some issues in genetics later. However, they did not develop in a social vacuum and it is important to understand how their use emerges from their history.

The rise of bioethics 1945–2000

There were periodic concerns about clinical and research ethics in the nineteenth century. These are illustrated in Britain by the riots over the Anatomy Act 1832, which licensed the supply of human bodies for dissection in medical education (Richardson 1987), and the anti-vivisection movements, which led to the first regulation of animal experiments in 1876 (Harrison 1967). However, the contemporary regime has its origins in the Allied reaction to the medical experiments conducted by German doctors during the Second World War and exposed by the Nuremberg Medical Trial of 1946–47. (Although there were comparable Japanese medical atrocities, these were covered up at the time and have had less influence on subsequent developments.)

At Nuremberg in 1946, twenty-three German doctors were accused of murdering inmates of concentration camps in the course of medical experiments (Annas and Grodin 1992: 70–86). Although the trial was conducted by a US military tribunal and is often seen as a purely American affair, Hazelgrove's (2002) work has shown the extent of British involvement. For all practical purposes, this was an Allied trial designed to distance Allied research from these atrocities committed in the name of science. The trial also served to exonerate the bulk of the German medical profession, distancing this handful of doctors from the 'normal science' of democratic societies (Ernst and Weindling 1998).

Hazelgrove describes how the prosecution team and their scientific witnesses decided in July 1946 to formulate 'some broad principles . . . for the use of humans as subjects in experimental work' to prevent the trial from stirring 'public opinion against the use of humans in any experimental manner whatsoever that a hindrance will thereby relate in the progress of science'. The defence focused on the lack of any generally accepted standards governing medical experimentation on human subjects. However, the prosecution argued that such standards could be formulated, at least implicitly, and used to judge the defendants' actions. The precise authorship of the 'Nuremberg Code', ten statements of principle set out by the tribunal in presenting its judgement, remains unknown (Annas and Grodin 1992: 102–3, 132–7). However, its enduring influence can be seen by comparing its ten points with the four principles laid out by Beauchamp and Childress, which are, effectively, more abstract versions of the same statements (the full Code can be found at http://ohsr.od.nih.gov/Nuremberg.php3).

As Hazelgrove (2002) shows, the clean moral story that has often been told about the Nuremberg Code is really somewhat murky. Although reference was made to guidelines published by the American Medical Association, these did not appear until nineteen days after the trial's start and seem to have been inspired by the prosecution's expert witnesses. The defence made considerable play with the US history of eugenic interventions and of experiments conducted on criminals, where voluntary consent seems to have been absent. Recent historical work has also raised questions about some of the Allies' research on their own soldiers and civilians. The Allies were quick to consider what scientific lessons could be learned from the Nazi experiments and to re-employ doctors who were not included in the trial, much as they did with German missile engineers and scientists.

The Nuremberg principles were widely adopted internationally during the immediate post-war years. However, Hazelgrove notes that their impact on medicine in the USA and Britain was limited. The Americans continued to make questionable use of prisoners and there is increasing evidence of the abuse of military personnel in the UK in experiments relating to radiation and poison gas. Some critics have claimed that the Allies simply assumed that the Nuremberg Code did not apply to them. There was growing unease among sections of the medical and scientific communities on both sides of the Atlantic by the end of the 1950s.

This unease was crystallized in the whistle-blowing of two men: Henry Beecher and Maurice Pappworth. Beecher was a member of the US medical elite, a Harvard anaesthesiologist, who attacked the ethical standards of clinical research in leading US institutions through two widely read papers in 1959 and 1966 (see also Rothman 1993). Pappworth was more of an outsider, whose knowledge was gained from the clinicians who came to the cramming courses that he ran for the Membership examination of the Royal College of Physicians – analogous to a specialty licensing board in the USA. Hazelgrove describes how this information came to form the basis first of a 1962 article and then of a book, *Human Guinea Pigs*, in 1967. These concerns coincided with a review of the Nuremberg Code by the World Medical Association. Despite its title, European and North American interests dominated the Association and the review focused on their agenda. Hazelgrove notes that the original draft of what became the Declaration of Helsinki in 1964 was significantly tightened on the issue of consent. (The text of the Declaration and its revisions in 1975, 1983 and 1989 can be found in Annas and Grodin (1992). The latest version, incorporating the 1996 and 2000 revisions, can be found at http://www.wma.net/e/policy/17-c_e.html.) However, it still took several years for both the US and the British medical establishments to urge their colleagues to comply with these principles. Further revelations, about US experiments that had deliberately infected children in Willowbrook, a residential care institution for learning disabilities, with hepatitis (Rothman 1993) and about the US Public Health Service Tuskegee Study, where black men with syphilis had been left untreated for forty years to observe the natural history of the disease (Jones 1981), finally provoked more explicit regulatory interventions, including the development of the US structure of Institutional Review Boards and the UK structure of Local Research Ethics Committees.

International approaches to research on animals are more variable (Brody 1997: 378–80). Most developed countries have regulatory schemes that involve independent review to ensure that the interests of animals are weighed against the benefit to humans. They aim to secure humane living conditions for research animals, to minimize suffering during the actual research even where this leads to the sacrifice of the animal, and to limit the number of animals actually used. There is, though, considerable divergence over the extent to which animal suffering can weigh against potential human benefit. The UK and European position tends to suggest that some experiments benefiting humans may be unacceptable because of the extent of animal suffering involved. US regulations tend towards a human priority position that heavily discounts animal suffering.

Although clinical bioethics adopted the same fundamental principles and draws inspiration from the Nuremberg Code and the Declaration of Helsinki, the idea that these principles should be explicitly applied to ordinary medical practice did not emerge until the 1960s. *The Hastings Center Report*, the bulletin of one of the leading US bioethics think tanks, published a special supplement to its November–December 1993 issue reporting the discussion at a 1992 conference in Seattle to mark 30 years since 'The Birth of Bioethics' (Jonsen 1993).

The contributors, all of whom had worked in the field since the 1970s, acknowledged that the main source for its creation was an article in *Life* magazine, on 9 November 1962, describing the work of a committee that had been created to decide which patients should get access to the haemodialysis programme at a Seattle hospital. Kidney dialysis was a newly available technology and the equipment and facilities were in short supply. This hospital had tried to ration access by creating a 'God Committee', mainly composed of people who were not doctors, to review the medical records and to decide, quite literally, who should have a chance to live and who would die. Should this judgement rest on personality, wealth, social acceptability, past or future contribution to society, or family support obligations? The conference also referred to Beecher's work, described above, and to the development of heart transplantation. In 1967, a South African surgeon, Christiaan Barnard, had transplanted a heart from a dead, or dying, patient into another patient with terminal cardiac disease. The immunological mechanisms of tissue rejection were poorly understood and the recipient only lived for a few days. This provoked widespread concern about the definition of death, the nature of consent, from the donor's point of view, and the risk–benefit ratio, from the recipient's. Was the donor 'really' dead when the heart was removed or had he been killed by the surgeon's intervention? Had the donor consented to the use of his heart? Did the recipient understand the risks of this heroic intervention and its almost certain outcome? Was Barnard morally, if not legally, guilty of murdering two people?

Alongside technical developments went cultural changes. The struggle to ensure equal civil rights for Black Americans in the early 1960s set a pattern of challenges to discrimination and social hierarchies that marked US politics for the rest of the twentieth century. Successive groups – women, people with disabilities, gays and lesbians, other ethnic and cultural minorities – attacked real or perceived forms of discrimination and denial of the rights to equal protection and equal participation in society apparently guaranteed by the Constitution. Medicine, seen – with some justification – as the preserve of relatively affluent white men, was one of the challenged institutions. Medical paternalism came to be seen as an oppressive rather than a caring use of social power. Rather than sparing patients the stress of making difficult decisions or dealing with painful knowledge, like diagnoses of terminal illness, paternalism made the physician's life easier by preventing patient questioning of the values concealed by his judgements. It concealed the extent to which access to care depended upon the 'wallet biopsy', the patient's wealth. Finally, the emerging evidence of the direct abuse of patients in research led to questions about whether the trust implied by paternalism was really justified. If research subjects were being treated in the ways documented by Beecher and others, what was happening in routine clinical practice?

These challenges were picked up intellectually by the generation of philosophers and theologians represented at the Seattle conference. They used the traditional tools of moral theory to explore the implications of thinking about patients as people who had rights, in contrast to the Hippocratic tradition of concentrating on doctors' obligations.

Box 9.1: The Hippocratic Oath

I SWEAR by Apollo the physician, and Aesculapius, and Health, and All-heal, and all the gods and goddesses, that, according to my ability and judgment, I will keep this Oath and this stipulation to reckon him who taught me this Art equally dear to me as my parents, to share my substance with him, and relieve his necessities if required; to look upon his offspring in the same footing as my own brothers, and to teach them this art, if they shall wish to learn it, without fee or stipulation; and that by precept, lecture, and every other mode of instruction, I will impart a knowledge of the Art to my own sons, and those of my teachers, and to disciples bound by a stipulation and oath according to the law of medicine, but to none others. I will follow that system of regimen which, according to my ability and judgment, I consider for the benefit of my patients, and abstain from whatever is deleterious and mischievous. I will give no deadly medicine to any one if asked, nor suggest any such counsel; and in like manner I will not give to a woman a pessary to produce abortion. With purity and with holiness I will pass my life and practice my Art. I will not cut persons laboring under the stone, but will leave this to be done by men who are practitioners of this work. Into whatever houses I enter, I will go into them for the benefit of the sick, and will abstain from every voluntary act of mischief and corruption; and, further from the seduction of females or males, of freemen and slaves. Whatever, in connection with my professional practice or not, in connection with it, I see or hear, in the life of men, which ought not to be spoken of abroad, I will not divulge, as reckoning that all such should be kept secret. While I continue to keep this Oath unviolated, may it be granted to me to enjoy life and the practice of the art, respected by all men, in all times! But should I trespass and violate this Oath, may the reverse be my lot!

Their approach drew strongly on Protestant theology and its model of humans as active participants in relationships with God. Reformation thinking was used to challenge the divinity of the physician, just as it had once challenged the power of Popes. Although the movement became both more secularized and more ecumenical, some version of the Protestant Ethic remains central. At the same time, bioethics changed the practice of American philosophy and theology (Toulmin 1982). Although these had traditionally been more applied than their European counterparts – as in the work of the Pragmatists who influenced the Chicago School of sociology between 1900 and 1940 – they now had an opportunity to become directly involved in real-world events of great practical significance. Philosophers who joined committees about the definition of brain death were asked to make decisions of an importance that they had never previously experienced. Suddenly, there were new career opportunities, jobs in medical centres, courses to teach, consulting to undertake. Bioethics was embraced by medicine, to an extent that has begun to concern some of its leaders.

Bioethics is substantially an American invention. We shall look later at some of the implications of its transplantation to countries like the UK, whose health care systems operate on different principles. Although this account has stressed its Protestant roots, Continental European bioethics has also been strongly influenced by Catholic thought. This has defended the Church's deontological approach, arguing that the Protestant emphasis on the rights of believers to make their own accommodation with God, or their doctor, must be constrained by other fundamental values. This clash is most evident over issues like abortion or euthanasia, where the asserted rights of autonomous citizens to self-determination may conflict with the claim that these are intrinsically wrong and should not be choices permitted to anyone.

Bioethics as a social movement

As Bosk (2000) notes, sociologists were slow to give much attention to bioethics. However, they have increasingly begun to express concern about its implications. This concern has three dimensions: the implicit ideology of bioethics; the professionalization of bioethics; and the reasons for its adoption by hospitals and research establishments.

Bioethics as ideology

Although Beauchamp and Childress saw their four principles as having equal weight, there is a growing view that autonomy has become pre-eminent (Wolpe 1998). As a result, the autonomy of patients and the autonomy of medicine become mutually supportive against the claims of justice or community. The liberal individualism embedded in US law and political culture reinforces this. Autonomous patients do not need an apparatus of regulation and quality assurance to guide purchasing decisions. Managed care becomes subject to a joint challenge by physicians and patients: it constrains the autonomy of both. Physicians cannot supply the care they choose to and patients cannot obtain the care they desire.

Box 9.2: Managed care

Traditionally, US health care had been provided on a fee for service basis, where patients, or their insurers, simply paid whatever medical bills were presented. This led to considerable upward pressure on costs because there was little check on doctors' decisions to order tests, prescribe drugs or carry out operations, at least for those who could pay. Since the 1960s, there have been various attempts at institutional innovation to limit costs and make care more affordable, which are known generically as managed care. These usually involve some kind of monitoring over doctors' decisions intended to ensure that only necessary expenditure is incurred.

Patient litigation has increasingly undermined the attempts of managed care to constrain costs and to achieve a measure of justice in the delivery of US health care. This problem is also visible in UK debates about the NHS, which can be seen as a nation-wide managed care organization. Successive governments' attempts to limit costs by the rational practice of evidence-based medicine, a form of central planning, have been paralleled by a growing rhetoric of consumerism, that the NHS should provide customized care for each individual patient. Local providers are squeezed, in the same way as US managed care organizations, by assertions of patient rights to treatments that the providers may not consider that they have a duty to supply (Richards *et al.* 2001).

The professionalization of bioethics

The Irish playwright George Bernard Shaw once famously described all professions as a conspiracy against the laity. The eighteenth-century social theorist, Adam Smith, put it slightly more formally when he observed that 'people of the same trade seldom meet together, even for merriment and diversion, but the conversation ends in a conspiracy against the public...' (Smith 1976: i, 144). This view has dominated most sociological writing on the professions since the 1960s. DeVries and Conrad (1998) describe how US bioethics has moved from a diverse interdisciplinary movement towards a professionalized specialty. In the early 1990s, most leaders in the field had been sceptical about such a development, arguing that bioethics drew strength from its diverse, inter-disciplinary nature and open recruitment. By the end of the decade, a large number of specialized graduate programmes had been created and the four main associations had merged. The specialty was well on the way to developing a certification regime that seemed likely to become *de facto* licensing.

> **Box 9.3: Certification and licencing**
>
> *Certification* means that some people are allowed to make a special claim of competence in a field; *licencing* means that only people certified as competent are allowed to practice in that field.

The whole process looks like a classic story of professionalization and is being repeated elsewhere. Members of the growing number of UK hospital ethics committees are under increasing pressure to attend formal training courses and to obtain recognition of their competence to make moral judgements. The small number of bioethics centres in the UK are developing graduate programmes and short training courses, which both serve and stimulate demand and which provide further resources for the development of these centres.

However, the classic story of professionalization is an incomplete one. Professional status is not purely the achievement of a well-organized group that can lobby for special resources and privileges but must also be supported by a demand for their services (Dingwall 1999). Why do health care providers want the services of bioethicists? Why do they want credentialled bioethicists?

Bioethics and defensive practice

Why did organized medicine so rapidly come to terms with bioethics? Part of the answer lies in the ideological convergence encouraged by the emphasis on autonomy and part in the desire of bioethicists to be useful. This desire has led to increasing problems for bioethicists. Arthur Caplan, one of the field's current leaders, was cited as a co-defendant in the civil action brought against the University of Pennsylvania over the 1999 death of Jesse Gelsinger during a gene therapy trial. Although the action was settled, Caplan was criticized by other bioethicists for having become so closely involved in the design and management of trials. Part of the University's response to the lawsuit and the parallel Federal investigation was to restructure his group to increase its organizational distance from practising clinicians and researchers.

Caplan's entanglements may offer some clues to the growth in demand for bioethicists. It might be argued that they have become a substitute for the solution of the real problems of US medicine. Instead of addressing the various concerns of women and ethnic, cultural, social or sexual minorities about the lack of accountability for its practice, the institutional incorporation of bioethics may have diluted or deflected these concerns. The fundamental regulatory structures and culture of the US medical profession and its health care organizations are left untouched but the house bioethicists affirm their moral cleanliness. This may also be useful in resisting litigation, where the defendants can show that they have taken expert moral advice on apparently questionable decisions. Like all specialists in modern health care, however, bioethicists must be able to demonstrate that they are the 'right kind of people'. They do this by acquiring the right kind of certification, which affirms that they have absorbed the prevailing scholarly paradigm and its accommodation with the established interests of the institutions to which they will be affiliated.

This is not to disparage the contributions that bioethicists have made to changing normative debates in health care. However, it is to question the extent to which the everyday cultures of clinical practice and science have actually altered as a result of their interventions. This chapter's author, for example, has served on a panel for the ethical review of proposals to the European Union's research programme in biosciences. In each funding round under the Fifth Framework (1998–2002), around 15–20 per cent of the proposals judged by peer review to be scientifically acceptable and fundable are identified by programme officers as ethically problematic and forwarded to this interdisciplinary panel. Their review seems frequently to involve significant redesigns of the research, which indicate the limited awareness of both the original proposers and the scientific peer reviewers. Scientists with an adequate ethical training would simply not conceive that they could do certain things to human subjects. Although there is a growing body of sociological work on how people actually deal with ethical dilemmas in medical practice and research, much still needs to be understood about how those processes can be influenced and made socially accountable.

Bioethics and genetics

The remainder of this chapter will look at three case studies arising from the new genetics. It is worth reminding ourselves, however, about the character of genetic knowledge. Many ways in which this knowledge will be used are actually quite conventional. One of the main benefits will be our ability to do some things more efficiently or more effectively. This, of course, may pose some challenges in itself: where we have evolved social institutions for managing uncertainty about individual people's futures, any reduction in uncertainty is bound to have implications for those institutions. If, however, we are simply using a genetic therapy to replace a conventional one, the issues are not really new. The problem about Jesse Gelsinger's death during a gene therapy trial was not the therapy itself, but whether the risk–benefit ratio had been properly defined and explained to him and to his father before he agreed to take part (see Box 6.4). Had the investigators been clear that the therapy would not do this young man any harm (non-maleficence) and that his autonomy had been properly respected? The questions would have been no different if his death had resulted from a conventional medication. The unique potential of genetic intervention, however, is its application to reconstruct germ lines, to make changes in organisms that can be passed on to descendants. Of course, a germ line changed in one generation can always be changed again in the next, a point that is often forgotten. If we do not like the results, we can modify the organism again, although, as some will argue, we may have let a genie out of the bottle – with a range of other consequences that are less easily reversed.

We have listed our case studies below and you may like to take the four core principles of bioethics – non-maleficence, beneficence, autonomy and justice – and see how you would analyse the questions before looking at our suggestions.

1 Should genetic screening in pregnancy be banned?
2 Should parents be allowed to design their babies?
3 Should employers be allowed to ban people with certain genotypes from certain jobs?

Screening in pregnancy

This is an example where genetic knowledge makes it possible to achieve current goals more efficiently and effectively. We already use indirect means of screening pregnancies for congenital problems, notably neural tube defects (spina bifida) and Down's syndrome. Screening fetal tissue for genetic markers would extend the range of conditions that could be identified with a high degree of certainty. However, none of these interventions can repair the problems that are revealed and the only remedy available to pregnant women is the therapeutic termination of their pregnancy and the opportunity to try again.

Non-maleficence

Who is harmed by genetic screening and in what way? First, there are small risks that the sampling procedure will lead to a miscarriage and that a therapeutic abortion will impair a woman's ability to get pregnant again in the future. However, the main harm is obviously done to a fetus found to have a genotype unacceptable to the pregnant woman and, potentially, her husband or partner. A potential life is terminated. The extent to which we should be concerned about this depends upon whether we regard potential lives as having the same value as actual lives and upon whether we regard some actual lives as less worth living than others. If you think that a potentially impaired life is less valuable, then you may not see the termination of a pregnancy as the result of genetic screening as a harm. However, if you think that all potential lives are as valuable as actual lives and that all actual lives are of equal value, regardless of genotype, you may decide that screening fails the test of non-maleficence. You might also argue that some degree of moral or psychological harm is done to parents who are asked even to confront the choice of whether or not to terminate the pregnancy. There is a further claim that permitting the termination of pregnancy on the basis of genotype may have wider implications for the value that we place on people who are born or become disabled for reasons that we cannot control or as a result of a decision by their parents to reject the choice of termination. Finally, it should not be forgotten that genetic information does not simply give information about people who are tested but also about their close kin, who may not have the same choice about whether they want to know this information or not. Of course, testing may also reveal that they are actually not the close kin that had been assumed! Genetic testing is an unequivocal way of establishing whether people who think they are biological parents actually are.

Beneficence

Who benefits from genetic screening and in what way? Three potential beneficiaries can be identified. First, the parents of the fetus can avoid whatever economic, psychological or other costs are associated with the birth of a child whose 'genotype' does not fall within the range of socially acceptable variation. Second, and more controversially, the fetus may be spared the physical pain, psychological distress and social exclusion that go with a socially unacceptable genotype. Can there be such a thing as a 'life not worth living'? Finally, others in society as a whole may be spared the costs of social solidarity, paying additional taxes or insurance premiums to subsidize those caring for the genotypically unacceptable. Social solidarity may also involve payments to people who are genotypically unacceptable and may, as a result, be unable to generate sufficient income by their own efforts to meet their needs. Additionally, other citizens are spared whatever costs may arise from the adaptation of their society to accommodate those who are genotypically unacceptable. These adaptations may be physical – making buildings accessible to people in wheelchairs – or cultural – including people with learning disabilities on the board of charities working for their interests.

Autonomy

The complexity of the group of beneficiaries makes the question of autonomy particularly difficult to resolve. Conventionally, the autonomy principle would emphasize the right of parents, particularly mothers, to choose. It is, after all, the pregnant woman who will have to carry to term what has now been defined as an imperfect baby and who is highly likely to have to bear most of the long-term consequences, whether in terms of care or courtesy stigma. However, this principle discounts the possible interests of others affected. Does the fetus have any claim to autonomy? Should there be some general social constraint on parental decisions about which potential lives are worth living? For example, could we declare that termination for a serious hereditary disorder, like beta-thalassemia, which will lead to an early death with considerable suffering, is acceptable but that termination on the grounds of gender, that a girl will be born into a society that disvalues women, is not. The practical difficulties around these issues are discussed in more detail in Chapter 4. Should we, in any case, be comfortable with the idea that some women might be forced to complete pregnancies that they do not want to?

Justice

Allowing the principle of autonomy to triumph may also raise questions of justice. Is it just that other people in a society should have the costs of genotypes they find unacceptable imposed on them as a result of decisions that they play no part in making? Do parents have an unlimited right to make an autonomous decision to give birth to children predicted to be genotypically unacceptable regardless of the costs imposed on those who currently recognize a relationship of social solidarity with them? Social solidarity might have been sustainable when the incidence of disability could be seen as the result of a natural lottery in which all parents participated. Since no parent could predict the outcome of pregnancy with any certainty in their particular case, then it might be just for the 'winners', with acceptable babies, to compensate the 'losers', with unacceptable babies, for some part of their losses. Is this argument as persuasive when the 'losers' have incurred their loss as a result of their own choice? Could we, however, justify requiring women with a genotypically unacceptable pregnancy to terminate this in the interests of us retaining more of our own wealth or income? Remember that we may also have a moral claim, based on autonomy, to the enjoyment of our earnings or property that would assert that these can only be taxed to the minimum extent necessary for the achievement of broadly consensual social goals.

Unrestricted autonomy may also lead to unjust results for people who are born disabled as a result of unidentifiable causes or become disabled as a result of accidents, illnesses or ageing. The 'weak eugenics' of parental choice discussed in Chapter 4 can subtly devalue the status of those who still end up disabled as a result of nature's lottery. Should this group have some right to constrain the decisions taken by parents? Might this, however, not lead to problems with the autonomy-claim that no woman should be forced to carry a baby that she does not want to?

Designer babies

One way to avoid some of the ethical difficulties of prenatal screening would be to intervene at a pre-implantation or even pre-fertilization stage. At present, there are only limited technical possibilities for this and their use is closely regulated. In the UK, the Human Fertilization and Embryology Authority (HFEA) currently allows fertilized embryos to be screened before implantation where there is a family history of a serious genetic disorder that can be identified by screening the DNA contained in a cell removed at a very early stage of the embryo's development. At the time of writing (Summer 2001), the HFEA was considering requests to extend such screening to select embryos that were more likely to implant successfully, increasing the otherwise low success rate of IVF pregnancies. From an ethical point of view, however, some would argue that discarding a fertilized embryo that has only grown to a few cells and has no structures that permit nervous activity or consciousness, is not significantly different from terminating an established pregnancy. Suppose, though, we were able to manipulate the embryo's DNA at this early stage and 'edit' the faulty sections – a theoretical, if distant, possibility. The process would be enormously risky in its early stages and would also depend upon considerable advances in the ability to re-implant embryos once removed from the womb. Nevertheless, it could remove some of the objections to the termination of life, if you believe that life begins at the moment of fertilization. However, many people would argue that it should still be banned, because the result would be a 'designer baby'. Would this be so bad?

Non-maleficence

Who would be harmed? As we have stressed, there would obviously be considerable physical risks in the early stages of such a technology and these might make us reluctant to proceed. Suppose these can be solved, though. Would a designed child be harmed? If the technology were applied successfully, presumably the child would benefit from not growing up with some serious disorder. If the technology became popular, then the child's appearance might be selected for fashion. Maybe in 2101, there will be a fashion for blonde children with green eyes, while the following year everyone wants a dark child with dark eyes. Is this very different from the fashions in first names – if you are called Kylie, this says something about your age and your parents' aspirations for you, just as much as if you are called Fiona. If you do not want to follow the fashion with your own children, then you can use the same technology to design them differently. Would parents be harmed? It is not obvious how. Would other people in society be harmed? There might be some implications for people with disabilities just as there are now and you might want to think how they would apply in this case. There might also be implications for some activities that currently rest on the lottery of gene mixing – sports are a good example. Would basketball be as watchable if the teams were made up of people designed for that sport rather than searched out from the population as a whole for their physical and mental characteristics?

Beneficence

Who would benefit? In part, the answer is already given by your answers to the questions about harm. If children benefit physically, how much does their possible embarrassment about their parents' tastes matter?

Autonomy

This technology certainly increases parental autonomy. Instead of the lottery of fertilization, they get a chance to control its terms and outcome in a way that they have not previously been able to do. They can still choose to play the roulette of natural conception but they have a new opportunity to exercise their tastes and preferences. On the other hand, they also become accountable both for their choices and, even more importantly, for rejecting the chance to choose. Maybe autonomy is not such a good deal when your tastes are so publicly and permanently displayed: you can change a child's name but you cannot remake its body.

Justice

In the nature of things, this technology would almost certainly be available at first only to rich people in rich nations. Does this matter? Is it not always the case, that the rich get technological innovations first and pay the development costs until economies of scale lead prices to fall and make products available to mass markets? Would there ever be a case, though, for delivering this technology as a public service, funded by taxation or social insurance? Would we need to distinguish between 'serious' and 'frivolous' interventions, as we do in the UK with cosmetic surgery? How would we do this? Would the results not lead us back to the questions of discrimination against people with disabilities as we noted earlier? Could the results further cement existing structures of inequality within and between countries as the rich tried to manipulate genotypes to their advantage?

Much of the opposition to 'designer babies' stems from confusion with reproductive cloning added to crude genetic determinism. The designed babies of *Brave New World* are the products of an authoritarian society that believes itself to be benign. (Actually, of course, these babies are designed by environmental interventions – the chemicals added to the artificial wombs in which they are grown.) However, babies might also be designed by consumer choices in a market. Does opposition to the first run the risk of creating an illiberal obstacle to the second?

Employment rights

One likely development from a greater understanding of human genotypes is a recognition of the bases on which people vary in their response to exposures to known workplace hazards, as discussed in Chapter 6. If your genotype places you at a higher risk of certain cancers, for example, then working in an industry that uses chemicals which are known to cause such cancers may not be a good idea. Pre-employment screening might detect this increased risk. Should that employer be allowed to discriminate against you because you are more likely to develop cancer than other people who could do this job? Alternatively, should you be allowed to make your own decision based on your assessment of the risks and benefits involved?

Non-maleficence

The main harm done by such discrimination is your exclusion from certain kinds of employment, which may have implications for your ability to generate income and for the welfare of those who are dependent on your earning capacity. However, the significance of this will depend upon the alternative employment opportunities available and their prevailing wage rates. Generally speaking, limitations on your freedom to move around in the labour market will tend to reduce your lifetime earnings because you may find yourself 'held captive' in those jobs that are safe for you and unable to improve your wages by the threat of movement to better-paid work. Pre-employment screening may also harm the interests of existing workers, if it allows employers to reduce their investment in protection against exposure to hazards. A workplace may become less safe for those who would not otherwise be at risk because the people whose greater vulnerability will provide an early signal of risks to others are excluded.

Beneficence

The main beneficiary is obviously the employer, who may have to invest less in safety and pay less in compensation to people like you who develop some disorder as a result of exposure to a workplace hazard. However, there may be some overall social benefit, if your greater fitness means that less has to be spent on your health and social care, for example. This might be offset by a loss of productivity resulting from your exclusion from an occupation where you might have made a greater social and economic contribution. Will genetic exclusions make us collectively better or worse off?

Autonomy

Your autonomy would clearly be compromised if employers were allowed to discriminate against you rather than allowing you voluntarily to assume the risks of the trade. However, we would then have to consider the extent to which you had full information about your risks and were in a position to make a free choice because equally good alternative occupations were available to you. Moreover, you might also want to think carefully about whether you could expect the same kind of compensation, whether from an employer or from social security, if you suffered an injury to your health as a result of a voluntary assumption of risk. Suppose that an employer knows that 1 per cent of their workforce will contract bladder cancer even though their exposure to benzenes is controlled as closely as practicable. A potential worker is warned that they have twice the risk of being part of that 1 per cent because of their genotype but they use an anti-discrimination law to force the employer to hire them. If the worker then gets bladder cancer, should the employer's liability to compensate them not be reduced?

Justice

Will everybody facing pre-employment discrimination be in the same position? What happens if some candidates have fewer alternative jobs available or a greater need for this job than other candidates, whether because of location, lack of skills, a larger number of dependants or whatever? Does autonomy lead to a just result in these circumstances? Would a pro-discrimination law actually favour justice, since no employer would be allowed to hire any genetically compromised worker, in the same way that no-one who is colour-blind can be a railway engine-driver?

The practical application of bioethical principles: a sociological perspective

As these case studies show, the application of bioethical principles rarely leads to simple answers. These four points cannot just be added up in a checklist and their implications often require a detailed investigation of the social context in which the decision is being made and of the interests involved in the operationalization of what are, after all, rather abstract criteria. Nevertheless, an appreciation of the ways in which bioethical debates are conducted may be helpful in ensuring that relevant issues are not overlooked or neglected. The use of these principles helps to systematize the way in which new issues can be explored. However, the manner in which they are then used needs to be examined for its unacknowledged values and interests in just the same way as any other set of social claims. The traditional sociological questions about who says this, how they are saying it, why are they saying it and what they hope to gain as a result remain as crucial as ever.

Summary points

- There are two main approaches to ethical questions: *consequentialist* approaches focus on the outcomes of actions and *deontological* approaches treat people as having certain inherent rights to protection from abuse, regardless of the intended outcome.

- The dominant approach in contemporary bioethics evaluates actions by reference to four principles: non-maleficence, beneficence, autonomy and justice. However, all of the principles are open to interpretation.

- Contemporary bioethics emerges from the Allied concerns about Nazi medical experiments in the Second World War. However, it was not until the 1960s that there was widespread recognition that some US and UK research was also morally problematic.

- Bioethics is as much a social movement as an application of philosophy. Its approach embeds the political assumptions of US liberalism and may be seen as a technocratic response to the challenges faced by established medicine since the 1970s.

- Bioethical principles are difficult to apply in particular cases and often lead to contradictory results. They cannot be used as a simple checklist but may help to structure debates and identify issues that need to be resolved.

Further reading

Anspach, R. (1993) *Deciding Who Lives: Fateful Choices in the Intensive-Care Nursery.* Berkeley, CA: University of California Press.

Chambliss, D. (1996) *Beyond Caring: Hospitals, Nursing and the Social Organization of Professional Judgement.* Chicago, IL: University of Chicago Press.

Fox, R.C. and Swazey, J. (1992) *Spare Parts.* Oxford: Oxford University Press.

Guillemin, J.L. and Holmstrom, L.L. (1986) *Mixed Blessings: Intensive Care for Newborns.* Oxford: Oxford University Press.

Heimer, C.A. and Staffen, L.R. (1998) *For the Sake of the Children: The Social Organization of Responsibility in the Hospital and the Home.* Chicago, IL: University of Chicago Press.

Zussman, R. (1992) *Intensive Care: Medical Ethics and the Medical Profession.* Chicago, IL: University of Chicago Press.

10

THE FUTURE OF
GENETIC RESEARCH
AND DEVELOPMENT

Introduction

This chapter begins by examining the results of surveys of public attitudes towards new genetic technologies, and then explores the ways that these vary across different applications and between economic and cultural circumstance. Public dissatisfaction with the regulation of technology is a key theme arising from these surveys, and some of the different strategies that may be utilized in policy making, and the advantages and disadvantages of each, are explored. The chapter moves on to consider how the new genetic technologies that are most positively viewed might be incorporated into health care and what barriers exist to their widespread adoption. It concludes with a sociological critique of the advances promised by the new genetics, drawing on themes that have been discussed throughout this book.

Public knowledge and attitudes towards the
new genetics

Alongside the development of what have come to be called the new genetic technologies over the last 30 years or so, there has been an increasing awareness of molecular genetics, and a significant change in public consciousness around issues relating to the new genetics. This change can be seen over relatively short periods of time – in 1988 in a survey of a random sample of the British public, only 43 per cent of respondents could state correctly that DNA had something to do with living things. When this survey was repeated in 1996, that figure had almost doubled, to 81 per cent (Durant 1999).

At the same time, there has been an increasing differentiation of public attitudes towards the new genetics. People are increasingly inclined to discriminate between different aspects of the field, and this is reflected in very different attitudes towards different applications of molecular genetics. A 1993 study of British people's views on the Human Genome Project showed that participants largely held two sets of contrasting images of the advances: a discourse of promise relating to potential benefits and a discourse of concern relating to actual or potential misuse of the technologies. These discourses were sometimes contradictory; for example, the ability to diagnose serious genetic disorders was seen as an important benefit, but any attempt to 'improve human nature' had powerful negative associations (Durant 1999). What they illustrate are contrasting views of the same technologies, demonstrating the fact that a particular genetic advance is unlikely to be viewed as straightforwardly 'good' or 'bad'. Instead, sophisticated conceptions of both the advantages and disadvantages of technologies are brought to bear. However, surveys of public attitudes also illustrate some consistencies in the differences in the ways varying applications of genetic technologies are perceived.

The difference in public attitudes towards medical and agricultural applications of new genetic technologies has been discussed in the course of this book, particularly in Chapter 7, and some of the theories underlying these different attitudes have been explored. Recent research continues to support these theories. For example, Mayor (2001b) draws on the results from a MORI survey carried out in 2000 to illustrate that most members of the UK general public are in favour of genetic research for medical purposes. This MORI survey (http://www.hgc.gov.uk/business_publications.htm#moriattitudes) asked 1038 members of a randomly recruited panel of the general public how they thought genetic research should be used and regulated. Ninety per cent of the respondents considered that genetic developments could and should be used to diagnose and achieve cures for disease. Over two-thirds expressed support for the use of gene therapy and almost all (94 per cent) thought genetic information should be used to help solve crime, by identifying and eliminating suspects. At the same time, however, about one-third of the sample were concerned that genetic research was interfering with nature, and 70 per cent had little or no confidence that rules and regulations were adequately keeping pace with new developments. In other words, then, while there is general hope about the benefits of some new genetic technologies, this is matched by concerns about the consequences. Even in the case of those medical applications that are more generally favoured, there are specific concerns over issues such as access to genetic information and consent.

Comparing attitudes in the UK to those in Europe and the USA

Probably the largest survey of public perceptions to date has been the Eurobarometer survey (1996), a survey funded by the European Commission and carried out in all member states (and also Norway and Switzerland). The total sample size was 16,246 (approximately 1000 from each EU country) and respondents were asked for their attitudes to six applications of biotechnology (Biotechnology and the European Public Concerted Action Group 1997):

- genetic testing;
- introducing human genes into bacteria to produce medicines/vaccines;
- GM crop plants – making these more resistant to pests;
- producing more nutritious foods or foods with longer shelf lives;
- developing GM animals for research;
- introducing human genes into other animals to produce xenotransplants.

In general terms, the first two of these applications received positive public endorsement in all 15 member states. At the other extreme, the last two animal biotechnologies were viewed as least acceptable. The food biotechnologies tended to be ranked somewhere in the middle; although they were perceived as more morally acceptable, they were also seen to be high risk. Across Europe, then, as in the UK, medical applications of genetic technology tend to have the most public support. Even within this group, however, not all medical applications are seen in the same way; applications with the most immediate and direct relevance to health care are seen as most acceptable. There are also differences dependent on how established biotechnology industries are in a particular country. The Eurobarometer survey results suggest a general picture of greatest support for genetic technologies in those countries where the science and industry is in its infancy, where the economic importance of new developments may be paramount (Biotechnology and the European Public Concerted Action Group 1997). This gives an illustration of the importance of taking account of contextual factors in any analysis of differences. Contrasting attitudes towards particular applications in the USA and UK further illustrate this point, demonstrating how economically and culturally specific factors may play a significant part in shaping public attitudes. The differences in relation to GM food have been discussed in Chapter 7, and it is often thought that the case of GM food mirrors attitudes more generally across the Atlantic. Interestingly, while the public climate in the USA is on the whole more receptive to new genetic technologies, there is more opposition to genetic testing in the USA than Europe. It is likely, as Durant (1999) suggests, that the financing of health care, and in particular the need in the USA for private health insurance based on an assessment of medical risk, plays an important role in determining these attitudes.

The opposition among the public to some applications of genetics raises once again the popular viewpoint that this opposition is based on a lack of understanding of the technology involved. As considered in Chapter 7, this viewpoint ignores sociological debates over risk and trust and the fact that lay cost–benefit analyses may be made individually in relation to different applications of genetic technology. Clearly, large sections of the European public hold deeply ambivalent attitudes about new genetic technologies. As the European Commission's Concerted Action Team suggests, 'the prevailing focus of this ambivalence appears to be moral, a collection of anxieties about unforeseen dangers that may be involved in a range of technologies that are commonly perceived to be unnatural' (Biotechnology and the European Public Concerted Action Group 1997: 847). They go on to argue that the language of objective risk assessment is inadequate when discussing new genetic technologies, precisely because the risks involved are seen as moral and political. A sociological approach, which enables an understanding of risk as subjective and collectively perceived, has much to offer in terms of examining these issues in more detail.

Regulating new genetic technologies

One of the key features of polls of public attitudes towards genetic technologies is a common concern that technology will not be controlled or regulated properly. Milewa (1999) cites the Eurobarometer survey of 1996 in noting that only 24 per cent of Britons (and 23 per cent of people in the EU) were happy with regulations as they stood at that time. However, there appears to be no clear consensus on how structures should be reformed, except for a prevailing view that experts should be involved. Additionally, as Milewa argues, for respondents to these kinds of surveys, regulation has a particular kind of meaning – it is most commonly associated with formal legal or professional interventions.

The differences in attitude that may be held towards the same applications of genetic technologies, often by the same individuals, is a clear illustration of the central dilemma facing regulators and policy makers. How is it possible to permit research that may have benefits for society, while preventing research that may create problems? The obvious difficulty is that there is no easy way of distinguishing the two, since in many cases they represent different views of the same research programmes. For policy makers, then, many of the problematic issues arise in the applications of the technology, rather than the technology itself. As well as social issues, there are also economic ones at stake here, since failure to develop biotechnology companies and to capitalize on research will have important economic consequences for countries that follow a restrictive approach. Zimmern et al. (2001: 1005) suggest that regulatory frameworks 'should be robust enough to protect patient and public interests but balanced enough to allow new developments, including predictive tests, gene therapies, and reproductive technologies'. However, it is clear that this ideal is easier espoused than achieved.

In terms of the possible ways of regulating new genetic technologies, Knoppers *et al.* (1999) argue that there are four emerging approaches to policy making. These may be outlined as follows:

Human rights approach

This approach relies on court challenges brought by interest groups and campaigning organizations through constitutions and international conventions. As Knoppers *et al.* (1999) suggest, these cases result in the clarification of issues and set far-reaching precedents as to how they are to be interpreted (for example, what the right to privacy means in practice, or what constitutes discrimination in relation to employment or insurance). However, individual cases do not constitute an integrated approach to policy making. On the whole, the policies that result are ad hoc in nature. Additionally, and importantly, they can only be achieved after the technology has already been integrated into research and practice and when its use has come into question in particular circumstances. Like all litigation, the process can also be costly, time-consuming and may not be successful.

Statutory approach

A statutory approach to regulation requires specific legislation in response to new technologies. This legislation commonly addresses the implications of technologies through prohibitions, constraints or moratoria. Knoppers *et al.* (1999) argue that this approach has the advantage of immediate certainty, clarity and precision. To some extent, for legislation to be approved, it also has to represent political consensus. However, legislation is limited to current issues and tends to close off debate. Intentionally or unintentionally, it can also close off avenues of research that may be important or legitimate. Likewise, it may fail to predict advances that fall outside its immediate remit (as was the case with the Human Fertilization and Embryology Act 1990 in the UK and the subsequent development of nuclear replacement cloning techniques in mammals). New knowledge and techniques may fall outside of the statutory definitions, and continual amendments to deal with this problem can be confusing. Since this type of regulatory approach tends to be the one uppermost in public thought (Milewa 1999), there is also the possibility of hasty reactions in the face of public outcry, which are not necessarily based on proper scientific assessment.

Administrative approach

An administrative approach regulates new developments through government or professional bodies. This kind of approach allows professional codes of conduct and self-regulation to be gradually developed and, where necessary, licensing, monitoring and quality assurance procedures to be implemented. Knoppers *et al.* (1999) describe how, since those groups involved in research are also involved in the regulatory process, this approach potentially results in greater compliance with guidelines and integration into practice. However, they also point out that ethical guidelines and codes of practice can be seen as self-serving and act as a way for those involved to avoid restrictive legislation. More fundamentally, there is a lack of public participation in this kind of approach, and it may not be publicly clear how or why particular choices have been made or constraints have been implemented.

Market driven approach

A liberal, market-driven approach maintains that, in an unrestricted marketplace, proper professional practices will, in the end, win out. Those bodies providing high-quality and ethical services will ultimately be favoured over those that do not. As Knoppers *et al.* (1999) suggest, this approach is most flexible and supportive of scientific research, but leaves the development of any given technology to the vagaries of the market and consumer choice. Some of the consequences of this type of approach to genetic testing can already be seen in the availability of mail order genetic testing and of tests with debateable predictive powers. Additionally, the market depends on investment from groups who may have particular agendas relating to the development or restriction of new genetic technologies. This kind of approach does nothing to protect the consumer from varying standards of technology and implementation, and any consensus as to these standards has no official outlet.

Clearly, all of these approaches have advantages and disadvantages and no one approach will solve all the problems potentially created by new genetic technologies. Some of them can co-exist more easily than others – a human rights approach can be brought to bear on existing frameworks where these are seen to create injustice, for example. In broad terms, regulation of new genetic technologies has been very fragmented to date both intra- and internationally, and there has tended to be a reliance on an administrative approach, through the use of advisory committees such as the Human Genetics Commission (www.hgc.gov.uk) in the UK and the Task Force on Genetic Testing in the USA. However, as Knoppers *et al.* (1999) warn, government caution towards legislation could be interpreted as endorsing a market-driven approach, and undermine important societal values of equity and access to services. Some critics (e.g. Holzman and Shapiro 1998) have suggested that both the USA and UK have been slow to respond to issues raised by new genetic technologies and, in particular, the issues raised by the most immediate implication – the potential spread of genetic testing. In the UK, developing a governmental framework has been a priority, which might be described as a 'top-down' approach to policy making. This framework has then been used to issue guidance on the provision of genetic tests direct to the public, and on the use of genetic test results by insurance companies, for example. The USA has taken a different approach, focusing on the substantive issues that arise as a result of testing, such as discrimination in employment and health insurance. This might be more accurately characterized as a 'bottom-up' approach, focusing on the possible consequences. As a result, laws have been passed at state and federal level to reduce this discrimination. Holzman and Shapiro (1998) suggest that each country could benefit by examining the approach the other has taken.

Integrating genetic services into medical care

In considering the implementation of new genetic technologies, particularly as they relate to health care, some consideration must be given to the role of the medical profession. The 1996 Eurobarometer survey highlighted the fact that, for Europeans, the medical profession is often described as the most trusted source of information on medical applications of new genetic technologies. In addition, Europeans tend to prefer the idea of regulating genetic technologies through international health care organizations such as the World Health Organization (WHO). Since doctors are reportedly the most trusted source of information in this context and are also in frequent contact with the public, there has been much debate over the expansion of their role to implement new genetic technology in health care.

As Emery and Hayflick (2001) argue, the increases in the availability of DNA testing promised by new genetic technologies will mean that non-specialist practitioners will need to become increasingly genetically literate. Currently, most genetic services in both the USA and UK are accessed through specialist centres. However, in the UK, genetic medicine appear increasingly likely to become part of primary care, through the availability of predispositional testing and screening. Primary care medicine already plays a role in identifying those at family risk of certain cancers or of common recessive disorders such as haemochromatosis, but as the field of pharmacogenetics develops this role is likely to expand. Even if counselling services remain the province of specialists, pharmacogenetic knowledge will have potentially profound implications on prescribing. Knowledge of the genetic basis of adverse drug reactions or of non-response to treatment will impact on prescribing without the need for the detailed communications that would be required in running screening and testing programmes.

In the UK, primary care is often described as the ideal home for an integrated genetics service, because of its traditional focus on the family and its largely computerized clinical records (Emery and Hayflick 2001). Some commentators have suggested that, rather than simply acting as a referral service for specialist genetic units, primary care is also where patients and their families ought to receive basic genetic information to help them understand a condition or possibility of a condition in the context of the family, and to make informed decisions about accessing further services or treatment. Equity of access could also potentially be improved if patients were to be referred to specialist national services by their own physician. Additionally, doctors could utilize genetic information to inform the advice that they already give to patients about behaviour or lifestyle. Some services that fall under the broad umbrella of genetics already operate on this community-based model. Antenatal screening, for example, is largely carried out in the community in some areas of the UK. The pre-screening consultation and sample collection for maternal serum alphafetoprotein screening is often carried out by community midwives, in liaison with general practitioners. The results of this screening are used to decide who should be offered further specialist testing, and it is this kind of initial screening role that could most easily be expanded by community physicians. However, even this kind of expansion would require skills that it is not clear primary care physicians currently have, in terms of recognizing patterns of inheritance, communicating risk and understanding the broader implications of testing. Since many of the new genetic advances under discussion are so recent, many doctors have not received appropriate clinical training in genetics to prepare them for this new role. Educational processes are notoriously slow to change, and there will be a time lag before the implementation of any educational changes takes effect in practice.

In considering the impact of new genetic technologies on the way health services are delivered, however, there is a risk of using the information we already have and the services we already provide as a model for future advances. As many commentators have cautioned, most of our knowledge to date concerns monogenic disorders (e.g. Huntington's disease), where the genetic factors involved are clear and where they have a huge and direct impact. It is important to remember that much of the knowledge of the role genes play in disease that is subsequently uncovered will be less definite and dependent on social and environmental variables. As a result, these advances are more likely to fall under the heading of public health.

Genetics and public health

Preventative medicine is a cornerstone of public health policies, and the advances that genetic technologies promise are argued to represent great advances in the field of preventative medicine (e.g. Duff, quoted in Richards 2001). From this viewpoint, genomic medicine, where treatment is tailored to individual characteristics and susceptibilities, is seen as the best route to preventing disease. Screening for genetic susceptibilities will bring with it the possibility of identifying and attempting to modify risk, through drug treatment, lifestyle interventions and dietary manipulation. However, while there is broad agreement that preventative action is a common focus of a public health agenda (for example, in relation to HIV infection or smoking cessation), this particular view of prevention encompasses a subtle shift in the way public health problems are perceived. As Petersen (1998: 59) notes, the new genetics promises a version of public health in which 'the health of populations is defined by freedom from risk of genetic disease'. This risk is inherent to the individual and cannot in itself be prevented, but once identified it can be used to inform lifestyle and treatment decisions. For it to be cost-effective, implementing this kind of preventative programme will require large-scale and widespread screening programmes. This potentially creates another problem in relation to more traditional notions of public health, in that this type of widespread screening is only likely to be an option in developed countries. Although it has been argued that future impacts (such as the development of vaccines as a result of genetic research) will also benefit developing countries, these are long-term goals.

Genetics and developing countries

Even in developed countries, the demand for services such as genetic testing is likely to exceed current resources. Where there is a lack of resources for health care more generally, this problem is likely to be exacerbated. However, it has been argued that this lack of resources does not mean that there will be no benefits from genetic advance seen in the developing world. Family histories can reveal much of what new genetic technologies can tell us (e.g. family predisposition to breast cancer; Bloom and Trach 2001). Knowledge of how a disease may be inherited offers the potential for identifying those who are at risk and monitoring their progress, even in the absence of genetic testing. However, although new developments in genetic technologies may improve diagnosis of conditions with a genetic component in the developing world, they are unlikely to impact, in the absence of other interventions, on the availability of treatment. The impact on health and medical care in developing countries will be hugely varied, depending on health care systems, financial resources and the burden of disease in particular areas. For the full benefits to be seen, we need to recognize that a more traditional public health agenda of global health is a priority.

At the same time, in discussing the worldwide impact of the new genetics, we need to be aware that there is a lesson in humility to be learnt from the Human Genome Project that has particular resonance for developing countries. Blom and Trach (2001) give the example of sickle cell anaemia, a disease for which we have already identified the gene and its mutations, and the mechanism by which the condition manifests itself. However, we can still do little for patients, wherever they are located or whatever health care systems they have access to, in the way of treatment or cure. More fundamentally, as Zimmern *et al.* (2001) note, we cannot think of the issues raised by the new genetics simply in terms of health care and health services. As the cases that have been discussed throughout the course of this book illustrate, the consequences for society reach far beyond these boundaries.

Summarizing the sociological critique

The rise of the genetic paradigm has been accompanied by an increased sociological scrutiny of new genetic technologies and their consequences. Many of the specific social issues that are raised by the application of the new genetics have been considered in earlier chapters of this book, for example the impact of genetic testing on access to insurance, or the effects of routinization on uptake of antenatal screening procedures. At a deeper level, however, many of the varying applications of genetic knowledge touch upon broader sociological concerns. Some of these are related more generally to the way in which scientific knowledge is and has been constructed by different societies and groups within them, and the legitimacy and significance that is often afforded to it. More specifically, recurring themes in the debate over the rise of the genetic paradigm itself encompass questions of what it is to be human, how societies are organized and stratified, and how health and disease are conceptualized. Genetic science has profound implications for how these distinctions are created and legitimized. These concerns may be summarized under three broad headings.

Geneticization

Lippman (1992) eloquently describes the drama inherent in stories of mapping the human genome, with their compelling messages and seductive promises. At the same time, these stories also reflect the ongoing process of geneticization – the way in which differences between individuals are reduced to their DNA. Human characteristics, and the differences in these characteristics, become equated with differences in their biological make-up. Lippman (1992: 1470) suggests that these genetic stories, and the way they are presented, 'clearly extend the Cartesian tradition of reductionism (and dualism)'. The presentation of bodies as machines, made up of identifiable and (in the case of gene therapy, for example) interchangeable parts, takes apart the linkages between body and self. Health itself becomes the subject of different biological categories, each to be addressed individually. In this way, Lippman argues that the body is objectified and it is the genome, rather than the person, that becomes the focus of medical attention. This objectification leads to distinctions being made between those genomes that are considered to be more or less desirable. Ettore (2000) illustrates this point when she highlights the distinctions that are made, discussed in Chapter 4, between women who are perceived as 'good' or 'bad' reproducers on the basis of their genes. Additionally, Lippman (1992) notes how this reconceptualization of disease as a change or fault in DNA enables the dialogue of 'fixing' and 'replacement' that pervades the discussion of genetic advances in health care. Faulty genes can be fixed or replaced in the same way that faulty joints or organs can be fixed or replaced. As a result, good health becomes a straightforward matter of having good genes.

Changing the boundaries between health and disease

This last point illustrates how the way in which we view health and disease is also altered by viewing them through a genetic lens. From this perspective, health is no longer defined by an absence of symptoms, feelings or the bodily effects of disease. Predictive testing means that individuals who currently have no physical symptoms or pathology can be redefined as ill on the basis that they may or will become so in the future. More fundamentally, genetics also has the potential to change our notions of normality, restricting the definition to those with 'normal' genes. However, normality is a problematic concept for genetic science, given that there is no accepted objective definition of the term at a societal level. Since no individual has a 'perfect' genome and only tiny genetic variations exist between individuals, using these differences as the basis of 'abnormality' is problematic. Not all of these variations are associated with recognized disease states and, from a sociological point of view, the concept of normality is only meaningful in terms of its relationship with what is defined as abnormal. This relationship is not constant, either through time or across groups and societies. These difficulties of definition are illustrated by the contrasting claims that are made for new genetic knowledge. Supporters of the programme to identify a genetic basis for homosexuality, for example, argue that if a biological cause can be found, homosexuality must be accepted as a natural and, therefore, 'normal' state. Opponents argue that identifying a biological variation in gay men and women will lead to justification for their consideration as 'abnormal'. More subtly, antenatal screening and testing is designed to detect fetal abnormalities on the basis of chromosomal analysis. However, identifying what is regarded as a biological abnormality gives prospective parents little information as to the severity of expression of this disorder in their particular case or the long-term consequences of living with this disorder. In other words, it cannot help them in assessing the *social* abnormality of a child, in terms of society's reactions to and interactions with them. Once again, this highlights how normality only has a meaning in relation to what is considered 'abnormal' at any point in time in a society, and by particular groups within that society. The example of deaf parents who assert a preference for having deaf children, discussed in Chapter 5, clearly illustrates how biologically based definitions of abnormality may be turned on their head in different social contexts.

Reducing society to individuals

The third key strand of the sociological critique concerns the way that exaggerating the clinical benefits of the Human Genome Project and the advances related to it may raise false hopes and divert attention from important issues. As Holzman puts it, 'Exaggerating the importance of genetic factors stops people thinking about the need to clean up the environment and tackle socioeconomic inequity' (Holzman, quoted in Richards 2001: 1016). More broadly, stressing the importance of genetic factors also means that collective problems are seen as having individual causes. In terms of health, as Lippman (1992) argues, an individual with a genetic label can be isolated from the context in which they became ill, since the source of the problem is located firmly inside that individual's body. Viewing the cause as internal means that contributory or exacerbating factors – for example, poverty, stress or available resources – can be dismissed. This approach can be extrapolated from health problems to social problems more widely, where it follows that, if the individual is seen as the source of problems, it is the individual, and not the society, that requires change to remedy these problems. As Chapters 2 and 3 of this book have described, this individualist view of society is by no means new, but advances in genetic science, and particularly the research programmes aimed at finding genes associated with particular traits or behaviours, potentially gives it a powerful new legitimization. Petersen (1998) describes how much of the new genetics is based on the premise that science can and will reveal all that is to be known about human health and behaviour: an extreme form of reductionism in which the individual is the same as and no more than the sum of their traits. These traits include not only those that predispose us to good or poor health, but also to crime, welfare dependency, homosexuality, and so on. In this sense, genetic medicine itself may be conceptualized as a form of social surveillance and control, under the guise of 'public health'.

In considering these themes of reductionism and biological determinism, and the way in which they have become entwined with the new genetics, we need to look back as well as forwards. Why, for example, do we continue to seek a genetic basis for human homosexuality, when there is no comparable research programme into less contentiously viewed traits such as altruism? In addressing this question, Duster (1990) describes the role that historical context has played in determining which human traits will be considered to be hereditary at particular points in time. Viewing pauperism as a hereditary problem at the beginning of the twentieth century enabled the proposal of particular solutions to the pressing social problems of the time, just as viewing low IQ as hereditary did at the end of the century. These solutions both reflected and reinforced particular social and political climates that existed at these times. As Duster stresses, then, lessons from history should be borne in mind when considering the genetic causes we currently seek.

Nevertheless, it would be short-sighted and simplistic to consider new genetic technologies only in terms of the threat they pose to the existing social order. At the same time, new technologies also offer an opportunity. Cunningham-Burley and Kerr (1999) describe how technological change is interlinked with social change and how it can force us to confront new questions, or to revisit old ones from different perspectives. But, as the title of this book suggests, we cannot consider 'genetic issues' or 'social issues' in isolation from each other. Genetics is a rapidly growing *part* of society and needs to be considered as such. This need is clearly expressed by Ramsay (1994: 258): 'If we reduce societies to individuals and individuals to their genes, we cannot put the pieces back together again and expect to understand them, for we deny the interaction between genes and the environment, the individual and society'.

Summary points

- Surveys show an increasing awareness by the public of new genetic technologies, together with an increasing tendency to discriminate in their attitudes to different applications.

- These different attitudes can be linked to the risks and benefits that particular applications are seen to have, and also to social and cultural factors such as the need for health care insurance, food scares, the importance of the biotechnology industry, and so on.

- Regulation of new genetic technologies is a common concern voiced by survey respondents. A variety of approaches to regulation are possible, but the central dilemma of how to restrict ill effects without restricting benefits remains.

- Integrating new genetic technologies into medical care means that non-specialist practitioners will have to become increasingly genetically literate. However, this will require a change in education processes and will also impact on the way health and disease are viewed.

- From a sociological point of view, the applications of genetic knowledge touch upon three key themes: geneticization, changing the boundaries between health and disease, and reducing society to individuals. Since genetic science is a rapidly growing *part* of society, it needs to be considered in its social context.

GLOSSARY OF TERMS

Alphafetoprotein A protein made in the liver of the developing fetus which reaches the maternal circulation. Maternal serum alphafetoprotein (MSAFP) concentrations, as measured by a blood test, are used as a predictor of developmental abnormalities in the fetus.

Amniocentesis A method by which cells from the amniotic fluid surrounding the fetus are withdrawn using a needle. These cells are used for the diagnosis of genetic abnormalities.

Autosome Any chromosome that is not a sex chromosome.

Carrier A person with one unaffected and one affected copy of a gene associated with a recessive disorder. Carriers do not usually display signs of the disorder themselves, but can pass the affected gene on to their offspring.

Chorionic villus sampling A method by which cells are taken from the placenta surrounding the developing fetus using a needle. These cells are used for the diagnosis of genetic abnormalities.

Chromosome A linear structure found in all cells of an organism that contains the DNA of that organism. In humans there are 46 chromosomes, arranged in 23 pairs.

Clone An organism genetically identical to its parent.

Dizygotic twins Non-identical (fraternal) twins produced from two embryos conceived simultaneously. Dizygotic twins share no more genetic material than other siblings.

DNA (deoxyribonucleic acid) The carrier of genetic material in all cells. DNA comprises a linked string of four possible bases: adenine (A), cytosine (C), guanine (G) and thymine (T).

DNA sequencing The process of determining in which order the four bases A, C, G and T occur along the DNA structure.

Dominant disorder A disorder that develops in a person with a single copy of the affected gene. Dominant genes result in characteristics seen in the *phenotype*.

Down's syndrome A human disorder, present from birth, that affects both mental and physical development. It is caused by an extra copy of chromosome 21, sometimes called 'trisomy 21'.

Eugenics The intent to improve the quality of the human race, often in terms of selective breeding. Positive eugenics aims to encourage the breeding of particular groups in a society. Negative eugenics aims to discourage particular groups from breeding and, historically, has often involved an element of coercion.

Evolution Cumulative change in the genetic characteristics of a population through time.

Gamete A reproductive cell, such as sperm or egg in animals. Gametes have only one set of chromosomes, which are joined after fertilization.

Gene The basic hereditary unit. Located on chromosomes, genes are regions containing DNA that contain instructions for cell function.

Genetic engineering The transfer of parts of the genetic material from one cell to another, or the introduction of changes into this genetic material.

Gene therapy The insertion of genetic material into cells to alter or modify their function.

Genetically modified organism An organism that has undergone *genetic engineering*.

Genetic screening Screening all members of a population (e.g. pregnant women) for a genetic condition where there is no prior evidence of its presence.

Genetic testing Testing to identify a genetic alteration or mutation associated with a genetic disorder. Testing is usually carried out where other evidence suggests the disorder may be present.

Genome The total genetic make-up of an organism.

Genotype The genetic constitution of an individual organism (see *phenotype*).

Germ cells The cells that develop into reproductive cells, e.g. sperm and egg.

Mitochondrial DNA Cell structures called mitochondria contain small amounts of DNA. When DNA from the *nucleus* is removed from an egg cell in *nuclear transplantation cloning*, this mitochondrial DNA will remain in the egg.

Monogenic disorder A disorder caused by an abnormality on a single gene.

Monozygotic twins Identical twins produced from a single embryo and sharing a genotype.

Multifactorial disorder A disorder arising from the effects of several genes combined with environmental factors.

Mutation A heritable alteration in a gene or chromosome (or the process by which this alteration happens).

Nuclear replacement cloning Technique by which the complete genetic material of one organism is transferred into the fertilized egg of another.

Nucleus The part of a cell containing genetic material.

Phenotype The physical constitution of an individual organism, e.g. height, eye colour.

Polygenic disorder A disorder arising from the effects of more than one gene.

Predictive testing Testing to identify an individual who will develop a genetic condition at some point in the future.

Predispositional testing Testing to identify an individual who has an increased risk, but not a certainty, of developing a genetic condition at some point in the future.

Pre-implantation diagnosis Procedure where cells are removed from *in vitro* embryos and tested for genetic disorders before implantation in the uterus.

Presymptomatic testing Testing to identify an individual who may develop a genetic condition before any symptoms are present.

Recessive disorder   A disorder that only manifests itself in individuals who have two copies of an affected gene. Individuals with only one copy are termed *carriers*.

Reproductive cloning   The application of cloning technologies to produce identical fetuses or animals.

Single nucleotide polymorphism   A mutation or variation in DNA sequence occurring in at least 1 per cent of the population. A single polymorphism involves a change in a single base of a DNA sequence (e.g. TGCA becomes TGGA).

Somatic cells   All body cells with the exception of the gametes and the germ cells from which the gametes develop.

Stem cells   Undifferentiated cells from which specialized cells such as blood cells subsequently develop.

Therapeutic cloning   The application of cloning technologies not intended to produce identical fetuses or animals. Therapeutic cloning may be used to produce genetically identical body cells (e.g. skin cells) for transplantation purposes.

Transgenic   organisms are organisms that have had genetic material from another species added to them through genetic engineering.

X-linked gene   A gene located in the X-chromosome. X-linked disorders are the result of X-linked genes.

Xenotransplantation   Transplantation of cells or organs across species, e.g. from pigs to humans.

REFERENCES

Alderson, P. (1993) *Children's Consent to Surgery*. Buckingham: Open University Press.

Allison, P. (1954) Protection afforded by sickle-cell trait against subtertian malarial infection, *British Medical Journal*, 1: 290–4.

Annas, G.J. and Grodin, M.A. (eds) (1992) *Nazi Doctors and the Nuremberg Code: Human Rights in Human Experiments*. Oxford: Oxford University Press.

Atkinson, P., Batchelor, C. and Parsons, E. (1997) The rhetoric of prediction and chance in the research to clone a disease gene, in M.A. Elston (ed.) *The Sociology of Medical Science and Technology*. Oxford: Blackwell.

Ball, D.M. and Murray, R.M. (1994) Genetics of alcohol misuse, *British Medical Bulletin*, 50(1): 18–35.

Beauchamp, T.L. and Childress, J.F. (2001) *Principles of Biomedical Ethics*, 2nd edn. New York: Oxford University Press.

Beauchamp, T.L. and Walters, L. (eds) (1999) *Contemporary Issues in Bioethics*. Belmont, CA: Wadsworth.

Beck, U. (1992) *The Risk Society: Towards a New Modernity*. London: Sage.

Beecher, H. (1959) Experimentation in man, *Journal of the American Medical Association*, 169: 461–78.

Beecher, H. (1966) Ethics and clinical research, *New England Journal of Medicine*, 24: 1345–60.

Berg, P. and Singer, M. (1998) Regulating human cloning, *Science*, 282: 413.

Berger, A. (2001) UK genetics database plans revealed, *British Medical Journal*, 322: 1018.

Biotechnology and the European Public Concerted Action Group (1997) Europe ambivalent on biotechnology, *Nature*, 387: 845–7.

Blom, B.R. and Trach, D.D. (2001) Genetics and developing countries, *British Medical Journal*, 322: 1006–7.

Blum, K., Noble, E.P., Sheridan, P.J. *et al.* (1990) Allelic association of human dopamine D2 receptor gene in alcoholism, *Journal of the American Medical Association*, 263: 2055–60.

Bosk, C. (1992) *All God's Mistakes: Genetic Counseling in a Pediatric Hospital*. Chicago, IL: University of Chicago Press.

Bosk, C.L. (2000) The sociological imagination and bioethics, in C.E. Bird, P. Conrad and A.M. Fremont (eds) *Handbook of Medical Sociology*, 5th edn. Upper Saddle River, NJ: Prentice-Hall.

Bredahl, L. (1999) Consumers' cognitions with regard to genetically modified food: results of a qualitative study in four countries, *Appetite*, 33: 343–60.

British Medical Council (1998) *Human Genetics: Choice and Responsibility*. Oxford: Oxford University Press.

Brody, B.A. (1997) Research ethics: international perspectives, *Cambridge Quarterly of Healthcare Ethics*, 6: 376–84.

Butler, D. (1997) Calls for human cloning ban 'stem from ignorance', *Nature*, 387: 324.

Butler, D., Reichhardt, T., Abbot, A. *et al.* (1999) Long term effects of GM crops serves up foods for thought, *Nature*, 398: 651–6.

Caplan, P., Keane, A., Willetts, A. and Williams, J. (1999) Studying food choice in its social and cultural contexts: approaches from a social anthropological perspective, in A. Murcott (ed.) *The Nation's Diet: The Social Science of Food Choice*. London: Addison Wesley Longman.

Cardon, L.R. and Watkins, H. (2000) Waiting for the working draft from the human genome project (editorial), *British Medical Journal*, 320: 1223–4.

Carter, S. (1995) Boundaries of danger and uncertainty: an analysis of the technological culture of risk assessment, in J. Gabe (ed.) *Medicine, Health and Risk: Sociological Approaches*. Oxford: Blackwell.

Cavalieri, P. and Singer, P. (eds) (1993) *The Great Ape Project: Equality Beyond Humanity*. London: Fourth Estate.

Clarke, A., Parsons, E. and Williams, A. (1996) Outcomes and process in genetic counselling, *Clinical Genetics*, 50: 462–9.

Cole Turner, R. (1995) Religion and gene patenting, *Science*, 270: 52.

Collins, H.M. (1992) *Changing Order: Replication and Induction in Scientific Practice*, 2nd edn. Chicago, IL: University of Chicago Press.

Conrad, P. (1997) Public eyes and private genes: historical frames, news constructions and social problems, *Social Problems*, 44(2): 139–54.

Conrad, P. (1999a) A mirage of genes, *Sociology of Health and Illness*, 21(2): 228–41.

Conrad, P. (1999b) Genes, mental illness and the media. Paper presented to the 84th Annual Meeting of the American Sociological Association, Chicago, IL, 10 August.

Cotton, N.S. (1979) The familial incidence of alcohol, *Journal of Studies of Alcohol*, 40: 89–116.

Cox, S. and McKellin, W. (1999) 'There's this thing in our family': predictive testing and the social construction of risk for Huntington's disease, in P. Conrad and J. Gabe (eds) *Sociological Perspectives on the New Genetics*. Oxford: Blackwell.

Cunningham-Burley, S. and Kerr, A. (1999) Defining the 'social': towards an understanding of scientific and medical discourses on the social aspects of the new human genetics, *Sociology of Health and Illness*, 21(5): 647–68.

Darwin, C. (1859) *On the Origin of Species by Means of Natural Selection*. London: John Murray.

Dawkins, R. (1976) *The Selfish Gene*. Oxford: Oxford University Press.

Decruyenaere, M., Evers-Kiebooms, G., Denayer, L. and Van den Berghe, H. (1992) Cystic fibrosis: community knowledge and attitudes towards carrier screening and prenatal diagnosis, *Clinical Genetics*, 41: 189–96.

Denayer, L., Evers-Kiebooms, G., De Boek, K. and Van den Berghe, G. (1992) Reproductive decision making of aunts and uncles of a child with cystic fibrosis: genetic risk perception and attitudes towards carrier identification and prenatal diagnosis, *American Journal of Medical Genetics*, 44: 104–11.

DeVries, R. and Conrad, P. (1998) Why bioethics needs sociology, in R. DeVries and J. Subedi (eds) *Bioethics and Society: Constructing the Ethical Enterprise*. Upper Saddle River, NJ: Prentice-Hall.

Dickenson, D. (1999) Can children and young people consent to being tested for adult onset genetic disorders?, *British Medical Journal*, 318: 1063–6.

Dingwall, R. (1999) Professions and social order in a global society, *International Review of Sociology*, 9(1): 131–40.

Dobson, R. (2000) Gene therapy saves immune deficient babies in France, *British Medical Journal*, 320: 1225.

Durant, J. (1999) Public understanding of the significance of genomics, in P. Williams and S. Clows (eds) *Genomics, Healthcare and Public Policy*. London: BSC Print.

Duster, T. (1990) *Backdoor to Eugenics*. London: Routledge.

Duster, T. (1995) The Bell Curve (review), *Contemporary Sociology*, 24(2): 158–61.

Elston, M.A. (ed.) (1997) *The Sociology of Medical Science and Technology*. Oxford: Blackwell.

Emery, J. and Hayflick, S. (2001) The challenge of integrating genetic medicine into primary care, *British Medical Journal*, 322: 1027–30.

Ernst, E. and Weindling, P. (1998) The Nuremberg Medical Trial: have we learned the lessons?, *Journal of Laboratory and Clinical Medicine*, 131(2): 130–5.

Ettore, E. (1999) Experts as 'storytellers' in reproductive genetics: exploring key issues, *Sociology of Health and Illness*, 21(5): 539–59.

Ettore, E. (2000) Reproductive genetics, gender and the body: 'Please doctor, may I have a normal baby', *Sociology*, 34(3): 403–20.

Evans, D., Burnell, L., Hopwood, P. and Howell, A. (1993) Perception of risk in women with a family history of breast cancer, *British Journal of Cancer*, 67: 612–14.

Evers-Kiebooms, G., Denayer, L., Decruyenaere, M. and Van den Berghe, H. (1993) Community attitudes towards prenatal testing for congenital handicap, *Journal of Reproductive and Infant Psychology*, 11: 21–30.

Faiola, A. (1999) Is it 'biopiracy' or just business?, *The Seattle Times*, 18 April.

Farrant, W. (1985) Who's for amniocentesis? The politics of prenatal screening, in H. Homans (ed.) *The Sexual Politics of Reproduction*. Aldershot: Gower.

Fernbach, D. (1998) Biology and gay identity, *New Left Review*, 228: 47–66.

Ferriman, A. (2001) UK approves preimplantation genetic screening technique, *British Medical Journal*, 323: 125.

Flinter, F.A. (2001) Preimplantation genetic diagnosis, *British Medical Journal*, 322: 1008–9.

Frewer, L.J. and Shepherd, R. (1995) Ethical concerns and risk perceptions associated with different applications of genetic engineering: interrelationships with the perceived need for regulation of the technology, *Agriculture and Human Values*, 12: 48–57.

Frewer, L., Howard, C. and Shepherd, R. (1996) Public concerns in the United Kingdom about general and specific applications of genetic engineering, *Science, Technology and Human Values*, 22: 98–124.

Fujimura, J. (1996) *Crafting Science: A Sociohistory of the Quest for the Genetics of Cancer*. Cambridge, MA: Harvard University Press.

Gabe, J. (ed.) (1995) *Medicine, Health and Risk: Sociological Approaches*. Oxford: Blackwell.

Giddens, A. (1990) *The Consequences of Modernity*. Cambridge: Polity Press.

Gilbert, G.N. and Mulkay, M. (1984) *Opening Pandora's Box: A Sociological Analysis of Scientists' Discourse*. Cambridge: Cambridge University Press.

Gill, M. and Richards, T. (1998) Meeting the challenge of genetic advance, *British Medical Journal*, 316: 570.

Goddard, H.H. (1912) *The Kallikak Family: A Study in the Heredity of Feeble Mindedness*. New York: Macmillan.

Gofton, L. and Haimes, E. (1999) Necessary evils? Opening up closings in sociology and biotechnology, *Sociological Research Online*, 4(3) (http://www.socresonline.org. uk.socresonline/4/3/gofton.html).

Goode, E. and Ben Yehuda, N. (1994) *Moral Panics: The Social Construction of Deviance*. London: Blackwell.

Gould, S.J. (1978) Biological potential *vs* biological determinism, in A. Caplan (ed.) *The Sociobiology Debate: Readings on the Ethical and Scientific Issues Concerning Sociobiology*. New York: Harper & Row.

Gould, S.J. (1997) *The Mismeasure of Man*, expanded edition. Harmondsworth: Penguin.

Green, J. (1999) Serum screening for Down's syndrome: experiences of obstetricians in England and Wales, *British Medical Journal*, 309: 769–72.

Green, J. and Statham, H. (1996) Psychosocial aspects of prenatal screening and diagnosis, in T. Marteau and M. Richards (eds) *The Troubled Helix: Social and Psychological Implications of the New Human Genetics*. Cambridge: Cambridge University Press.

Green, J.M., Statham, H. and Snowdon, C. (1994) *Pregnancy: A Testing Time*. Report of the Cambridge Prenatal Screening Study. Cambridge: Centre for Family Research, University of Cambridge.

Grinyer, A. (1995) Risk, the real world and naive sociology, in J. Gabe (ed.) *Medicine, Health and Risk: Sociological Approaches*. Oxford: Blackwell.

Hadden, S. (1979) DES and the assessment of risk, in D. Nelkin (ed.) *Controversy: Politics of Technical Decisions*. Beverly Hills, CA: Sage.

Hamer, D., Hu, S., Magnuson, V.L. *et al.* (1993) A linkage between DNA markers on the X chromosome and male sexual orientation, *Science*, 261: 321–7.

Harper, P.S. (1997) What do we mean by genetic testing?, in P.S. Harper and A.J. Clarke (eds) *Genetics, Society and Clinical Practice*. Oxford: BIOS Scientific.

Harris, J. (1997) 'Goodbye Dolly?': the ethics of human cloning, *Journal of Medical Ethics*, 23: 353–60.

Harrison, B.H. (1967) Religion and recreation in nineteenth century England, *Past and Present*, 38: 108–19.

Hauser, R.M. (1995) The Bell Curve (review), *Contemporary Sociology*, 24(2): 149–53.

Hawkes, N. (2000) Allow GM crops to feed poor, say top scientists, *The Times*, 12 July.

Hazelgrove, J. (2002) The old faith and new science: the Nuremberg Code and human experimentation ethics in Britain 1946–73, *Social History of Medicine*, 15(1): 109–35.

Henson, G., Gregory, S., Hamilton, M. and Walker, A. (1999) Food choice and diet change within the family setting, in A. Murcott (ed.) *The Nation's Diet: The Social Science of Food Choice.* London: Addison Wesley Longman.

Herrn, R. (1995) On the history of biological theories of homosexuality, in J.P. De Cecco and D.A. Parker (eds) *Sex, Cells and Same-Sex Desire: The Biology of Sexual Preference.* New York: Haworth Press.

Herrnstein, R.J. and Murray, C. (1994) *The Bell Curve: Intelligence and Class Structure in American Life.* New York: Free Press.

Hobbes, T. ([1651] 1976) *Leviathan.* Harmondsworth: Penguin.

Holden, C. (1991) Probing the complex genetics of alcoholism, *Science*, 251: 163–4.

Holm, S. (1998) A life in the shadow: one reason why we should not clone humans, *Cambridge Quarterly of Healthcare Ethics*, 7: 160–2.

Holzman, N. and Shapiro, D. (1998) Genetic testing and public policy, *British Medical Journal*, 316: 852–6.

House of Commons Science and Technology Committee (1995) *Human Genetics: The Science and Its Consequences.* London: HMSO.

House of Commons Science and Technology Committee (1997) *The Cloning of Animals from Adult Cells.* London: HMSO.

Howe, D.T., Gornal, R., Wellesley, D., Boyle, T. and Barber, J. (2000) Six year survey of screening for Down's syndrome by maternal age and mid-trimester ultrasound scans, *British Medical Journal*, 320: 606–10.

Huggins, M., Bloch, M., Wiggins, S. *et al.* (1992) Predictive testing for Huntington's disease in Canada: adverse effects and unexpected results in those receiving a decreased risk, *American Journal of Medical Genetics*, 42: 508–14.

Hutchings, B. and Mednick, S.A. (1973) Biological and adoptive fathers of male criminal adoptees, in World Health Organization, *Major Issues in Juvenile Delinquency.* Copenhagen: WHO.

Huxley, A. (1932) *Brave New World.* London: Chatto and Windus.

Jacobs, P.A., Brunton, M., Melville, M.M. *et al.* (1965) Aggressive behaviour, mental subnormality and the XYY male, *Nature*, 208: 1351–2.

Jensen, A. (1969) How much can we boost IQ and scholastic achievement?, *Harvard Educational Review*, 39: 1–123.

Jones, J.H. (1981) *Bad Blood: The Tuskegee Syphilis Experiment.* New York: Free Press.

Jones, L. (1999) Genetically modified foods, *British Medical Journal*, 318: 581–4.

Jonsen, A.R. (ed.) (1993) The birth of bioethics, special supplement, *The Hastings Center Report*, 23(6): S1–S15.

Kahn, A. (1997) Clone mammals . . . clone man, *Nature*, 386: 119.

Kaprio, J. (2000) Genetic epidemiology, *British Medical Journal*, 320: 1257–9.

Kaye, J. and Martin, P. (2000) Safeguards for research using large scale DNA collections, *British Medical Journal*, 321: 1146–9.

Kelly, T.E. (1986) *Clinical Genetics and Genetic Counselling.* Chicago, IL: Year Book Medical Publishers.

Kerr, P. (1992) *A Philosophical Investigation.* London: Chatto & Windus.

Kessler, S. (1997) Genetic counselling is directive? Look again, *American Journal of Medical Genetics*, 61: 466–7.

Kettlewell, H.B.D. (1973) *The Evolution of Melanism.* Oxford: Oxford University Press.

Kevles, D. (1995) *In the Name of Eugenics: Genetics and the Uses of Human Heredity.* Cambridge, MA: Harvard University Press.

Khor, M. (1996) The worldwide fight against biopiracy, *Race and Class*, 37(3): 73–7.

Kmietowicz, Z. (2001a) Insurers will not use test results from research, *British Medical Journal*, 322: 1018.

Kmietowicz, Z. (2001b) MPs demand action to prevent 'genetic underclass', *British Medical Journal*, 322: 883.

Knoppers, M.M., Hirtle, M. and Glass, K.C. (1999) Commercialization of genetic research and public policy, *Science*, 286: 2277–8.

Lane, B., Challen, K., Harris, H.J. and Harris, R. (2001) Existence and quality of written antenatal screening policies in the United Kingdom: postal survey, *British Medical Journal*, 322: 22–3.

Latour, B. (1987) *Science in Action.* Cambridge, MA: Harvard University Press.

Latour, B. and Woolgar, S. (1979) *Laboratory Life: The Social Construction of Scientific Facts.* London: Sage.

Lave, J. (1988) *Cognition in Practice: Mind, Mathematics and Culture in Everyday Life.* Cambridge: Cambridge University Press.

Lazarou, J., Pomeranz, B.H. and Corey, P.N. (1998) Incidence of adverse drug reactions in hospitalised patients: a meta-analysis of prospective studies, *Journal of the American Medical Association*, 279: 1200–5.

Leeder, S.R. (2000) Genetically modified foods – food for thought, *Medical Journal of Australia*, 172(4): 173–4.

Lenaghan, J. (1998) *Brave New NHS? The Impact of the New Genetics on the Health Service.* London: Institute for Public Policy Research.

Levin, I. (1976) *The Boys from Brazil.* London: Pan.

Light, D. and McGee, G. (1998) On the social embededness of bioethics, in R. DeVries and J. Subedi (eds) *Bioethics and Society: Constructing the Ethical Enterprise.* Englewood Cliffs, NJ: Prentice-Hall.

Lippman, A. (1992) Led (astray) by genetic maps: the cartography of the human genome and health care, *Social Science and Medicine*, 35(12): 1469–76.

Losey, J.E., Rayor, S.L. and Carter, M.E. (1999) Transgenic pollen harms monarch larvae, *Nature*, 399: 214.

Low, L., King, S. and Wilkie, T. (1998) Genetic discrimination in life insurance: empirical evidence from a cross-sectional survey of genetic support groups in the UK, *British Medical Journal*, 317: 1632–5.

Lowrance, W.W. (2001) The promise of human genetic databases, *British Medical Journal*, 322: 1009–10.

Lynch, M. (1985) *Art and Artifact in Laboratory Science: A Study of Shop Work and Shop Talk in a Research Laboratory.* London: Routledge.

MacAndrew, C. and Edgerton, R.B. (1969) *Drunken Comportment: A Social Explanation.* Chicago, IL: Aldine.

McGuire, T.R. (1995) Is homosexuality genetic? A critical review and some suggestions, in J.P. De Cecco and D.A. Parker (eds) *Sex, Cells and Same-Sex Desire: The Biology of Sexual Preference.* New York: Haworth Press.

Macintyre, S., Reilly, J., Miller, D. and Eldridge, J. (1999) Food choice, food scares, and health: the role of the media, in A. Murcott (ed.) *The Nation's Diet: The Social Science of Food Choice.* London: Addison Wesley Longman.

MacKenzie, D. and Wajcman, J. (eds) (1999) *The Social Shaping of Technology.* Buckingham: Open University Press.

McKinlay, J.B. (1982) From 'promising report' to 'standard procedure': seven stages in the career of a medical innovation, in J.B. Milbank (ed.) *Technology and the Future of Health Care*, Milbank Reader, Vol. 8. Cambridge, MA: MIT Press.

Maddox, J. (1993) Has nature overwhelmed nurture?, *Nature*, 336: 107.

Malik, K. (2000) *Man, Beast and Zombie: What Science Can and Cannot Tell Us about Human Nature*. London: Wiedenfeld & Nicolson.

Markens, S., Browner, C.H. and Press, N. (1999) 'Because of the risks': how US pregnant women account for refusing prenatal screening, *Social Science and Medicine*, 49: 359–69.

Martin, P. (1999) Genes as drugs: the social shaping of gene therapy and the reconstruction of genetic disease, *Sociology of Health and Illness*, 21(5): 517–38.

Mathew, C. (2001) Postgenomic technologies: hunting the genes for common disorders, *British Medical Journal*, 322: 1031–4.

Mayor, S. (2001a) House of Lords supports human embryonic stem cell research, *British Medical Journal*, 322: 189.

Mayor, S. (2001b) UK survey shows public confusion about human genetic research, *British Medical Journal*, 322: 576.

Mazumdar, P. (1992) *Eugenics, Human Genetics and Human Failings: The Eugenics Society, its Sources and its Critics in Britain*. London: Routledge.

Mazur, A. (1981) Media coverage and public opinion in scientific controversies, *Journal of Communication*, Winter: 106–15.

Merton, R.K. (1973) *The Sociology of Science: Theoretical and Empirical Investigations*. Chicago, IL: University of Chicago Press.

Michie, S., Bron, F., Bobrow, M. and Marteau, T. (1997) Nondirectiveness in genetic counselling: an empirical study, *American Journal of Human Genetics*, 60: 40–7.

Middleton, A., Hewison, J. and Mueller, R.F. (1998) Attitudes of deaf adults towards genetic testing for hereditary deafness, *American Journal of Human Genetics*, 63: 1175–80.

Milewa, T. (1999) Public opinion and regulation of the new human genetics: a critical review (http://www.medinfo.cam.ac.uk/phgu/info_database/Policy/milewa.asp).

Mills, C.W. (1959) *The Sociological Imagination*. Oxford: Oxford University Press.

Morrison, P. (1998) Implications of genetic testing for insurance in the UK, *The Lancet*, 352: 1647–9.

Moseley, B.E.B. (1999) The safety and social acceptance of novel foods, *International Journal of Food Microbiology*, 50(1–2): 25–31.

Murcott, A. (1999) 'Not science but PR': GM food and the makings of a considered sociology, *Sociological Research Online*, 4(3) (http://www.socresonline.org.uk/socresonline/4/3/murcott.html).

Murphy, E., Parker, S. and Phipps, C. (1999) Food choices for babies, in A. Murcott (ed.) *The Nation's Diet: The Social Science of Food Choice*. London: Addison Wesley Longman.

National Bioethics Advisory Committee (1998) The science and application of cloning, in M.C. Nussbaum and C.R. Sunstein (eds) *Clones and Clones: Facts and Fantasies about Human Cloning*. New York: W.W. Norton.

Nature (1999) GM foods debate needs a recipe for restoring trust (editorial), *Nature*, 398: 639.

Nelkin, D. (1979) *Controversy: Politics of Technical Decisions*. Beverly Hills, CA: Sage.

Nelkin, D. (1987) *Selling Science: How the Press Covers Science and Technology*. New York: W.H. Freeman.

Nelkin, D. and Lindee, M.S. (1995) *The DNA Mystique: The Gene as a Cultural Icon*. New York: W.H. Freeman.

Nelkin, D. and Lindee, M.S. (1998) Cloning in the popular imagination, *Cambridge Quarterly of Healthcare Ethics*, 7: 145–9.

Nerlich, B., Clarke, D. and Dingwall, R. (1999) The influence of popular cultural imagery on public attitudes towards cloning, *Sociological Research Online*, 4(3): (http://www.socresonline.org.uk/socresonline/4/3/nerlich.html).

Nuffield Council on Bioethics (1993) *Genetic Screening: Ethical Issues*. London: Nuffield Foundation.

Nuffield Council on Bioethics (2000) *Stem Cell Therapy: The Ethical Issues*. London: Nuffield Foundation.

Nukaga, Y. and Cambrosio, A. (1997) Medical pedigrees and the visual production of family disease in Canadian and Japanese genetic counselling practice, in M.A. Elston (ed.) *The Sociology of Medical Science and Technology*. Oxford: Blackwell.

Oakley, A. (1984) *The Captured Womb: A History of the Medical Care of Pregnant Women*. Oxford: Blackwell.

Oliver, M. (1990) *The Politics of Disablement*. Basingstoke: Macmillan.

Osler, W. (1892) *The Principles and Practice of Medicine*. New York, Appleton.

Pappworth, M.H. (1962) Human guinea pigs: a warning, *Twentieth Century*, 171: 67–75.

Pappworth, M.H. (1967) *Human Guinea Pigs: Experimentation on Man*. London: Routledge & Kegan Paul.

Parsons, E. and Atkinson, P. (1992) Lay constructions of genetic risk, *Sociology of Health and Illness*, 14: 437–55.

Parsons, E. and Clarke, A. (1993) Genetic risk: women's understandings of carrier risks in Duchenne muscular dystrophy, *Journal of Medical Genetics*, 30: 562–6.

Petersen, A. (1998) The new genetics and the politics of public health, *Critical Public Health*, 8(1): 59–71.

Pilnick, A. (2002) There are no rights and wrongs in these situations: identifying interactional difficulties in genetic counselling, *Sociology of Health and Illness*, 25(1): 66–88.

Pilnick, A. and Dingwall, R. (2001) Research directions in genetic counselling: a review of the literature, *Patient Education and Counselling*, 44: 95–105.

Pilnick, A., Dingwall, R., Spencer, E. and Finn, R. (2000) *Genetic Counselling: A Review of the Literature*, discussion paper 00/01. Nottingham: Trent Institute for Health Services Research, Universities of Leicester, Nottingham and Sheffield.

Pilnick, A., Dingwall, R. and Starkey, K. (2001) Disease management: definitions, difficulties and future directions, *Bulletin of the World Health Organization*, 79(8): 755–63.

Press, N. and Browner, C.H. (1997) Why women say yes to prenatal diagnosis, *Social Science and Medicine*, 45(7): 979–89.

Ramsay, M. (1994) Genetic reductionism and medical genetic practice, in A. Clarke (ed.) *Genetic Counselling: Practice and Principles*. London: Routledge.

Regan, T. and Singer, P. (eds) (1989) *Animal Rights and Human Obligations*. Englewood Cliffs, NJ: Prentice-Hall.

Renfrew, J.W. (1997) *Aggression and Its Causes: A Biopsychosocial Approach*. Oxford: Oxford University Press.

Richards, C., Dingwall, R. and Watson, A. (2001) Should NHS patients be allowed to contribute extra money to their care? A debate from the Nottingham ethics of clinical practice committee, *British Medical Journal*, 323: 563–5.

Richards, M. (1996) Families, kinship and genetics, in T. Marteau and M. Richards (eds) *The Troubled Helix: Social and Psychological Implications of the New Human Genetics*. Cambridge: Cambridge University Press.

Richards, M.P.M. and Green, J. (1993) Attitudes towards prenatal screening of fetal abnormality and detection of carriers of genetic disease: a discussion paper, *Journal of Reproductive and Infant Psychology*, 11: 49–56.

Richards, T. (2001) Three views of genetics: the enthusiast, the visionary and the sceptic, *British Medical Journal*, 322: 1016.

Richardson, R. (1987) *Death, Dissection and the Destitute*. London: Routledge & Kegan Paul.

Rose, S., Lewontin, R.C. and Kamin, L.J. ([1984] 1990) *Not in Our Genes: Biology, Ideology and Human Nature*. Harmondsworth: Penguin.

Rothman, B.K. (1988) *The Tentative Pregnancy: Prenatal Diagnosis and the Future of Motherhood*. London: Pandora.

Rothman, B.K. (1998) *Genetic Maps and Human Imaginations: The Limits of Science in Understanding Who We Are*. New York: W.W. Norton.

Rothman, D.J. (1993) *Strangers at the Bedside: A History of How Law and Bioethics Transformed Medical Decision-Making*. New York: Basic Books.

Russo, E. and Cove, D. (1998) *Genetic Engineering: Dreams and Nightmares*. Oxford: Oxford University Press.

Senior, V., Marteau, T.M. and Peters, T.J. (1999) Will genetic testing for predisposition for disease result in fatalism? A qualitative study of parents' responses to neonatal screening for familial hypercholesterolaemia, *Social Science and Medicine*, 48: 1857–60.

Shakespeare, T. (1998) Choices and rights: eugenics, genetics and disability equality, *Disability and Society*, 13(5): 655–81.

Shakespeare, T. (1999) 'Losing the plot'? Medical and activist discourses of contemporary genetics and disability, *Sociology of Health and Illness*, 21(5): 669–88.

Shaw, A. (1999) 'What are "they" doing to our food?': public concerns about food in the UK, *Sociological Research Online*, 4(3) (http://www.socresonline.org.uk/socresonline/4/3/shaw.html).

Shiels, P., Kind, A., Campbell, K. *et al.* (1999) Analysis of telomere lengths in cloned sheep, *Nature*, 399: 316–17.

Singer, P. (1990) *Animal Liberation*. London: Jonathan Cape.

Smith, A. ([1776] 1976) *An Inquiry into the Nature and Causes of the Wealth of Nations*. Chicago, IL: University of Chicago Press.

Smith, D.K., Shaw, R.W. and Marteau, T.M. (1994) Informed consent to undergo serum screening for Down's syndrome: the gap between policy and practice, *British Medical Journal*, 309: 776.

Sneddon, R. (1999) Background paper to the Pharmacogenetics Workshop, 29 October, The Wellcome Trust (http://www.wellcome.ac.uk/en/images/pharmacogenetics_workshop_2438.pdf).

Sneddon, R. (2000) The challenge of pharmacogenetics and pharmacogenomics, *New Genetics and Society*, 19(2): 145–64.

Sociobiology Study Group of Science for the People (1978) Sociobiology – another biological determinism, in A. Caplan (ed.) *The Sociobiology Debate: Readings on the Ethical and Scientific Issues Concerning Sociobiology*. New York: Harper & Row.

Spallone, P. and Wilkie, T. (2000) The research agenda in pharmacogenetics and biological sample collections – a view from the Wellcome Trust, *New Genetics and Society*, 19(2): 193–205.

Spencer, H. ([1865] 1898) *The Principles of Biology*. London: Williams & Nurgate.

Stein, E. (1998) Choosing the sexual orientation of children, *Bioethics*, 12(1): 1–24.

Stimson, G. (1974) Obeying doctor's orders: a view from the other side, *Social Science and Medicine*, 8(2): 97–104.

Stockdale, A. (1999) Waiting for the cure: mapping the social relations of human gene therapy research, *Sociology of Health and Illness*, 21(5): 579–96.

Suslak, C., Price, D. and Deposito, F. (1985) Transmitting balanced translocation carrier information within families: a follow-up study, *American Journal of Medical Genetics*, 20: 227–32.

Taylor, H.F. (1995) The Bell Curve (review), *Contemporary Sociology*, 24(2): 153–8.

The Lancet (1999) Health risks of GM foods (editorial), *The Lancet*, 353: 1811.

Thomson, B. (1998) Time for reassessment of use of all medical information by UK insurers, *The Lancet*, 352: 1216–18.

Todd, A.D. (1989) *Intimate Adversaries: Cultural Conflict Between Doctors and Women Patients*. Philadelphia, PA: University of Pennsylvania Press.

Toulmon, S. (1982) How medicine saved the life of ethics, *Perspectives in Biology and Medicine*, 25(4): 736–50.

Warren, V. (2001) Genetics and insurance: a possible solution, *British Medical Journal*, 322: 1060.

Wellcome Trust (1998) *Public Perspectives on Human Cloning*. London: Wellcome Trust.

Wexler, N.S. (1979) Genetic 'Russian roulette': the experience of being 'at risk' for Huntington's disease, in S. Kessler (ed.) *Genetic Counselling: Psychological Dimensions*. New York: Academic Press.

White, C. (2001) Xenotransplantation unlikely to solve organ shortage in near future, *British Medical Journal*, 322: 510.

Wilkie, T. and Graham, E. (1998) Power without responsibility: media portrayals of Dolly and science, *Cambridge Quarterly of Healthcare Ethics*, 7: 150–9.

Wilkins, A. (1993) Jurassic Park and the 'gay gene': the New Genetics seen through the distorting lens of the media, *The FASEB Journal*, 7: 1203–4.

Williams, G., Popay, J. and Bissell, P. (1995) Public health risks in the material world: barriers to social movements in health, in J. Gabe (ed.) *Medicine, Health and Risk: Sociological Approaches*. Oxford: Blackwell.

Willis, E. (1998) Public health, private genes: the social context of genetic bio-technology, *Critical Public Health*, 8(2): 131–40.

Wilmut, I., Schnieke, A.E., McWhin, J., Kind, A.J. and Campbell, K.H.S. (1997) Viable offspring derived from fetal and adult mammalian cells, *Nature*, 385: 810–13.

Witkin, H.A. (1976) Criminality in XYY and XXY men, *Science*, 193: 547–55.

Wolf, C.R., Smith, G. and Smith, R.L. (2000) Pharmacogenetics, *British Medical Journal*, 320: 987–90.

Wolpe, P.R. (1998) The triumph of autonomy in American bioethics: a sociological view, in R. DeVries and J. Subedi (eds) *Bioethics and Society: Constructing the Ethical Enterprise*. Upper Saddle River, NJ: Prentice-Hall.

Wood-Harper, J. and Harris, J. (1996) Ethics of human genome analysis: some virtues and vices, in T. Marteau and M. Richards (eds) *The Troubled Helix: Social and Psychological Implications of the New Human Genetics*. Cambridge: Cambridge University Press.

Zimmern, R., Emery, J. and Richards, T. (2001) Putting genetics in perspective, *British Medical Journal*, 322: 1005–6.

INDEX